Nonproliferation Issues for Weapons of Mass Destruction

PUBLIC ADMINISTRATION AND PUBLIC POLICY

A Comprehensive Publication Program

Executive Editor

JACK RABIN
Professor of Public Administration and Public Policy
School of Public Affairs
The Capital College
The Pennsylvania State University—Harrisburg
Middletown, Pennsylvania

Assistant to the Executive Editor
T. Aaron Wachhaus, Jr.

1. *Public Administration as a Developing Discipline,* Robert T. Golembiewski
2. *Comparative National Policies on Health Care,* Milton I. Roemer, M.D.
3. *Exclusionary Injustice: The Problem of Illegally Obtained Evidence,* Steven R. Schlesinger
5. *Organization Development in Public Administration,* edited by Robert T. Golembiewski and William B. Eddy
7. *Approaches to Planned Change,* Robert T. Golembiewski
8. *Program Evaluation at HEW,* edited by James G. Abert
9. *The States and the Metropolis,* Patricia S. Florestano and Vincent L. Marando
11. *Changing Bureaucracies: Understanding the Organization before Selecting the Approach,* William A. Medina
12. *Handbook on Public Budgeting and Financial Management,* edited by Jack Rabin and Thomas D. Lynch
15. *Handbook on Public Personnel Administration and Labor Relations,* edited by Jack Rabin, Thomas Vocino, W. Bartley Hildreth, and Gerald J. Miller
19. *Handbook of Organization Management,* edited by William B. Eddy
20. *Organization Theory and Management,* edited by Thomas D. Lynch
22. *Politics and Administration: Woodrow Wilson and American Public Administration,* edited by Jack Rabin and James S. Bowman
23. *Making and Managing Policy: Formulation, Analysis, Evaluation,* edited by G. Ronald Gilbert

Nonproliferation Issues for Weapons of Mass Destruction

Mark A. Prelas
University of Missouri-Columbia

Michael S. Peck
University of Missouri-Columbia

Boca Raton London New York Singapore

A CRC title, part of the Taylor & Francis imprint, a member of the Taylor & Francis Group, the academic division of T&F Informa plc.

Library of Congress Cataloging-in-Publication Data

Prelas, Mark Antonio, 1953-
Nonproliferation issues for weapons of mass destruction / Mark A. Prelas and Michael S. Peck.
p. cm. — (Public administration and public policy ; 114)
Includes bibliographical references and index.
ISBN 0-8247-5339-9 (alk. paper)
1. Nuclear nonproliferation. 2. Nuclear arms control. 3. Biological arms control. 4. Chemical arms control. 5. Weapons of mass destruction. I. Peck, Michael S. II. Title. III. Series.

JZ5675.P73 2005
327.1'745--dc22 2004058250

Direct all inquiries to CRC Press, 2000 N.W. Corporate Blvd., Boca Raton, Florida 33431.

International Standard Book Number 0-8247-5339-9
Library of Congress Card Number 2004058250

For my parents Jure and Kati'ca Beck Prelas,
for my children Sarah, Jessica, and Josiah Peck,
and to future generations.

Contents

Preface

Weapons of Mass Destruction (WMDs) are a direct consequence of 20th century technology. Individually and corporately, we must face the challenges and threats presented by the awesome destructive power of WMDs. As citizens living within a pluralist sociality, we each have an obligation to gain a realistic understanding of the relative risks WMDs present to our way of life. This knowledge enables us to make informed decisions leading to the mitigation of these destructive forces. The intent of this book is to provide an alternative to the WMD misinformation propagated by the media.

Misinformation has permeated the popular media for various reasons. For example, when Dwight D. Eisenhower left the presidency of the United States, he warned of the growing Military-Industrial Complex. Eisenhower illuminated that military supplies would benefit from overestimations of Soviet capabilities. These overestimations were used to generate fear and facilitate inflated budgets and justification of "pet" projects. It is within human nature to exaggerate the truth in order to persuade others to our own point of view. However, when over exaggeration occurs on a large scale, it can be harmful or dangerous. A solid knowledge base allows us to identify what is true or an exaggeration. The knowledge base is our best defense against allowing others to manipulate our fears.

Our goal in presenting this book was to provide the reader with an understanding of proliferation risks of WMDs. Knowledge helps us dispel the myths and recognize the facts. It is especially critical for choosing the issues that are most important to stem proliferation and prevent possible use of WMDs. We will also recommend a strategy to limit WMD-proliferation by addressing the underlining reasons for driving continued development and deployment.

Historically speaking, any weapon technology has ultimately found its way into the public domain given enough time. For example, at one point, fully automatic assault weapons were reserved for the elite militaries of the world. Now the Russian-designed fully automatic Kalashaikov AK-47 assault rifle is widely available on many street corners of Third World countries for as little as $50. The factors that determine the rate of migration of a weapon technology are knowledge, cost, and motivation. The flow of knowledge has never been successfully controlled, and with the Internet streamlining information, the rate of dissemination will only increase. Cost has two components, the first being what you can afford, and the second being the inherent cost of the technology. The global redistribution of wealth is being driven by the oil-based economy. This redistribution to unstable regions of the world provides the resources for some nations, groups, or individuals to explore the acquisition of WMDs. However, the inherent cost of the various WMD technologies prices some out of the marketplace and makes others affordable. Motivations include the desire for security and protection (of people, land, wealth, and resources) against perceived threats or for the purpose of becoming an aggressor (to acquire people, land, wealth, or other resources). Knowledge and cost are very difficult to control, as one might expect, leaving motivation as the most effective lever for stemming proliferation of WMD technologies.

Humanity has arrived at a historically significant point. The oil that has fueled our unprecedented world economic growth is under the pressures of increasing demand from the growing economies of the world, specifically China and India, and a decreasing supply. World population continues to grow, putting pressures on food production, water, and other resources. The gulf between the affluent peoples and the disenfranchised continues to widen. Historically, the most common cause of war has been for the control of scarce resources. One might define modern proliferation as the conversion of oil to weapons of mass destruction. Clearly the forces driving proliferation of WMDs continue to grow.

Long-term U.S. and global strategies and policies are needed to stem the tide of proliferation of WMDs. This will require leadership and vision on the part of our political institutions.

1

Introduction

Contemporary life has taught us that the double-edged technological sword can be swung in the direction of either good or evil. Individual risks due to technology misuse are greater today than ever before. Our potential of becoming a victim of a weapon of mass destruction (WMD) is accelerating at a rate comparable with the exponential advances in technology and knowledge. During the 1940s the world witnessed the dawn of the nuclear age, leaving some to fear that nuclear weapons would lead to the end of mankind. The 20th century also ushered in the development of two other WMDs: chemical and biological weapons. The risks of these weapons may have been overstated in the past, but recent advances in science and technology provide validity for the concern that mankind is poised for self-destruction.[1]

Recent political change has left the world only one remaining superpower. Nations continue to compete for dwindling resources such as potable water, oil for energy, and food-production needs in the face of unprecedented population growth. This environment is ripe for escalation of conflicts and chaos. Coupled with advancements in science, the potency of the tools of war and WMDs will only increase, while more frequent conflicts and world chaos escalate fear. But understanding what to fear is critical. We must focus on the opportunities to quell these forces and develop solutions to ensure future world stability.

Coming from a science background, the authors view the current world political structure as "monopolar," with only one dominant superpower. In nature, the concept of a monopole is used when describing electrical charges. Negatively charged electrons and positively charged ions can exist separately but are unstable. They are attracted to one another to form stable structures called atoms. In nature, monopoles are inherently unstable. Political structures are much like the natural world. When the world's political structure began to change during the early 1990s with the collapse of the Union of Soviet Socialist Republics (USSR), it created a political monopole. We define a political monopole as a world with a single dominant superpower coexisting among many other nations of less capability. That dominant superpower is the United States of America (U.S.). This "monopole" status has provided the U.S. and its citizens many indulgences. Leaders of the U.S. have increasingly seen themselves as the moral conscience of the world, leading humanitarian efforts and combating oppression in countries such as Kuwait (1991), Bosnia (1994–1995), Somalia (1992–1993), and Kosovo (1999).[2] Since emerging as the world's sole superpower, the U.S. has enjoyed unprecedented economic growth due to significant reductions in military spending, a budget surplus, and low oil prices.

Monopole states have existed in the past. Rome emerged as the dominant superpower of the ancient world following the destruction of Carthage. Britain became a dominant superpower with the defeat of Napoleon. In each case, the world political stability increased after an adjustment period. The adjustments were caused by complex mechanisms. In a natural system, the forces that act on monopoles are well understood, such as electromagnetic fields. In a political structure, these forces are far more complex. Political stability is dependent on factors such as the distribution of wealth, technology advances, methods of warfare, and the competition for resources (e.g., land, food, water, energy). The adjustment periods following monopolar emergence appear to have spurred competition and conflict. Oftentimes this conflict was embodied in the fostering of scientific developments in new technologies and new weapons.

In the same way, the seeds of change have also been sown as the world adjusts to the U.S. as the dominant superpower.

1.1 THE SHIFTING OF WEALTH

Economics plays a significant role in the fortunes of a superpower. The U.S. economy has seen rapid changes over the last 15 years. During the 1990s the U.S. had unprecedented economic growth relative to other nations. This increased both the national wealth and the personal wealth of U.S. citizens. A significant shift in wealth occurred with the dramatic burst of the dot-com or tech bubble beginning in the late 2000s. Many individual retirement and savings accounts were devastated. The Internet played a major role in the gains of technology stocks, which grew the various markets at a much higher rate than at any other time in history.[3] The U.S. was both the main beneficiary of the wealth generated by the bubble and the main loser when the bubble burst. The bubble burst initiated a three-year deflation in the U.S. stock market, paralleling the market crash of the 1930s.[4] In addition, the dot-com bubble provided states with enormous tax revenues, and this revenue growth led to accelerated rates in state spending.[5] After the bubble burst, states encountered revenue problems, leading to a projected $60 billion shortfall for 2004 for the combined 50 states. After a time of federal budget surpluses, the budget slipped back into deficits of $165 billion in 2002 and over $400 billion in 2003.[6] This shift in economic fortunes leaves dim the prospects for future budget surpluses.[7] In 2004 (at the time of this writing), despite the stimulus of enormous tax cuts, the economy was weighed down by the Iraq War, the war on terror, and oil prices of $40 or more per barrel.

Energy producers, corporate scandals, and terrorist activities also played an important role in the shifting of wealth. The California energy crisis of 2000–2001 resulted in a significant shortfall in electricity supply and a controversy about the effectiveness of deregulation.[8] The crisis resulted in a significant loss of public confidence and led one of the largest U.S. utilities, Pacific Gas and Electric, to declare bankruptcy.[9] Corporate scandals, such as the collapse of Enron, Global Crossing, WorldCom, Williams Communications, and XO Communications; and the insider-trading scandal at ImClone; and the accounting scandal of Arthur Anderson, illuminated the greed and corruption that existed at the highest corporate levels. These events eroded the confidence of domestic and foreign investors in U.S. companies and the U.S. stock market.[10] The sharp rise in oil prices caused by the Iraq War of 2003 also impacted the world economy.[11] Terrorist activities — including the devastating September 11, 2001, attacks on the World Trade Center and Pentagon and anthrax spores being sent through the U.S. mail[12] — further eroded confidence.[13] These events had an impact on the markets, and investors continue to be unsettled and fearful that if one more calamity strikes, the market could nosedive again.

1.2 THE PROLIFERATION OF TECHNOLOGY

Information technology has become widely available, providing an unprecedented access to knowledge. The development of the Internet in the 1990s significantly enhanced the means of free exchange of information and ideas. The Internet has had a positive influence on economic and technological productivity. However, information technology has also been used for destructive purposes. Terrorist organizations, such as al Qaeda, maintain Web sites that disseminate propaganda rhetoric as well as technical information, such as how to build bombs. Cellular and satellite phones have also become a common feature throughout the world, and these new telecommunication technologies have been extensively used by organizations such as al Qaeda for command and control purposes.[14] The potential use of WMDs by a terrorist group is a growing concern to all as terrorism escalates.[15]

Computer advances have also added to the proliferation of technology and capability. Over the past decade, remarkable advances and price reductions have significantly increased the computational power accessible to anyone in the world. For example, in 1992 a computer with a 25-MHz (megahertz) processor, such as the NEXT computer,[16] was under strict U.S. export control. At the same time, supercomputers were integral for the design of advanced nuclear weapons. The supercomputer was one of the significant advantages the U.S. had over the USSR toward the end of the Cold War. Maintaining this advantage was the driving force behind our export control policy. Today, computers with 3-GHz (gigahertz) processors are readily available on the world market. Contemporary laptop computers have about the same capability as the supercomputers used by nuclear weapon designers of a decade or so ago.

Technology proliferation is of great concern to the U.S. government.[17] Nuclear technology was dramatically introduced at the end of World War II with the U.S. bombing of Hiroshima and Nagasaki. Despite subsequent peaceful use of nuclear technology, the violent images of nuclear weapons persist in the public's mind. The technology used in nuclear weapons is significantly different from that used in nuclear power or in medical applications. Despite these differences, the peaceful uses of nuclear science are still viewed with suspicion. The five nuclear powers that are permanent members of the United Nations (UN) Security Council — the U.S., England, France, China, and Russia — have managed to keep nuclear weapons under reasonable control. A nuclear weapon has not been used since World War II. However, nuclear power and medical technologies have remained widely available within the public domain.

Nuclear weapons production is highly dependent upon attaining quality fissile material. A modern nuclear weapon can be constructed of either highly enriched uranium (HEU) or weapons-grade plutonium. Both of these materials are very difficult and expensive to produce. Isotope-separation technology is required to produce HEU. Plutonium is a human-made element that is produced by specially designed nuclear reactors. The plutonium is chemically separated from the other elements found in spent nuclear fuel. The technologies used to produce HEU and plutonium are complex and expensive, and the use of such technologies is detectable using standard intelligence methods. Chapter 3 describes the steps and processes necessary for manufacturing these materials. The sophisticated technology and expertise required to produce a nuclear weapon limit this type of enterprise to entities with a wealth of available resources. However, it is also possible for the technology and materials to be obtained on the world market. For example, North Korea recently obtained isotope separation technology from Pakistan in exchange for missile technology.[18]

The fall of the USSR also brought a reduction in the control of its highly sophisticated nuclear, missile, aerospace, biological, and chemical technologies.[19] Over 40% of the USSR's gross national product was allocated to the Soviet military complex. The Soviet weapon industry employed many more scientists, engineers, and technicians than did the Western nations. Weapons engineers and scientists were among the most prestigious Soviet professions. However, the USSR collapse left the huge weapons infrastructure in shambles. Many Soviet scientists, engineers, and technicians were reduced to poverty, leading to significant Western concerns about the proliferation of weapons technology to rogue states and terrorist groups.

Missile technology has also proliferated. North Korea, with the help of China and Russia, has developed both short- and long-range missiles.[20] The sale of this missile technology and hardware has been one of the ways that North Korea generates hard currency. These missiles have the capability to deliver conventional payloads or WMDs.

Chemical weapons have been available to most industrialized nations since World War I. The infrastructure for chemical weapons production is very similar to the industry processes involved in the manufacture of pesticides and fertilizers. However, the dissemination and dispersion technologies for chemical weapons are complex and not widely available.

Finally, biological weapons have a long history in the annals of warfare. The tactic of polluting water and food during long sieges of cities has been used since the beginning of recorded military history. During the 1346 siege of a Genoese-controlled city, Caffa, located in present-day Ukraine, the Tartars believed the Europeans were responsible for a plague epidemic in Asia. The Tartars laid siege to Caffa and catapulted the cadavers of plague victims into the city.[21] The attempt to spread plague by cadaver was probably not as significant a contributor to the subsequent plague outbreak as the rats and fleas that the Tartar army brought with them. One of the significant hazards of using biological weapons was illustrated during the siege of Caffa. A few Genoese merchants escaped Caffa and sailed home, taking the illness with them. Ships with infected rats and fleas arrived at the port of Messina, Sicily. In 1347, the disease spread from Messina and plunged Europe into a major pandemic, creating 25 million casualties, or about one-fourth of the European population, after five years. The effect of the plague was magnified by European superstitions that cats were witches. Cats, the natural predators of rats, were killed because of this superstition. This epidemic was referred to in European history as the "black death."[22] One of the most effective military uses of a biological agent occurred during the French and Indian War. Sir Jeffery Amherst supplied enemy Indians with blankets and handkerchiefs from a smallpox hospital. Amherst was able to successfully conqueror Fort Ticonderoga after the Indians were weakened from smallpox.

Biological weapons have gained the reputation of being the "poor man's atomic bomb." Indeed, much work has been completed this century to optimize the infectiousness, lethality, and delivery of biological agents. As will be discussed in later chapters, the power of nuclear weapons to destroy life may pale compared with that of biological weapons. In the eyes of the authors, the proliferation of biotechnology potentially presents humankind with the greatest challenge it has ever faced.

1.3 THE CHANGE IN THE METHODS OF WARFARE

The strength and technological capability of the U.S. military make it difficult to defeat in a conventional war. Unfortunately, this strength increases the prospects for asymmetric, or unconventional, warfare to be used against the U.S. In 1999, when the pro-independence party government was securing its election in Taiwan, two Chinese colonels speculated on how to wage war with a superpower.[23] China views Taiwan as a renegade province and has stated in the past that it would invade Taiwan if Taiwan declared itself independent. The apparent goal of the report was to send a "less than subtle message" to the U.S. that China had the means of waging war against a superior military force.

Asymmetric warfare opens up the possibility of using sleeper agents, commandos, or state-supported terrorist organizations as a means of attacking targets on the soil of the superpower. These tactics include the delivery of WMDs and cyberterror attacks. A cyberterror attack could potentially disrupt the government operations and the economy of the targeted superpower. The world has now become dependent upon computers and databases and, as a result, has become more vulnerable to cyberterrorism.

We have seen the effects of state-supported terrorism in the Middle East. Hamas, for example, has a strong relationship with Iran.[24] There have been charges that some Islamic charities have taken money intended for humanitarian aid and used it to sponsor Hamas,[25] which has been active in targeting Israel.

After the Gulf War, Saddam Hussein released 40 two-man terrorist teams to attack U.S. targets.[26] The plan failed because the teams were poorly trained, and the U.S. and world intelligence networks were effective in deterring the attacks.

Al Qaeda was organized by Osama bin Laden and associates during the 1980s to wage *jihad* (holy war) in Afghanistan against the USSR. After the Afghan victory, the experienced *mujahedin* (freedom fighters) returned to their home countries of Egypt, Algeria, and Saudi Arabia with the desire to continue jihad. Their antagonism refocused against the U.S. and its allies after the U.S. established military bases in Saudi Arabia following the first Gulf War. Al Qaeda and affiliated terrorist groups were involved in the first World Trade Center attack (1993) through Sheik Omar Abdel Rahman. Rahman was convicted in the first World Trade Center bombing. Other terrorist operations credited, or partially credited, to al Qaeda include the killing of 18 U.S. servicemen in Operation Restore Hope in Somalia in 1994; the August 7, 1998, bombings of the U.S. embassies in Nairobi, Kenya, and Dar es Salaam, Tanzania; the October 12, 2000, bombing of the *USS Cole*; and the September 11, 2001, World Trade Center and Pentagon attacks.

Al Qaeda has demonstrated that successful asymmetric warfare can be waged against the U.S. by staging large-scale attacks and causing mass casualties.

Al Qaeda has sought to expand its capabilities by research into chemical, biological, and nuclear weapons. Al Qaeda members have also received specialized training from the Iranian government and the terrorist group Hezballah.[27] On February 5, 2003, Secretary of State Colin Powell presented evidence to the United Nations of Iraq's long history of support for the Palestine Liberation Front and the terrorist network headed by Abu Musab Zarqawi, an associate and collaborator of Osama bin Laden and his al Qaeda lieutenants.[28] What is clear is that there is a great deal of concern about the ties between rogue nations (with WMD capabilities) and groups such as al Qaeda. Indeed, this fear was used in part as justification for the invasion of Iraq by a coalition led by the U.S. on March 20, 2003.[29]

1.4 THE SEEDS OF CHANGE

The world is rapidly being driven toward change by

- The redistribution of wealth
- The rapid pace at which knowledge is distributed through the Internet
- The development of new technologies
- The competition for and the depletion of scarce resources
- The ability of rogue states and terrorist groups to wage asymmetric warfare

There are many suitors willing to fill the power vacuum left by the fall of the former USSR. This results in a globally destabilizing force affecting many of the world's institutions. China, the most populated country in the world, has a rapidly developing economy. India may soon surpass China in total population, and it also has a strongly developing economy and a good educational system. The European community (EU) has also banded together to form an economic and trade association of nation states that may rival the U.S.

As the world evolves, the EU may give us a glimpse of future economic and trading alliances. New alliances have been created around the world, demonstrating that even ancient enemies can cooperate for the common good and live in harmony. The natural breakdown of spheres of influence may be Europe and Africa, Asia and the Pacific Rim, and North America and South America. The key questions are: Can change take place without a revolution, and can this change occur without disruption of institutions through the use of WMDs? The September 11, 2001, attack significantly impacted the U.S. economy and resulted in the loss of civil liberties for U.S. citizens and detainees held as suspects in the war on terror.[30] Inflicting mass U.S. casualties with a WMD would result in economic and social chaos of unprecedented proportions, far greater than the aftermath of September 11, 2001. For this reason, proliferation of WMDs remains a critical issue.

Seemingly unrelated global problems may also drive radical change.[31] The world's population is expected to increase from the current 6 billion people to 8 billion people by the year 2025. The expanding world economy continues to threaten the environment and stress our resources. Twenty key issues were identified by J. F. Rischard in his book *High Noon*,[33] and these need solutions within the next 20 years. These issues include

- Environmental: global warming, loss of biodiversity, depletion of fisheries, water deficits
- Institutional: poverty, terrorism, infectious diseases, natural disasters
- Structural: taxing Internet commerce, biotechnology ethics, global economy, trade policies, intellectual property rights, energy supplies

The depletion of nonrenewable, finite resources critical to the global economy is one force that will dominate the future. As limited resources stress the fabric of world order, the rift between the wealthy and poorer nations will widen. This lays the foundation for breeding contempt and hatred, resulting in the increased potential for the use of WMDs by disfranchised groups against affluent nations and against the U.S. in particular.

1.5 ENERGY AND THE VOLATILE MIX

The world's increasing dependence on oil reinforces the continued strategic importance of the Middle East. Table 1.1 lists the world's known oil reserves as of 1997. The Middle East accounted for over 65% of the total. Saudi Arabia alone had more than 25% of the world's known oil reserves. Oil is graded based on viscosity. Light oil flows easily, while heavy oil is viscous, like molasses. The lighter Middle Eastern oil is easy to pump, reducing the well recovery

Table 1.1 Proved Reserves of Oil

	Thousand million barrels				Share of total
	At end 1977	At end 1987	At end 1996	At end 1997	At end 1997
USA	35.5	35.4	30.2	29.8	2.9%
Canada	7.4	9.0	6.9	6.8	0.7%
Mexico	14.0	48.6	48.8	40.0	3.8%
Total North America	**56.9**	**93.0**	**85.8**	**76.6**	**7.4%**
Argentina	2.5	2.3	2.4	2.6	0.2%
Brazil	0.9	2.3	4.8	4.8	0.5%
Colombia	1.0	1.6	2.8	2.8	0.3%
Ecuador	1.6	1.6	2.1	2.1	0.2%
Peru	0.7	0.5	0.8	0.8	0.1%
Trinidad and Tobago	0.7	0.6	0.6	0.6	+
Venezuela	18.2	56.3	64.9	71.7	6.9%
Other South and Central America	0.8	0.5	0.8	0.8	0.1%
Total South and Central America	**26.4**	**65.7**	**79.1**	**86.2**	**8.3%**
Denmark	0.1	0.4	1.0	0.9	0.1%
Italy	0.6	0.7	0.7	0.7	0.1%
Norway	6.0	14.8	11.2	10.4	1.0%
Romania	n/a	n/a	1.6	1.6	0.1%
United Kingdom	19.0	5.2	4.5	5.0	0.5%
Other Europe	4.6	3.1	1.5	1.6	0.1%
Total Europe	**30.3**	**24.2**	**20.5**	**20.2**	**1.9%**
Azerbaijan	n/a	n/a	7.0	7.0	0.7%
Kazakhstan	n/a	n/a	8.0	8.0	0.8%
Russian Federation	n/a	n/a	48.7	48.6	4.7%
Uzbekistan	n/a	n/a	0.6	0.6	0.1%
Other Former Soviet Union	n/a	n/a	1.2	1.2	0.1%
Total Former Soviet Union	**75.0**	**59.0**	**65.5**	**65.4**	**6.4%**
Iran	62.0	92.8	93.0	93.0	9.0%
Iraq	34.5	100.0	112.0	112.5	10.8%
Kuwait	70.1	94.5	96.5	96.5	9.3%
Oman	5.7	4.0	5.1	5.2	0.5%
Qatar	5.6	3.1	3.7	3.7	0.4%
Saudi Arabia	153.1	169.6	261.5	261.5	25.2%
Syria	2.1	1.8	2.5	2.5	0.2%
UAE	32.4	98.1	97.8	97.8	9.4%

TABLE 1.1 (continued) Proved Reserves of Oil

	Thousand million barrels				Share of total
	At end 1977	At end 1987	At end 1996	At end 1997	At end 1997
Yemen	–	0.6	4.0	4.0	0.4%
Other Middle East	0.3	0.2	0.2	0.2	+
Total Middle East	**365.8**	**564.7**	**676.3**	**676.9**	**65.2%**
Algeria	6.6	8.5	9.2	9.2	0.9%
Angola	1.2	1.2	5.4	5.4	0.5%
Cameroon	0.1	0.5	0.4	0.4	0.1%
Republic of Congo (Brazzaville)	0.4	0.7	1.5	1.5	0.1%
Egypt	2.4	4.3	3.7	3.8	0.4%
Gabon	2.0	0.6	1.3	2.5	0.2%
Libya	25.0	21.0	29.5	29.5	2.8%
Nigeria	18.7	16.0	15.5	16.8	1.6%
Tunisia	2.7	1.8	0.3	0.3	+
Other Africa	0.1	0.7	0.7	0.6	0.1%
Total Africa	**59.2**	**55.3**	**67.5**	**70.0**	**6.7%**
Australia	2.0	1.7	1.8	1.8	0.2%
Brunei	1.5	1.4	1.4	1.4	0.1%
China	20.0	18.4	24.0	24.0	2.3%
India	3.0	4.3	4.3	4.3	0.4%
Indonesia	10.0	8.4	5.0	5.0	0.5%
Malaysia	2.5	2.9	4.0	3.9	0.4%
Papua New Guinea	–	0.2	0.3	0.3	+
Vietnam	–	–	0.6	0.6	0.1%
Other Asia Pacific	0.7	0.5	1.0	1.0	0.1%
Total Asia Pacific	**39.7**	**37.8**	**42.4**	**42.3**	**4.1%**
Total World	**653.3**	**899.7**	**1037.1**	**1037.6**	**100.0%**

Source: See Endnote 33, DOE, Annual Eng. Rev.. With permission.

costs. Crude oil from Saudi Arabia costs about $0.50 per barrel to extract, while some domestic oil (using tertiary recovery methods) may cost as much as $15 per barrel to recover. Oil production is tempered not only by the amount of oil reserves, but also by extraction cost. The reduced expense of extracting Middle Eastern oil adds to its strategic significance.

The developing world economy has an enormous appetite for oil, as does the U.S. Global energy consumption is measured in quadrillion British thermal units (10^{15} Btu). A Btu is defined as the energy required to increase the temperature of 1 lb of water by 1°F. We call 10^{15} Btu a *quad*. The world currently consumes about 390 quads per year. Of these 390 quads, the U.S. uses 96 quads per year, or about one-quarter of the world's energy production. In contrast, the U.S. population is about 290 million people, less than 5% of the world's total population. Energy is fundamental to the economy of modern society. As the most advanced economy in the world, the U.S. uses more energy per capita than any other country. As developing countries aspire to match the U.S. standard of living, the world's energy usage is expected to increase at a rapid rate.

Energy is so intertwined with the fabric of U.S. society that it would be an impossible task to unravel. For example, the farm machinery, pesticides, and fertilizers used in food production are directly tied to the availability of oil and gas. Consider that each working U.S. farmer is capable of producing enough food to feed over 100 people. This high production rate is due to the efficiency of farm machinery and chem-agriculture. Farm machinery requires oil for fuel. Pesticides and fertilizer are also highly dependent on oil as a feed source for chemical processing. Without fundamental energy resources, the world's food production would decrease. However, any decrease in farm production with the increasing world population growth would be disastrous.

The U.S. is an energy-intensive society, as indicated by the following statistics of U.S. energy use:

- Total energy use in the U.S. is about 96 quads per year.
- The U.S. uses 43% of the world's oil.
- The U.S. uses 23% of the world's natural gas.
- The U.S. uses 24% of the world's coal.
- The U.S. uses 4% of the world's hydroelectric power.
- The U.S. uses 6% of the world's nuclear energy.

Nearly 40% of the energy used in the U.S. is petroleum, as shown in Figure 1.1, most of which is used in transportation, as shown in Figure 1.2.[33] Figure 1.3 shows the impact of the oil embargo and the Six-Day War on the Dow Jones Industrial Average (DJIA), resulting in one of the steepest declines in the DJIA and most-prolonged economic downturns in U.S. history.

The U.S. must continue to view the Middle East as a strategic resource because of the world's dependence upon oil. This oil dependence has manifested itself in the form of political and economic imperialism. Oil-driven imperialism has bred policies that have created contempt and hatred of the U.S. This hatred, in turn,

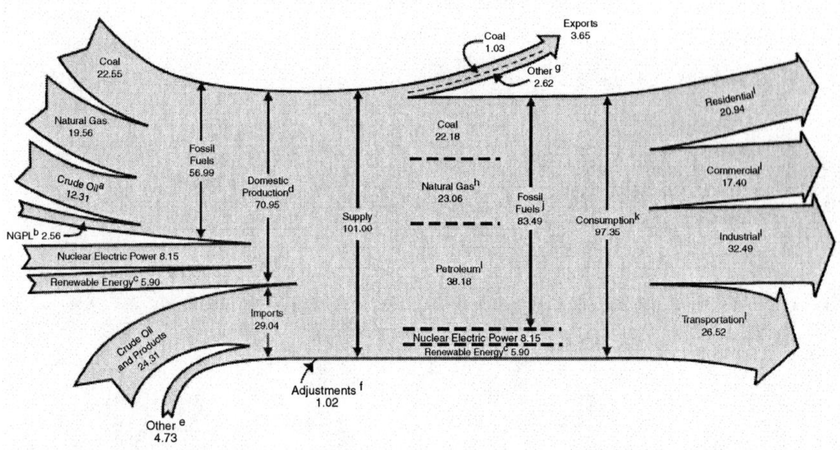

Figure 1.1 Energy flow in the U.S. (quadrillion Btus). (See endnote 33.)

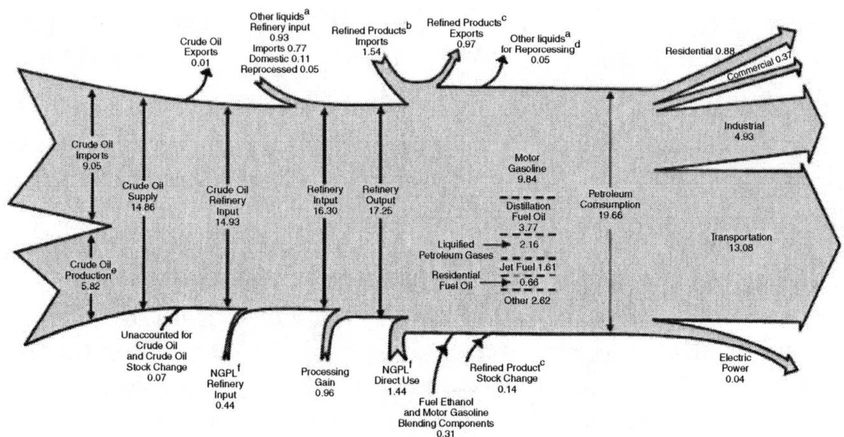

Figure 1.2 Breakdown of U.S. oil consumption (million barrels per day). (See endnote 33.)

has resulted in the rise to prominence of groups like al Qaeda. The U.S. still imports more oil than is domestically produced, even after all of the nation's conservation and self-sufficiency efforts following the 1973 oil embargo. What is surprising is where that oil comes from (Table 1.2). The Persian Gulf nations provide 23.5% of our imported oil (11.619 million barrels per day) and Iraq alone, despite sanctions after the first Gulf War, supplied 0.778 million

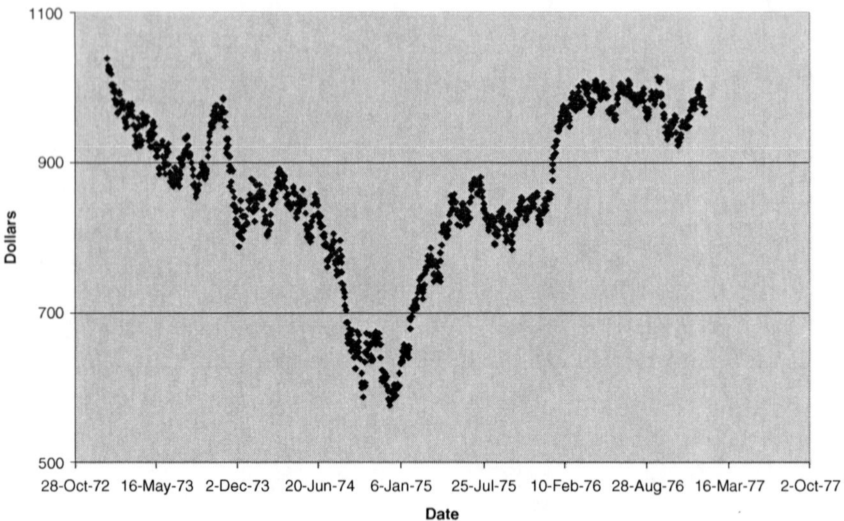

FIGURE 1.3 Impact of the oil embargo and Six-Day War on the Dow Jones Industrial Average.

barrels of oil a day to the U.S. during the year prior to the second Gulf War. In 2001 Iraq's oil revenue from sales in the U.S. alone was about $7 billion.

During the crisis leading up to the second Gulf War, the price of oil hovered above $30 per barrel. Even after the second Gulf War, the price of oil remained high because of increased demand for oil by China, terrorism fears, and unrest in Iraq. Oil costs the U.S. about $407 million per day or over $148 billion per year. These numbers will increase with time as prices rise and demand for imported oil increases.

Dr. M. King Hubbert developed a model for the depletion of a finite resource.[34] The application of this model to oil resources predicts that the world peak production of oil will occur near the end of the first decade of the 21st century and will rapidly decline afterward. The political reality is that when the oil production rate reaches a downward trend, greater price instability will result. Given that oil is involved in virtually every aspect of our economy, price instability will result in reduced economic stability. Past economic crises have been driven by energy supply problems. For example, on October 15, 1973, the Yom Kippur War began with an

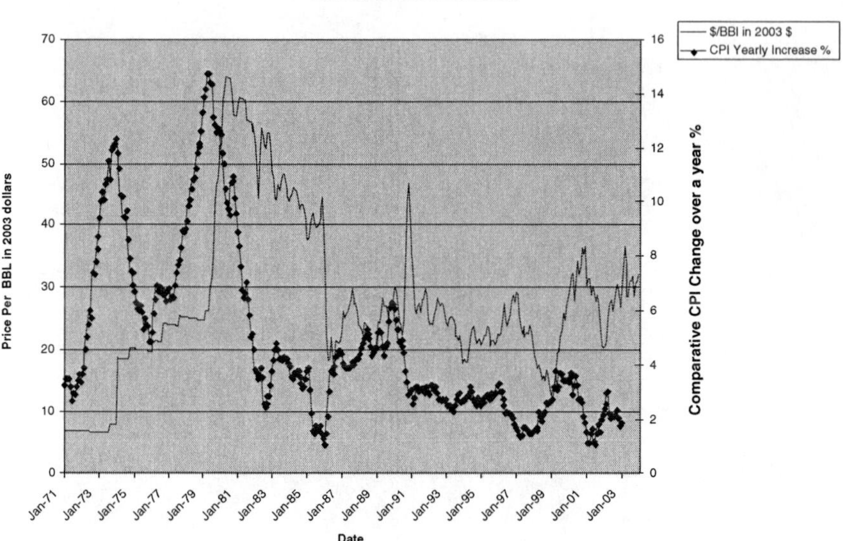

FIGURE 1.4 Comparison of the consumer price index (CPI) with the cost of oil from January 1971 to January 2003.

attack by Syria and Egypt on Israel. The U.S. and many other countries supported Israel. Because of the U.S. support of Israel, several Arab exporting nations imposed an embargo. This embargo caused Arab nations to curtail production by 5 million barrels of oil per day. Other countries were able to make up 1 million barrels of oil per day. The net loss of 4 million barrels of oil production per day extended through March of 1974. This represented 7% of the free world's oil production. For comparison, the 1972 price of crude oil was about $3 per barrel. By the end of 1974, the price of oil had risen by a factor of four to over $12. One only need look at the Dow Jones average to see the impact that the embargo had on the U.S. economy (Figure 1.3). A recession followed the energy crisis, and it was one of the most severe in U.S. history. As the oil price increases, the consumer price index also increases (Figure 1.4). The consumer price index changes most rapidly when the price of oil rises rapidly.

The gross domestic product is impacted by inflation. An increase in oil prices impacts the consumer price index. As the consumer price index increases, the gross domestic product decreases (Figure 1.5). Prior to the embargo of 1973–1974, the

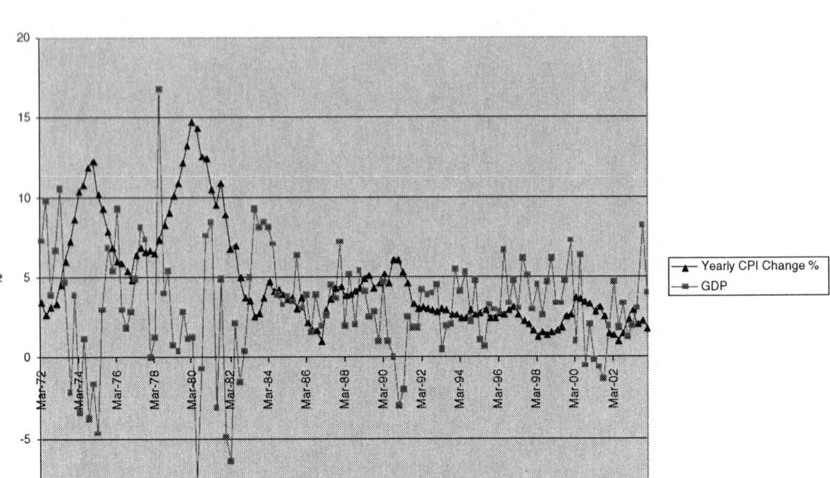

FIGURE 1.5 Comparison of the consumer price index (CPI) with the gross domestic product (GDP) from March 1972 to March 2002.

total energy expenditures in the U.S. constituted 8% of gross domestic product (GDP). The share of petroleum expenditures was just under 5%, and natural gas expenditures accounted for 1%. The oil price shocks of the 1970s and early 1980s resulted in energy costs rising dramatically to 14% of GDP overall, with 8% going to oil and 2% to natural gas by 1981. Since 1981, the percent of expenditures on energy has fallen consistently over the last two decades to the current levels of about 7% for total energy, petroleum to 3.5%, and natural gas to just over 1%.

The U.S. dependence on imported oil has increased substantially since 1973 (Figure 1.6). Although the U.S. has reduced the cost of petroleum as a share of its economy, the amount of oil that the U.S. imports has risen to over 50% and is expected to reach 64% by 2020.

U.S. dependence on Middle Eastern oil has been increasing at an alarming rate (Table 1.2). This dependence on imported oil creates a focus for U.S. policy on the Middle East and increases the likelihood of continued conflict in the region. In an ironic twist, some of the money that flows to Middle Eastern countries through

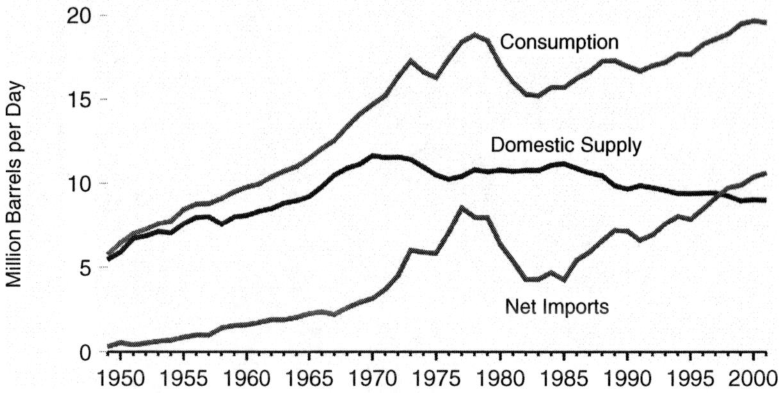

FIGURE 1.6 U.S. petroleum overview. (See endnote 33, DOE.)

the sale of oil ends up supporting the development of WMDs or terrorist groups.[35] The only long-range solution is for the U.S. and other countries to reduce their dependence on oil. Solutions that can minimize the degree of dependence on Middle East oil would have an impact on reducing the proliferation of WMDs.[36]

1.6 CONCLUSIONS

Forces are already in place that are profoundly changing the world order. The effect of these forces will become increasingly apparent over the next few decades. The proliferation of information and technology will continue to impact the world in many positive ways, but there are also negatives. The technology and knowledge for the production of WMDs such as chemical, biological, and nuclear weapons will proliferate. There is an increasing risk that this proliferation will go beyond states to terrorist groups. It is for this reason that the focus of this book is on nonproliferation issues for WMDs. We will explore the types of WMDs in Chapter 2. In order to understand the overall impact of nuclear, biological, and chemical weapons, we will look at the characteristics of these weapons in Chapters 3, 4, and 5. In Chapter 6, we will examine the effectiveness of arms control in containing weapons of mass destruction. Finally, in Chapters 7 and 8, we will conclude by examining the future of weapons of mass destruction and how we can reduce the threat they represent.

TABLE 1.2 Petroleum Imports by Country of Origin, 1972–2001

Year	Persian Gulf nations	Selected OPEC countries: Iraq	Nigeria	Saudi Arabia	Venezuela	Total OPEC	Selected Non-OPEC countries: Canada	Colombia	Mexico	Norway	United Kingdom	Total non-OPEC	Total imports	Imports from Persian Gulf nations as share of total imports	Imports from OPEC as share of total imports
	Thousand barrels per day														
1972	471	4	251	190	959	2,063	1,108	5	21	0	9	2,678	4,741	9.9	43.5
1973	848	4	459	486	1,135	2,993	1,325	9	16	1	15	3,263	6,256	13.6	47.8
1974	1,039	0	713	461	979	3,280	1,070	5	8	1	8	2,832	6,112	17.0	53.7
1975	1,165	2	762	715	702	3,601	846	9	71	17	14	2,454	6,056	19.2	59.5
1976	1,840	26	1,025	1,230	700	5,066	599	21	87	36	31	2,247	7,313	25.2	69.3
1977	2,448	74	1,143	1,380	690	6,193	517	17	179	50	126	2,614	8,807	27.8	70.3
1978	2,219	62	919	1,144	646	5,751	467	20	318	104	180	2,612	8,363	26.5	68.8
1979	2,069	88	1,080	1,356	690	5,637	538	18	439	75	202	2,819	8,456	24.5	66.7
1980	1,519	28	857	1,261	481	4,300	455	4	533	144	176	2,609	6,909	22.0	62.2
1981	1,219	(s)	620	1,129	406	3,323	447	1	522	119	375	2,672	5,996	20.3	55.4
1982	696	3	514	552	412	2,146	482	5	685	102	456	2,968	5,113	13.6	42.0
1983	442	10	302	337	422	1,862	547	10	826	66	382	3,189	5,051	8.8	36.9

1984	506	12	216	325	548	2,049	630	8	748	114	402	3,388	5,437	9.3	37.7
1985	311	46	293	168	605	1,830	770	23	816	32	310	3,237	5,067	6.1	36.1
1986	912	81	440	685	793	2,837	807	87	699	60	350	3,387	6,224	14.7	45.6
1987	1,077	83	535	751	804	3,060	848	148	655	80	352	3,617	6,678	16.1	45.8
1988	1,541	345	618	1,073	794	3,520	999	134	747	67	315	3,882	7,402	20.8	47.6
1989	1,861	449	815	1,224	873	4,140	931	172	767	138	215	3,921	8,061	23.1	51.4
1990	1,966	518	800	1,339	1,025	4,296	934	182	755	102	189	3,721	8,018	24.5	53.6
1991	1,845	0	703	1,802	1,035	4,092	1,033	163	807	82	138	3,535	7,627	24.2	53.7
1992	1,778	0	681	1,720	1,170	4,092	1,069	126	830	127	230	3,796	7,888	22.5	51.9
1993	1,782	0	740	1,414	1,300	4,273	1,181	171	919	142	350	4,347	8,620	20.7	49.6
1994	1,728	0	637	1,402	1,334	4,247	1,272	161	984	202	458	4,749	8,996	19.2	47.2
1995	1,573	0	627	1,344	1,480	4,002	1,332	219	1,068	273	383	4,833	8,835	17.8	45.3
1996	1,604	1	617	1,363	1,676	4,211	1,424	234	1,244	313	308	5,267	9,478	16.9	44.4
1997	1,755	89	698	1,407	1,773	4,569	1,563	271	1,385	309	226	5,593	10,162	17.3	45.0
1998	2,136	336	696	1,491	1,719	4,905	1,598	354	1,351	236	250	5,803	10,708	19.9	45.8
1999	2,464	725	657	1,478	1,493	4,953	1,539	468	1,324	304	365	5,899	10,852	22.7	45.6
2000	2,487	620	896	1,572	1,546	5,203	1,807	342	1,373	343	366	6,257	11,459	21.7	45.4
2001^P	2,731	778	854	1,657	1,538	5,447	1,786	280	1,423	327	306	6,172	11,619	23.5	46.9

Source: See endnote 33, DOE..

REFERENCES

1. Rees, M., *Our Final Hour*, Basic Books, New York, 2003.
2. Wars and Conflicts: 1950's to Present; Reunion High, http://www.yearbookhigh.com/history/wars%20and%20conflicts.htm; accessed 10/08/04.
3. Leonhardt, D., Japan and U.S.: Bubble, Bubble, Toil and Trouble, *New York Times*, Oct. 2, 2002. http://www.nytimes.com/2002/10/02; accessed 1/11/03.
4. Berenson, A., The Markets: Stocks; Wall St. down a 3rd Year, Leaving Fewer Optimists, *New York Times*, Jan. 1, 2003.
5. Broder, J.M., California Ups and Downs Ripple in the West, *New York Times*, Jan. 6, 2003. http://www.nytimes.com/2003/01/06; accessed 1/11/03.
6. CNN, States Face Deeper Budget Pressures in '03, Dec. 24, 2002; http://www.cnn.com/2002/ALLPOLITICS/12/24/state.budget.ap/index.html; accessed 1/11/03.
7. CNN, White House Projects Higher Budget Deficit, July 12, 2002; http://www.cnn.com/2002/ALLPOLITICS/07/12/budget.deficit/; accessed 1/11/03.
8. CNN, Greg LaMotte on California's Energy Crisis, Dec. 20, 2000; http://www.cnn.com/2000/US/12/20/lamotte.debrief/; accessed 1/11/03.
9. Pacific Gas and Electric Co., Chapter 11 Reorganization; http://www.pge.com/006_news/current_issues/reorganization/court_docs/index.shtml; accessed 1/11/03.
10. Eichenwald, K., Corporate Conduct: News Analysis: Pushing Accounting Rules to the Edge of the Envelope, *New York Times*, Dec. 31, 2002.
11. CNN, Iraq, Venezuela Push up Oil Price, Jan. 3, 2002; http://www.cnn.com/2003/BUSINESS/01/03/oilprices.update/index.html; accessed 1/11/03.
12. CNN, Sources: Anthrax Possibly Linked to Lab, Oct. 10, 2001; http://www.cnn.com/2001/HEALTH/10/09/gen.anthrax/index.html; accessed 1/10/03.
13. CNN, Bin Laden Hails September 11 Economic Losses, Apr. 18, 2002; http://www.cnn.com/2002/WORLD/asiapcf/central/04/17/bin.laden.tape/index.html; accessed 10/07/04; and Timeline: A Year of War, Anxiety and Questions, *New York Times*, Sep. 11, 2002; http://query.nytimes.com/search/article-page.html?res=9E00E0D91731F932A2575AC0A9649C8B63.

14. Anon., Traces Lead to Terror Cells, High-Technology Tactics Employed, *Columbia Daily Tribune*, Sep. 16, 2002; http://archive.columbiatribune.com/2002/sep/20020916news009.asp; accessed 10/07/04.

15. CNN, Blair Warns of WMD Terrorism Threat, Mar. 5, 2004; http://www.cnn.com/2004/WORLD/europe/03/05/uk.blair/index.html.

16. NEXT Computer Cube; available on-line at http://www.lowendmac.com/next/cube.html; accessed 10/07/04.

17. U.S. Department of Defense, Proliferation: Threat and Response, Jan. 2001; http://www.defenselink.mil/pubs/ptr20010110.pdf; accessed 5/15/04.

18. CNN, Pakistan Assures U.S. of No N. Korea "Nuke Deal," Nov. 25, 2002; http://www.cnn.com/2002/WORLD/asiapcf/south/11/25/pakistan.nkorea/index.html; accessed 1/11/03.

19. Prelas, M., Soviet High-Tech Bonanza, *Christian Science Monitor*, Feb. 3, 1992; http://www.csmonitor.com/cgi-bin/getasciiarchive?tape/92/feb/day03/03181; accessed 1/11/03.

20. CNN, Pyongyang's Missile Program, Dec. 11, 2002; http://www.cnn.com/2002/WORLD/asiapcf/east/12/10/nkorea.scuds/index.html; accessed 1/12/03.

21. Pringle, L., *Chemical and Biological Warfare: The Cruelest Weapons*, Enslow Publishers, Berkeley Heights, NJ, 1993.

22. Ghosh, T., Prelas, M., Viswanath, D., and Loyalka, S., *The Science and Technology of Terrorism and Counterterrorism*, Marcel Dekker, New York, 2002.

23. Pomfret, J., China Ponders New Rules of "Unrestricted War," *Washington Post*, Aug. 8, 1999. http://www.washingtonpost.com/1999/08/08; accessed 10/07/04.

24. CNN, Sources: U.S. to Accuse Iran of Sponsoring Terrorism, Apr. 7, 1998; http://www.cnn.com/WORLD/meast/9804/07/iran.terrorism/index.html; accessed 1/14/03.

25. CNN, Sources: Feds Raid Islamic Charity Groups, Dec. 15, 2001; http://www.cnn.com/2001/US/12/14/inv.raid.charity/index.html; accessed 1/14/03.

26. Kaplan, D. and Whitelaw, K., Saddam's Secret Weapon? *U.S. News & World Report*, Jan. 20, 2003. http://www.washingtonpost.com/2003/01/20; accessed 10/07/04.

27. Federal Bureau of Investigation, statement for the record of J.T. Caruso, acting assistant director, Counterterrorism Division, Federal Bureau of Investigation, on Al-Qaeda international, Dec. 18, 2001; http://www.fbi.gov/congress/congress01/caruso121801.htm; accessed 1/14/03.

28. CNN, transcript of Powell's U.N. presentation, Feb. 6, 2003; http://www.cnn.com/2003/US/02/05/sprj.irq.powell.transcript.09/index.html; accessed 2/6/03.

29. CNN, U.S. Launches Cruise Missiles at Saddam, Mar. 20, 2003; http://www.cnn.com/2003/WORLD/meast/03/19/sprj.irq.main/index.html; accessed 6/16/03.

30. CNN, Balancing Life and Liberty: Danger to Civil Liberties When Security Is Strengthened, Sep. 11, 2002; http://www.cnn.com/2002/LAW/09/10/ar911.civil.liberties/index.html; accessed 1/15/03.

31. Rischard, J.F., *High Noon*, Basic Books, New York, 2002.

32. See note 31 above.

33. U.S. Department of Energy, Annual Energy Review; http://www.eia.doe.gov/emeu/aer/diagrams/diagram1.html; accessed 1/16/03.

34. Hubbert Peak of Oil Production, The Coming Global Oil Crisis; http://www.hubbertpeak.com/; accessed 10/07/04.

35. New York Times, Subsidizing Terrorism, *New York Times*, Dec. 4, 2002; http://query.nytimes.com/gst/abstract.html?res=F70D16FC3C5F0C778CDDAB0994DA404482; accessed 10/07/04.

36. CNN, Spain Charity Terror Link Alleged, Dec. 8, 2002; http://www.cnn.com/2002/WORLD/europe/12/08/spain.alqaeda/index.html; accessed 1/17/03.

2

What Is a Weapon of Mass Destruction?

A weapon of mass destruction (WMD) is capable of inflicting great numbers of human casualties over a large area. We give this special status to certain nuclear, biological, and chemical weapons. This chapter provides a description, brief history, and synopsis of destructive potential for each of these WMD classes.[1]

2.1 NUCLEAR WEAPONS

When Dr. Albert Einstein first presented his special theory of relativity, which predicted that great amounts of energy could be produced by nuclear reactions ($E = mc^2$), little did the world appreciate the full implications of this relationship. Einstein's formula predicted that when certain particles are split, or fissioned, some of the original mass is transformed into energy. In 1937, German physical chemist Otto Hahn, along with coworkers Fritz Straussman and Lise Meitner, observed that neutron bombardment of uranium resulted in multiple radioactive species. They observed the formation of fission fragments. Meitner was Jewish and fled to Stockholm to escape Hitler's anti-Semitic policies. Meitner was the theoretical inspiration for the work on fission, but once in Stockholm, she had great difficulty in continuing her collaboration with Hahn and Straussman. She and colleague O.R. Frish described the possibility of nuclear fission which was published in *Nature* on February 11, 1939. The discovery of fission was the catalyst for the race to develop nuclear weapons. Word of the discovery of fission spread quickly. Dr. Niels Bohr went to the U.S. for a conference and discussed the possibility of fission with U.S. scientists.

2.1.1 Pursuit of the Fission Bomb

Hungarian-American physicist Dr. Leo Szilard began to think about the possibility of a nuclear chain reaction as early as 1934.[2] Shortly after the discovery of fission, Szilard was concerned that Germany could use the nuclear chain reaction to develop a powerful weapon. Given his status as a Jewish refugee from Nazi Germany, he was fully aware of the danger posed by a potential fission bomb in the hands of the Nazis. Szilard discussed his fears with physicist Eugene Wigner and Edward Teller. They sought to bring their concerns to the attention of the U.S. government. In order to do so, they enlisted the help of the world's most prominent scientist, Albert Einstein. They were able to persuade Einstein to write a letter to President Franklin D. Roosevelt. By 1941 Roosevelt had agreed to fund a massive research program to develop a weapon based on nuclear fission. Roosevelt approved the order on December 6, 1941, the day before the Japanese attacked Pearl Harbor.

The beginning of mankind's trek into nuclear energy began with fear while most of the world was embroiled in World War II. The Manhattan Project was the code name chosen for the development work leading to the first atomic bomb. The Manhattan Project was named for the U.S. Army Corps of Engineers, Manhattan Engineer District, because much of the initial research was done in New York City.

The major hurdle of the Manhattan Project was to produce enough fissile material to produce a weapon. The project pursued two parallel production paths. One path focused on development of a uranium device, while the other pursued a concept based on the newly discovered element, plutonium. The two suitable materials were uranium-235, a naturally occurring isotope of uranium, and plutonium-239. In nature, uranium consists of three isotopes, uranium-238 (99.2745%), uranium-235 (0.720%), and uranium-234 (0.0055%). In order to procure uranium with a high enough percentage of uranium-235 to be useful in a fission weapon, a very elaborate technology for isotope separation had to be developed. Plutonium-239, on the other hand, is not found in nature but can be produced in a nuclear reactor by bombarding uranium-238 with neutrons.[3] We illustrate this process by a notation used by scientists and engineers. An arrow (→) indicates the direction of the reaction or process. On the left side of the arrow are the reactants. In Equation 2.1, uranium-238 (U is the symbol for uranium and the shorthand representation for the isotope is U^{238}) absorbs a neutron (n is the symbol for a neutron) for the first half of the process, showing the reactants and the direction of the reaction:

$$U^{238} + n \xrightarrow[\text{Reactants...Direction}]{} \tag{2.1}$$

On the right side of the arrow, the products from the reaction — neptunium-239 (Np is the symbol for neptunium and the shorthand representation for the isotope is Np^{239}), a beta particle (β, an energetic electron), and an antineutrino (ν) are shown:

$$U^{238} + n \xrightarrow[\text{Reactants...Products}]{} Np^{239} + \beta + \nu \tag{2.2}$$

Neptunium-239 subsequently undergoes beta decay to form plutonium-239 (Pu^{239}).

$$Np^{239} \xrightarrow[\text{Reactants...Products}]{} Pu^{239} + \beta + \nu \tag{2.3}$$

To produce plutonium-239, a source of neutrons and uranium-238 is needed. A nuclear reactor is used to provide the large source of neutrons needed for plutonium-239 production.

A major challenge for the Manhattan Project was separation of the different isotopes found in natural uranium. The project evaluated three approaches:[4]

1. Magnetic separation, which exploits a force derived from the interaction of magnetic fields with charged particles, called the Lorentz force, to separate particles of differing mass
2. Gaseous diffusion, which is based on a process called "diffusion" that is related to particle motion through matter, which varies for particles of different mass
3. Gas centrifuge, which generates large centripetal forces to separate particles of different mass using high-speed spinning centrifuges

The Manhattan Project concluded that the gaseous diffusion approach was the most expeditious and reliable method to use for isotope separation (see Chapter 3). Gaseous diffusion used uranium hexafluoride, which is a gas at relatively low temperatures, as feedstock. The gaseous uranium was passed through a cascade of porous filters that allowed the lighter uranium-235 isotope to transport at a faster rate than the uranium-238 isotope. The diffusion plant, located at Oak Ridge, TN, produced a sufficient amount of "bomb grade" highly enriched uranium (HEU) after one year of production to build a nuclear weapon.

Plutonium production required the development and construction of the first large-scale nuclear reactor. The fission of uranium-235 contained in natural uranium produced, on average, more than two neutrons and two fission fragments. The actual average number of neutrons produced is about 2.44. The reason for the fraction is that there are a number of possible products. Some will release two neutrons or fewer, and some will release three neutrons or more. On average, this number is between two and three. These neutrons are capable of transmuting some uranium in the reactor core into plutonium. Equation 2.4 illustrates this reaction.

$$ {}^{A}_{N}X_{Z} + n_{th} \rightarrow {}^{A_1}_{N_1}f_{lZ_1} + {}^{A_2}_{N_2}f_{hZ_2} + \vartheta n_{fast} \tag{2.4} $$

where

- ϑ is the average number of neutrons given off per fission reaction (for U-235, ϑ is 2.44)
- n_{th} is the number of thermal neutrons (neutrons that have slowed down to the point of thermal equilibrium with the temperature of the reactor)
- n_{fast} is the number of fast (at greater energy than "thermal") neutrons
- A is the atomic mass number of an atom's nucleus
- N is the number of neutrons in the nucleus
- Z is the number of protons in the nucleus
- X is the fissile material (U-235, U-233, and Pu-239)
- f_l is the light fission fragment
- f_h is the heavy fission fragment

Szilard exploited observations that more than one neutron was produced for each uranium atom fissioned to come up with the idea of the chain reaction. Consider a simple method of neutron bookkeeping: if one thermal neutron initiates fission, and on average each fission generates an additional 2.44 neutrons, then each of these neutrons should result in fissions. Using this model, about six neutrons would be produced in the second generation. The third generation would produce about 14 neutrons. The neutron population grows geometrically from generation to generation. Mathematically, the growth of neutrons in one generation can be predicted by the formula

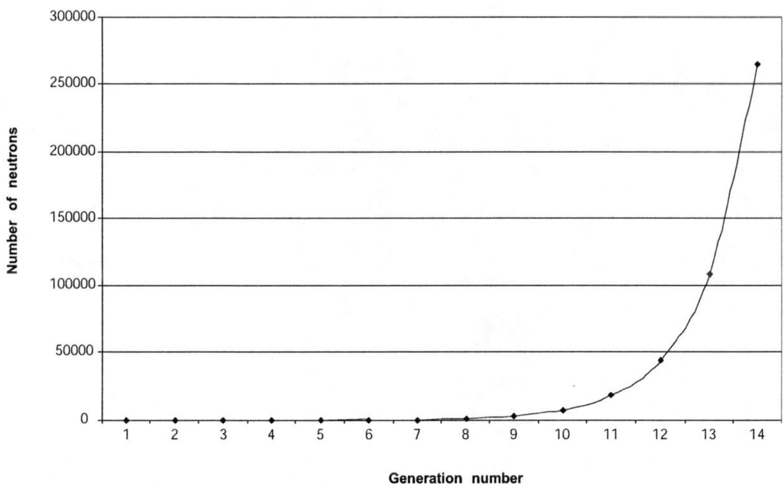

FIGURE 2.1 Geometrical buildup of neutrons in a chain reaction without neutron losses (e.g., k = 2.44).

$$N = 2.44^n \tag{2.5}$$

where

N is the number of neutrons in the generation
n is the number of the generation

Figure 2.1 illustrates how quickly the neutron population can increase. Szilard coupled geometric neutron growth with the very short time period between generations, about 1/10,000,000 of a second. Szilard predicted that considerable amounts of energy could be released over a very short time period when the amount of energy per fission was multiplied by the large number of total fissions possible during a chain reaction.

In practice, not all fission neutrons from one generation will result in fission in the subsequent generation because nuclear systems are not made up entirely of fissile materials. These systems, such as reactors or weapons, include structural and moderating materials. A moderating material is used to slow down a neutron through a series of elastic collisions (billiard ball type collisions). A neutron may be adsorbed into one of these materials (or be absorbed in the fuel) and not fission, or it may be lost by leaking outside the system. Nuclear engineers call the ratio of the number of neutrons in one generation to the past generation the "neutron multiplication factor," k_{eff}.

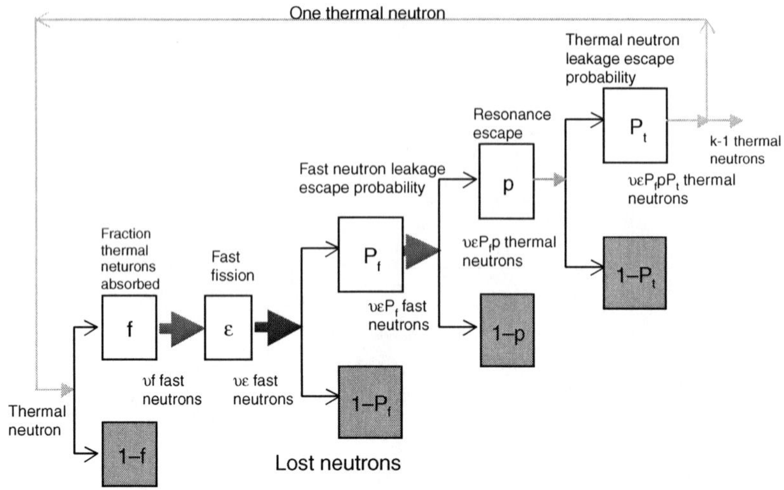

FIGURE 2.2 The neutron balance in a nuclear reactor. For the chain reaction to continue, the value k_{eff} must be greater than or equal to one. If k were less than one, the chain reaction would die.

Neutrons born from fission have a high energy. These high energy neutrons are often referred to as "fast neutrons," and they can collide with other materials in the nuclear system. As the neutrons collide, they lose energy or slow down. Neutrons will eventually slow down to the point where the neutron energy is at "thermal equilibrium" with the surroundings. These neutrons are referred to as "thermal neutrons." In some nuclear systems, such as most power reactors, the probability that the neutron will cause a subsequent fission increases dramatically as the neutron slows down, or approaches "thermal" energy. Many reactor systems are designed to maximize the population of thermal neutrons. Figure 2.2 illustrates how a thermal nuclear system works. Nuclear reactors are designed with "moderating" materials to provide a great number of elastic collisions to slow down neutrons and increase the population of thermal neutrons. Other nuclear systems, such as a nuclear weapon or a "fast" reactor, are designed to utilize neutrons at higher energies.

In describing the chain reaction, we use a mathematical relationship called the "six factor formula" shown in Equation 2.6 below.

$$k_{eff} = \nu f p \varepsilon P_f P_t \tag{2.6}$$

where

ν is the number of fast neutrons produced by the fission of a fissile atom

f is the fraction of thermal neutrons absorbed in the fissile fuel

p is the probability that a fast neutron will slow down without being first absorbed by another material

ε is a multiplier for additional fast neutrons that are created by fast fission

P_f is the probability that a fast neutron will not leak out of the system volume

P_t is the probability that a thermal neutron will not leak out of the system volume

The neutron multiplication factor, k_{eff}, provides a measure of how the neutron population in a nuclear system changes over time (measured in generations). If k_{eff} is greater than one, then the rate of fissions geometrically increase. If k_{eff} is equal to one, then the reaction is self-sustaining, with the fission rate remaining constant.[5] If k_{eff} is less than one, then the number of neutrons in each generation will decrease, and the neutron population is reduced with time. A nuclear power reactor operates with a k_{eff} equal to one. During start-up, reactor operators will maintain a k_{eff} slightly greater than one until the reactor reaches full power. After reaching full power, k_{eff} is reduced and held at a value of one. On the other hand, a nuclear explosive is designed to have a k_{eff} greater than 1.5. The neutron buildup with a multiplication factor greater than one is illustrated in Figure 2.3.

The power in a nuclear reactor is controlled by neutron absorbers. These controls are typically in the form of absorber rods or chemicals added to the reactor coolant. When the controls are inserted into the nuclear reactor, the k_{eff} value of the reactor is reduced to less than one. When the control rods are removed, then k_{eff} is greater than one, and the reactor is able to increase the number of reactions that take place or the power given off. When the reactor reaches a desired power level, the controls are adjusted so that the value of k_{eff} is one and the reactor sustains itself. The controls allow the operator to adjust or shut down the reactor power level.

The first nuclear reactor used natural uranium as fuel. Forming a critical system with natural uranium was difficult due to the relatively low amount of the fissile U^{235} isotope. For natural uranium

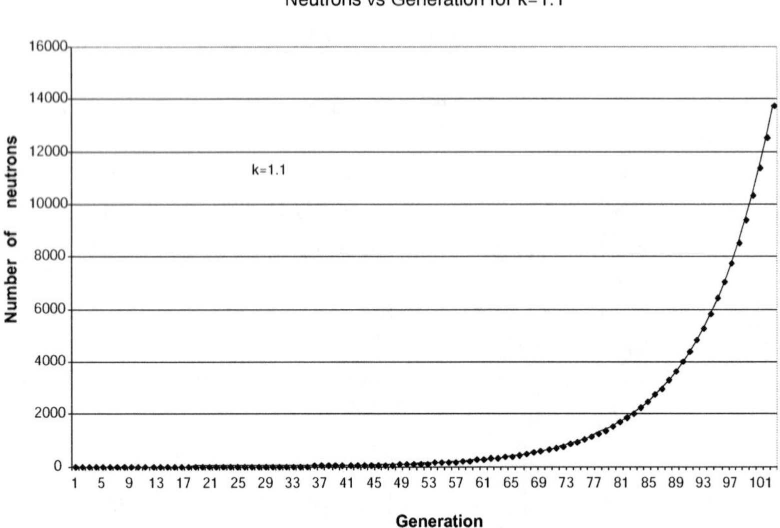

FIGURE 2.3 Number of neutrons in a generation for k = 1.1.

to support a self-sustaining nuclear reaction, several material science developments were required. One was to produce highly purified materials such as uranium metal and graphite that would minimize the number of neutrons lost due to absorption by materials other than the uranium fuel. Enrico Fermi and his colleagues were able to engineer the appropriate materials. Fermi undertook this challenge at the University of Chicago. He and his colleagues constructed and operated the first atomic pile in a volleyball field beneath the University of Chicago's sports stadium on December 2, 1942. The reactor consisted of highly purified graphite blocks, highly purified uranium fuel rods, and boron control rods.

Szilard explored how the energy from a large number of fission reactions could be used in a weapon.[6] Chemical explosives such as trinitrotoluene (TNT), cyclotrimethylenetrinitramine, (RDX), and high melting explosive (HMX) give off a relatively small amount of energy per chemical reaction. Fission reactions generated large amounts of energy, about 100 million times greater per reaction than chemical explosives. With a fissile assembly having a k_{eff} greater than one, it is possible to induce a huge number of reactions in several hundred neutron generations that would give off an enormous amount of energy. The two challenges facing the early weapon designers were (a) how to produce the quantity of fissile material necessary to sustain a chain reaction and (b) how to construct an assembly that could be held together long enough to produce the large number of reactions needed to maximize the energy release before blowing apart.

The Manhattan Project explored the use of two fissile materials: highly enriched uranium (HEU) and plutonium (Pu^{239}). HEU was an easier material to use in nuclear weapon design due to a higher fission rate and better physical properties. The HEU-type nuclear weapon used a "gun-type" detonator and consisted of two subcritical assemblies (each with $k_{eff} < 1$). The weapon was detonated by quickly bringing both assembles together, at about 1000 m/sec, to create a supercritical mass ($k_{eff} > 1$).[7] Working for the Manhattan Project, Richard Feynman calculated the mass of HEU needed to create a supercritical mass to be about 50 kg (110 lb).[8] The power of a large explosive was typically measured in equivalent tons of TNT. To see how nuclear explosives differ from conventional explosives, consider that the chemical explosive used to destroy the Alfred Murrah Federal Building in Oklahoma City was equivalent to about one-half ton of TNT. This explosive damaged a circular area with a radius of 150 ft. In contrast, the "Little Boy" nuclear bomb used to attack Hiroshima near the end of World War II had about 62 kg of HEU and produced an explosion of 17,000 tons (17 kton) of TNT.

Little Boy destroyed an area within a radius of one-half mile, measuring from the center of the explosion, by inducing a temperature of several thousand degrees Celsius.[9] The shock wave and high temperatures within 0.5 to 1 mile of the center destroyed all of the aboveground buildings and caused a 90% fatality rate. The shock wave within 1 to 1.75 miles caused large structures to collapse and bridges and roads to be damaged. In this region the mortality rate was 60%, with a morbidity rate of 30%. Severe heat damage resulted within a radius of 1.75 to 2.5 miles, with 50% fatalities and 45% injuries. Many fatalities occurred due to suffocation from the large number and intensity of secondary fires. Severe fire and wind damage occurred within a radius of 2.5 to 3 miles. Homes were damaged by the blast, and people suffered second- and third-degree burns. All told, about 66,000 people were instantly killed, and 69,000 people were injured. The residual effects of radiation also caused additional casualties.

Plutonium was the second fissile material explored by the Manhattan Project for use in a weapon design. The Manhattan Project built specially designed nuclear reactors at Hanford, WA, that produced the needed Pu^{239}. The gun-type detonation mechanism used for HEU was not applicable for a plutonium weapon due to a higher spontaneous fission rate. The plutonium had to be spherically imploded by a shock wave using conventional chemical explosives.[10] Richard Feynman and Hans Bethe estimated the supercritical mass of Pu^{239} to be about 16 kg (35.2 lb). The amount of needed plutonium was reduced to about 10 kg (22 lb) by blanketing uranium around the outside of the weapon. The plutonium bomb was called "Fat Man" by the Manhattan Project. A plutonium weapon was used for the first nuclear weapon test in Trinity, NM, on July 16, 1945, and in the subsequent attack on Nagasaki, Japan, on August 9, 1945. Fat Man yielded about 20 kton and produced damage similar to the described attack on Hiroshima. About 39,000 people died instantly and 25,000 were injured in Nagasaki. The implosion mechanism is the method used as a trigger for most modern nuclear weapons.

The U.S. spent $1.8 billion ($20 billion in 2004 dollars) on Manhattan Project activities between the years 1942 and 1946 to develop and build the first nuclear weapons. The Brookings Institute estimated that an investment of $1 billion to $9 billion would be needed today for a rogue nation to establish a program leading to production of a nuclear weapon.[11] The high cost of nuclear technology is the most effective proliferation deterrent for the weapon. This investment is too great for many countries to make. However, when compared with U.S. oil purchases of millions of barrels per day at up to $53 per barrel from Middle Eastern countries, the potential exists for diversion of these resources toward the development of nuclear weapons. The U.S. government has expressed concern over the evolution of nuclear programs in Iraq and Iran driven by oil revenues. As Middle Eastern oil revenues increase, so does the possibility that funds may be diverted toward the development or acquisition of WMDs. Also, countries that possess WMD technology or delivery systems, such as China, the Russian Federation, North Korea, and Pakistan, are a proliferation risk because they have been willing to sell critical technology in the past. Over the next few decades, as oil production declines and oil prices increase, the threat of some of this cash going into the WMD marketplace will increase, adversely affecting political stability.

2.1.2 Thermonuclear Weapons

The size of modern thermonuclear weapons has been reduced enough to fit into the payload volume of a missile (Figure 2.4).[12]

FIGURE 2.4 Multiple Independently Targetable Reentry Vehicle (MIRV). National Security Archive. http://www.gwu.edu/~nsarchiv/nsa/NC/mirv/mirv.html. Originally from Los Almano National Laboratory.

The development path to reduce these powerful weapons into such small packages was a difficult task. The history of thermonuclear weapons development in the U.S. illustrates the complexity of the technology.[13] Fermi and Teller began discussing the idea of using an atomic bomb to trigger a fusion bomb in the fall of 1941 while both worked on the Manhattan Project. Teller proposed using deuterium to construct a superbomb. Klaus Fuchs and John von Neumann built on this idea in May 1946 by proposing a two-core bomb, a key concept used in the design of modern thermonuclear weapons. In the two-core model, a fission core was used to ignite a deuterium-tritium fusion package. This concept led the two scientists to write a classified patent. Later in August, Teller proposed the "alarm clock" design using layered spherical shells of fission and deuterium-tritium fusion fuels. The alarm-clock design was a forerunner to another important concept later used in modern thermonuclear weapons design, the use of solid fusion fuel. Teller and Stunislas Ulam proposed that solid lithium deuteride (LiD) could be used as the fusion core. A third key concept was proposed in 1951, when Teller and Stanislaw Ulam added a two-stage system separating the fission and fusion cores. Radiation from the fission core was used to ignite the fusion core by a lensing effect through a conductive helix. By June, Teller and Frederic de Hoffmann had modified the approach by using lithium-6 deuteride (^{6}LiD) as the fusion fuel. Adapting the solid lithium deuteride fuel significantly reduced the size and weight from the cryogenically cooled (below –253°C) liquid deuterium-tritium system deployed in early tests.

The U.S. detonated the first thermonuclear bomb, "Ivy Mike," in November 1952. Ivy Mike used a cryogenically cooled deuterium-tritium fusion core employing the Teller–Ulam principle of separate staging. A fission bomb was used as the primary stage to trigger the liquid-deuterium fusion-fuel secondary stage. Ivy Mike yielded 10.4 million tons (10.4 Mton) of TNT, with 8 Mton coming from fission reactions and 2.4 Mton from fusion reactions. This device required a huge cryogenic refrigeration system and was far too large and heavy to be carried by conventional delivery systems, such as aircraft. The race to shrink the size of thermonuclear weapons became imperative due to gains within the Soviet Union's thermonuclear bomb program.

Subsequent development focused on reducing the weapon size by using a solid lithium deuteride fusion core. In March 1954, the "Bravo" device used LiD with 40% ^{6}Li along with the Teller–Ulam separate-staging design. In May 1956, the "Cherokee" test used pure ^{6}LiD for the fusion core along with the Teller-Ulam staging design. The Cherokee test demonstrated that the device could be dropped from an airplane. The U.S. continued to refine weapon designs and reduce the size of such weapons. Nuclear weapons have been made small enough to fit into the payload section of missiles and artillery shells.

The U.S. is a signatory of the Non-Proliferation Treaty (NPT).

2.1.3 USSR Nuclear Weapons Program

The Soviet Union began working on fission in 1938. Soviet scientists Zel'dovich and Khariton published a series of papers in 1939–1941 that laid the groundwork for later Soviet atomic weapons development. However, these early efforts received little support or interest from the Soviet government. In 1943, during World War II, physicist Igor Vasilievich Kurchatov convinced Stalin to begin a Soviet weapons program. Under Kurchatov, the program began modestly by sifting through reports collected by Soviet intelligence about the Manhattan Project.

The USSR commitment to develop an atomic bomb came immediately after the Hiroshima and Nagasaki attacks in August 1945. Stalin appointed Lavrenty Beria to head the project, with Igor Kurchatov as scientific director. The first Soviet nuclear reactor went critical on Christmas Day 1946, at the Kurchatov Institute in Moscow. The graphite-moderated F1, or Physics-1, reactor was based on the Hanford prototype 305 design and operated at 10 watts (W). The F1 prototype was used as the basis for subsequent large plutonium production reactors. The Soviets obtained detailed information about the U.S. production reactors and weapon design specifications through extensive use of espionage. The Soviets detonated their first nuclear weapon in August 1949. The weapon, called "First Lightning," was a plutonium bomb very similar in design to the U.S. Fat Man.[14]

The USSR thermonuclear superbomb program developed in parallel with the atomic weapons program. Again, espionage played a key part in the Soviet program. In September 1947, Klaus Fuchs betrayed U.S. thermonuclear bomb secrets by passing them along to a Soviet KGB agent named Feklisov. By December, Ya Zeldovich had developed the theory for a thermonuclear device using liquid D and LiD. During the following March, Fuchs passed a copy of the 1946 Fuchs–von Neumann patent to the KGB agent. Soviet scientist Andrey Sakharov probably used this information in his "Sloika" design, which was remarkably similar to Teller's "alarm clock." By January 1949, Sakharov had also developed a preliminary design for a two-stage thermonuclear device. Expanding upon the Sloika device, Vitali Ginzburg proposed the use of ^{6}LiD in the Sloika design in March 1949. Soviet Test No. 4, or Joe-4, tested the Sloika device and validated the ^{6}LiD approach on August 12, 1953. Even though the U.S. had demonstrated a hydrogen bomb in November 1952, the USSR claimed to have been the first to test a modern hydrogen bomb. The basis for their claim was that they were the first to use ^{6}LiD in a weapon.

By January 1954, Ya Zeldovich and Sakharov had developed a two-stage design. The design used energy from an atomic explosion to compress the fusion core. In April, Sakharov proposed a modification that achieved compression of the fusion core by radiation energy from the primary core. In November 1955, the RDS-37 device, using a two-stage ^{6}LiD design, was successfully deployed from an aircraft. In May 1956, six months later, the U.S. air-dropped a superbomb. At this point, the weapons designers' strategy focused on miniaturizing so that the hydrogen bomb could be carried on airplanes and missiles.

The USSR is a signatory of the Non-Proliferation Treaty.

2.1.4 British Nuclear Weapons Program

On January 8, 1947, Prime Minister Attlee headed a six-member committee that recommended Britain proceed with an atomic weapons program.[15] William G. Penney led the effort. Penney had been part of the British team that assisted with the Manhattan Project during World War II. The first British reactor went critical at Windscale in October 1950. The first fission weapon, named "Hurricane," was detonated on October 3, 1952. The British tested their first hydrogen bomb, named "Grapple 1" or "Short Granite," on May 15, 1957.

The U.K. is a signatory of the Non-Proliferation Treaty.

2.1.5 French Nuclear Weapons Program

The French had an active group of nuclear physicists prior to World War II. After WW II, France had to reestablish its nuclear expertise without U.S. or British help. The French sought the help of Israeli scientists who had fled France during the war. On February 13, 1960, the French tested their first fission bomb at Reganne, Algeria. On August 24, 1968, the French tested their first thermonuclear bomb at Fangataufa atoll in French Polynesia.[16]

France is a signatory of the Non-Proliferation Treaty.

2.1.6 China's Nuclear Weapons Program

China began its weapons program after Russia demonstrated its nuclear capability. China's first atomic bomb, Test Number 596, was detonated on October 16, 1964 (U^{235} bomb) at the Lop Nur Test Ground. China's first hydrogen bomb, Test Number 6, was detonated on June 17, 1967, also at the Lop Nur Test Ground.[17]

China is a signatory of the Non-Proliferation Treaty.

2.1.7 South Africa's Nuclear Weapons Program

South Africa developed U^{235} enrichment technology called UCOR during the 1960s and 1970s and began weapons research in 1971. The South Africans used the gun design because of the availability of U^{235} from their enrichment plants and the simplicity of the design. The "Y Plant" was built at Valindaba, next to the Pelindaba Research Center 25 km west of Pretoria, and was capable of enriching 60 kg of 90% U^{235} per year. In 1991 South Africa signed the Non-Proliferation Treaty. In a March 24, 1993, speech, President de Klerk announced that South Africa had produced nuclear weapons and that they had destroyed their arsenal before July 10, 1991, when South Africa joined the Non-Proliferation Treaty.

2.1.8 Israel's Nuclear Weapons Program

The Israeli government has never admitted to having nuclear weapons. On October 5, 1986, the London *Sunday Times* published a story attributable to Mordechai Vanunu, a former technician in Israel's clandestine nuclear program.[18] According to Vanunu,[19] the Israeli Dimona facility was the center of its nuclear weapons activity.[20] Ernst David Bergmann headed the Weizmann Institute of Science's chemistry program in 1949 with a nuclear focus.[21] In the 1950s and 1960s, Israel and France cooperated in their nuclear science programs. Israel's program took shape in October 1956 during the Suez Canal Crisis. Due to close collaboration between Israel and France, France agreed to build an EL-3 type reactor, with plutonium-separation technology, at the Dimona facility. Ground was broken in 1958. Norway sold Israel 20 tons of heavy water in 1959. The heavy water was loaded in 1961, and the Dimona reactor went critical in 1962. The French completed the plutonium-separation facility in 1964. According to the Israeli paper *Ha'aretz* on April 20, 1997,[22] Israel also assisted South Africa in developing nuclear weapons during the early 1980s.

Israel has not a signed the Non-Proliferation Treaty.

2.1.9 India's Nuclear Weapons Program

Driven by border tensions with China and China's pursuit of nuclear weapons, India decided to develop its own nuclear weapons program.[23] India began construction of a plutonium-separation facility during the 1950s at Trombay, near Bombay. The separation plant began operation in 1964. The plutonium probably came from a Canadian-built reactor at the Bhabha Atomic Research Center (BARC), a 40-MW Canadian–Indian heavy-water research reactor (also called "Cirus"). India detonated its first atomic bomb, called the "Smiling Buddha," on May 18, 1974, at Pokhran, Rajasthan Desert, India. India has several CANDU reactors (Canadian deuterium-moderated reactor; see Chapter 3) in addition to the Cirus.

During May 11–15, 1998, India tested several more nuclear weapons and declared itself a nuclear state.[24]

India has not signed the Non-Proliferation Treaty.

2.1.10 Pakistan's Nuclear Weapons Program

Due to strategic concerns generated from the Indian nuclear program, Pakistan initiated the Engineering Research Laboratories (ERL) in 1976.[25] The Pakistani program was based on a domestically engineered centrifuge uranium-enrichment plant. The facility used technology misappropriated from the European uranium centrifuge consortium URENCO (Britain, Germany, and the Netherlands are the participants). Dr. Abdul Qader Khan, who worked for Ultra-Centrifuge Nederland (UCN), the Dutch partner of URENCO, led the Pakistan program. In 1992 Foreign Minister Shahryrar stated that Pakistan had the components necessary to assemble nuclear weapons.

Pakistan has a Chinese-built power reactor. In addition, it has self-engineered a 50-MW heavy water–moderated nuclear reactor now under construction. After India's nuclear weapons tests of May 27–30, 1998, Pakistan also tested nuclear weapons and declared itself to be a nuclear state.[26]

Pakistan has not signed the Non-Proliferation Treaty.

2.1.11 Advanced Abilities

Countries that possess nuclear technology and have signed the Non-Proliferation Treaty are listed in Appendix 2.1

To build a nuclear weapon, a country must possess the financing, the technical expertise, and the industrial infrastructure to succeed. There are a number of countries that have not produced nuclear weapons but have demonstrated the technical capabilities required to produce HEU, nuclear reactors, plutonium-separation capability,[27] and the other necessary ingredients to produce a nuclear weapon. These countries are Germany, Japan, North Korea, South Korea, Taiwan, Ukraine, Canada, and Sweden. One of the most significant issues in 2003 was North Korea's pursuit of nuclear weapons in violation of a 1994 agreement with the U.S.[28] The danger of North Korea's gaining nuclear weapons is that other Asian nations such as Japan,[29] South Korea, and Taiwan could eventually be motivated to develop nuclear weapons of their own.[30] In 1998 North Korea launched the Taepo Dung I missile over

Japan. This action was highly destabilizing and has caused Japan to take a stance seemingly contrary to Article 9 of its constitution which states that it will "forever renounce war as a sovereign right of the nation" and would abandon their right to maintain "land, sea, and air forces, as well as other war potential." This concept had its roots in the 1929 Kellogg–Briand Pact. This pact had 62 signatories, including Russia, the U.S., Japan, China, and most of Europe. The basis of the agreement was to renounce war as a tool of national policy. The agreement was short-lived in that Japan invaded Manchuria in 1931. Shortly thereafter the Italians attacked Ethiopia, and the Germans occupied Austria in 1938. The world was soon to be plunged into World War II.

Article 9 did not stop Japan from spending $40.9 billion in 2002 on their military, the fourth highest military budget in the world. On February 13, 2003, the Japanese Defense Agency director General Shigeru Ishiba declared that Japan would "use military force as a self-defense measure if (North Korea) starts to resort to arms against Japan." Nuclear weapons in Japan are not out of the question, as Deputy Chief Cabinet Secretary Shinzo Abe warned in May 2002 that Japan could possess "small" nuclear weapons. He also stated that "in legal theory Japan could have intercontinental ballistic missiles and atomic bombs." On January 10, 2003, North Korea announced that it was withdrawing from the Non-Proliferation Treaty.[31]

2.1.12 Moderate Abilities

There are a number of countries that possess most of the required capabilities for producing nuclear weapons.[32] These countries include the Netherlands, Switzerland, Australia, Kazakhstan, Argentina, Brazil, Belarus, and Algeria.

2.1.13 Countries Working on Nuclear Weapons

A number of countries are pursuing or have pursued nuclear weapons despite signing the Non-Proliferation Treaty.[33] These countries include Iran, Libya, Iraq, and Syria. The concern arises that if a country is determined to accumulate weapons-grade plutonium or HEU, then it is feasible for that country to assemble a nuclear device.[34]

2.1.13.1 Iran

Iran began a nuclear program during the 1970s with considerable international help. The Chinese built a 27-kW research reactor, a zero-power reactor, and two subcritical reactors at the Isfahan Nuclear Technology Center. The U.S. completed a 5-MW reactor at Tehran University. The Siemens Corporation, from Germany, began the construction of two power reactors near Bushehr that have not been completed.[35] After the Iranian revolution in 1979, the nuclear program was stopped but revived in 1984. Iran tried to reach agreements with Germany, China, and France to finish the construction of the Bushehr reactors. In 1995 Russia signed an agreement with Iran to complete the reactors. This continuing relationship with Russia in the development of nuclear technology has received increasing attention[36] because there is a fear that de facto technology transfer will benefit Iran's ambition to produce nuclear weapons.

In March 2003, Iran announced that it intended to activate a uranium conversion facility near Isfahan. This facility is used to produce uranium hexafluoride gas, which in turn can be used in gas centrifuges to enrich uranium. *Time* magazine reported on March 8, 2003, that "the International Atomic Energy Agency (IAEA) has concluded that Iran actually introduced uranium hexafluoride gas into centrifuges at an undisclosed location to test their ability to work. This would be a blatant violation of the Nuclear Non-Proliferation Treaty, to which Iran is a signatory."[37]

2.1.13.2 Libya

Libya also had an ambition to develop weapons of mass destruction. Indeed, Libya used chemical weapons in its war against Chad in 1987. It acquired a 10-MW research reactor from the USSR in the 1970s. After the fall of the Soviet Union in 1991, Libya developed a strategic relationship with the Ukraine in nuclear technology, hoping to keep its nuclear program active.[38] In 1998 Russia provided Libya with funding to renovate the research reactor.[39] Libya has since agreed to renounce nuclear weapons, but the revelations made by Libya about the progress it had made has stunned experts.[40] Libya had produced small amounts of plutonium, primarily using technologies obtained through the black market. In addition, Libya had a uranium enrichment program that had obtained technologies and materials from Pakistan.

2.1.13.3 Iraq

Iraq had been aggressive in its pursuit of nuclear weapons.[41] Iraq's interest in nuclear technology dates back to the U.S. Atoms for Peace Program in 1956. In 1962 the USSR began building the 2-MW IRT-5000 research reactor at the Al Tuwaitha Nuclear Center located 17 km south of Baghdad. This facility used 80% enriched uranium[42] and was upgraded to run at 5 MW in 1978. The program became a high priority when Saddam Hussein took a personal interest in securing nuclear weaponry. A secret plan was initiated in 1971 to covertly violate the Non-Proliferation Treaty, which Iraq had signed in 1968. The goal of the plan was to secure a reactor capable of producing weapons-grade plutonium. In this quest, Iraq initially approached France in an effort to purchase a 500-MW, graphite-moderated, natural uranium–fueled, gas-cooled reactor (a design used by the U.K. and France to produce weapons-grade plutonium for their nuclear weapons programs). France rejected Iraq's proposal.

Iraq then approached Canada to purchase a CANDU reactor (a heavy water–moderated natural uranium–fueled reactor), the type of reactor that was used by India to produce weapons-grade plutonium for its program. Iraq's proposal was quickly rejected by Canada. The next step in the plan was to approach France to purchase a 40-MW materials–test reactor (fueled with 93% enriched uranium and moderated with light water). This type of reactor produces a large amount of neutrons and is used to test materials and components in high neutron-density environments as a simulation of the effects of nuclear weapons. Iraq planned to use the high neutron density from the reactor to irradiate natural uranium and produce weapons-grade plutonium. The plutonium production potential, using this reactor as an irradiation source, was about 11 kg of plutonium every 150 days. The reactor, called Tammuz-1 or Osirak, was to be built at Al Tuwaitha. In addition, Iraq contracted for a lower-power French-made Isis reactor called Tammuz-2. Both Tammuz-1 and Tammuz-2 used enough 93% enriched uranium fuel to produce a few gun-type nuclear weapons. Iraq contracted with the Italian company SNIA-Techint in 1979 for a pilot plutonium separation and handling facility and a uranium-refining and fuel-manufacturing plant, both of which were not covered by IAEA safeguards. They were also interested in acquiring a production-scale plutonium plant from Italy. Iraq aggressively procured uranium, including 100 tons of natural uranium from Portugal and about 400 tons of uranium from Brazil and Nigeria. The Iraqis also worked on electromagnetic isotope-separation facilities whose extent was unknown until after the post-First Gulf War inspections began.[43]

Israel was concerned about the Iraq nuclear program from the beginning. The Israeli Mossad initiated Operation Sphinx, an attempt to destroy the two reactor cores purchased by Iraq while they were stored at the facilities of the French firm of Constructions Navales et Industrielles de la Méditerranée in La Seyne-Sur-Mer near Toulon. The operation failed to destroy the cores. The damage was not severe, and both cores were repairable. The Mossad is then believed to have assassinated Yehia al-Meshad, the Egyptian nuclear engineer hired by Iraq to supervise the Iraqi-French reactor deal. Failing to deter the Iraqis, the Israelis initiated Operation Babylon, where at 6:35 P.M. local time on June 7, 1981, eight Israeli F-16 Falcons destroyed the Osirak reactor and the other nuclear facilities at Al Tuwaitha. Iraq is estimated to have invested between $10 billion and $20 billion in their nuclear program.[44] During the second Gulf War in 2003, it was determined that very little of the Iraqi nuclear infrastructure had survived the first Gulf War of 1991.[45]

2.1.14 Outlook

Nuclear technology has been sought after by many countries and groups beyond those that we have already discussed (e.g., Syria), and there are countries with nuclear weapons technology and expertise that have been willing to assist others for a price (North Korea, Pakistan, Russia, and China).[46] This is of considerable importance because it demonstrates a clear need for worldwide arms control. As will be discussed in Chapter 7, limiting the spread of WMDs has been a challenge, and the challenge will only continue to grow.

2.2 DIRTY BOMB

Recent claims have surfaced that al Qaeda has the capability of making a dirty bomb.[47] There have been persistent rumors of al Qaeda's nuclear ambitions and capabilities that date back to an article appearing in *Al-Watan Al-'Arabi* (November 13, 1998), which reported that bin Laden had purchased two nuclear warheads from Chechen and Russia mafia for $30 million in cash and 2 tons of Afghan heroin.[48] A dirty bomb uses conventional explosives to spread radioactive materials. According to a United Nations report, Iraq tested a 1-ton radiological bomb in 1987 but gave up on the idea because they could not generate high enough radiation levels to make it deadly. Even though a dirty bomb has not been used as a weapon of terror, there are examples of radiological incidents. First in 1987, at Goiânia, Brazil, highly radioactive cesium was removed from an abandoned clinic. Children noted that the material glowed and believed it to be miraculous. The children and some adults put the radioactive material on their bodies, and in the end, four individuals died. A second incident occurred in 1995, when Chechen separatists placed a canister of highly radioactive fission by-products in a Moscow park. There were no injuries.

2.3 BIOLOGICAL WEAPONS

Biological weapons are made from living organisms, or the toxins generated by living organisms, that cause disease in humans, animals, or plants. These agents can be bacteria, viruses, mycoplasmas, or toxins. The agent may be lethal or incapacitating. Biological agents can be used as proximity antipersonnel agents against humans; they can also be employed as antianimal, antiplant, and antimaterial agents. Antianimal agents are effective against domestic livestock. Antiplant agents are live organisms that cause disease or damage to crops, and antimaterial agents cause damage to or breakdown of materials such as rubber.

Potential bacterial agents that can be used in biological warfare include anthrax (*Bacillus anthracis*), plague (*Yersinia pestis*), tularemia (*Francisella tularensis*), typhoid fever, (*Salmonella typhi*), cholera (*Vibrio cholerae*), Rocky Mountain spotted fever (*Rickettsia rickettsii*), ehrlichiosis (*Ehrlichia chaffeensis*), and Q-fever (*Coxiella burnetti*). There are a host of other microbial agents that could be weaponized, as discussed in the U.S. Army Medical Research Institute of Infectious Disease, *Biological Casualties Handbook*, 2001.[49]

Viral agents require living cells to replicate and are composed of DNA (e.g., smallpox) or RNA (e.g., viral hemorrhagic fevers such as Ebola, Marburg, and Congo-Crimean). Examples of other viral agents are dengue fever, vireo encephalitides (e.g., Venezuelan equine, West Nile, Japanese, western equine, and eastern equine), monkey pox, white pox, Rift Valley fever, Hantaan virus, and yellow fever.

Toxins are poisonous chemicals that are produced by the metabolic activities of living organisms. These agents are organic chemical compounds such as proteins, polypeptides, and alkaloids. Toxins can be categorized in two ways: neurotoxins that affect nerve impulse transmission and cytotoxins that destroy or disrupt cells. Toxins can be derived from bacteria, and they can be either exotoxins (poisons that diffuse out of cells) or endotoxins (poisons contained in the cell but released when the cell disintegrates).

Toxins produced by fungi are called mycotoxins. Mycotoxins are exotoxins that include tichothecenes (which may be the source of the Cambodian yellow rain that occurred before the Vietnam War), aflatoxins (produced by *Aspergillus flavus*), and temorgens (which affect the nervous system). Toxins can be produced from plants such as castor beans (ricin), abrus seeds (abrin), or algae (anatoxin A from blue-green algae). Finally, a number of toxins are generated by animals, including batrachotoxin from a frog, palytoxin from soft corals, saxitoxin from shellfish, comotoxins from sea snails, tetrodotoxin from puffer fish, and venoms from snakes and spiders.

Biological weapons have a long history. In their earliest manifestation, the water or food supplies of an opposing army or of a city under siege were fouled. As early as 600 B.C., the Assyrians poisoned the wells of their enemies with a parasitic fungus called rye ergot that caused the disease ergotism.[50] This disease was incapacitating, leaving towns defenseless when the Assyrians invaded. History has also recorded the use of plague-infected corpses that were catapulted into cities under siege or into the ranks of an opposing army. Later, more-lethal agents were used. For example, smallpox was a threat to the American colonies during the Revolutionary War because the British were known to have employed smallpox against opponents. Scabs from smallpox patients were ground into a powder and then used to infect enemies. Sir Jeffery Amherst, for example, arranged for smallpox-infected blankets and handkerchiefs to be given to Native Americans during the French and Indian War. George Washington was concerned about the smallpox threat and ordered that the Continental Army be vaccinated in 1777. Vaccination against smallpox in 1777 involved the use of a weak strain of the disease.[51] There was a smallpox outbreak in the colonies soon after, but no one under Washington's command caught it. Biological weapons were used at least twice during the American Civil War.[52] During the Confederate retreat from Vicksburg, General Johnson contaminated wells with the carcasses of dead animals to slow down General Sherman's Union troops. A Confederate sympathizer who would later become the governor of Kentucky, Dr. Luke Blackburn, infected clothing with smallpox and yellow fever and then sold the goods to Union troops. In response to these acts, the Union specifically banned the use of poison and infectious disease by its troops.

At the end of the 1800s, Pasteur and others demonstrated that microorganisms were the cause of infectious disease. During World War I, German scientists had isolated some disease-causing microorganisms. A German sympathizer, Dr. Anton Dilger who lived near Washington, DC, grew *Bacillus anthracis* (the cause of anthrax) and *Pseudomonas mallei* (the cause of glanders) from cultures supplied by the imperial German government.[53] German agents posing as dockworkers in Baltimore obtained cultures of these bioagents from Dilger. The cultures were used to infect about 3000 head of livestock that were being shipped to Allied troops in Europe. In addition, several hundred Allied troops were also infected.

As science became more sophisticated during the 20th century, so did the understanding of disease and how it might be exploited as an effective military weapon. The Japanese began a program in 1937 to weaponize biological agents. The operation was housed in a complex in Manchuria called Unit 731. The scientists under the direction of Dr. Ishii Shiro in Unit 731 tested and weaponized plague, cholera, and anthrax under the guise of water purification research. By 1940, Japan had begun testing some of its creations on the civilian population of China, Chinese soldiers, and prisoners of war. In one such experiment, plague-infested rat fleas were dropped from the air, causing an epidemic with 10,000 deaths. Over the course of World War II, as many as 200,000 people died because of the experiments performed by Unit 731 scientists.

The U.S. began its own program in offensive biological weapons to counter potential threats from the German and Japanese programs in 1941, when Secretary of War Henry L. Stimson requested the National Academy of Sciences to review the feasibility of biological weapons. In 1942, the National Academy of Sciences concluded that biological weapons were feasible. Shortly thereafter, George W. Merck formed the War Reserve Service. Camp Detrick in Frederick, Maryland, was chosen as the War Reserve Service's primary site. The site became operational in 1943. In 1944 a site was developed for testing biological agents at the Dugway Proving Grounds in Utah, and a biological-agent production plant was built in Terre Haute, Indiana. From 1947 to 1949, the program conducted small-scale testing of *Bacillus globigii* (BG) and *Serratia marscens* (SM), nonlethal bacterial stimulants for anthrax, at Camp Detrick. In 1950 the biological weapons program was expanded due to the Korean War. By 1951, the U.S. had developed an anticrop bomb that was placed into production. In 1953 Camp Detrick was expanded, and in 1954 a biological weapons production facility in Pine Bluff, Arkansas, became operational. The Pine Bluff facility began producing the weaponized biological agent tularemia in 1954.

A statement in 1955 by Marshal Zhukov that the USSR would use both chemical and biological weapons in future wars provided additional impetus for the U.S. biological weapons program. From 1959 to 1969 the U.S. engaged extensively in the development of biological munitions. The military services submitted requirements for biological weapons munitions including artillery, missiles, and drones. In 1962 the U.S. biological weapons program established the Desert Test Center (DTC) at Ft. Douglas, Salt Lake City, Utah, as a testing ground for these new weapon systems. In the 1964 to 1966 time frame, the U.S. biological weapons program developed the capability to weaponize viruses and rickettsiae in special production plants at Pine Bluff. However, due to overriding military, humanitarian, and political factors, President Nixon renounced the use of biological weapons in 1969. The U.S. unilaterally dismantled its biological weapons program, and between 1970 and 1972, it destroyed all of its biological weapons. The U.S. action was the main force behind the Biological Weapons Convention that was signed in 1972 and ratified in 1975 by the U.S. Congress with the support of President Ford.

Ken Alibeck, a senior official of the USSR biological weapons program, defected to the U.S. in 1992. He provided a detailed description of this highly secretive program in his book *Biohazard*.[54] The USSR, one of the 140 signatories (see Appendix 2.2) of the 1972 biological weapons convention,[55] pledged not to develop, produce, stockpile, or otherwise acquire or retain biological agents for military weapons. The USSR had engaged in a massive developmental program in biological weapons that was far more extensive than the U.S. effort. The Russian program learned to weaponize antibiotic-resistant anthrax, plague, vaccine-resistant smallpox, Marburg variant U (a type of hemorrhagic fever), and many other agents. Facilities were built that were capable of producing tons of these agents on demand. Hundreds of tons of anthrax and dozens of tons of plague and smallpox were stockpiled.

Following the collapse of the USSR, there have been persistent rumors that unemployed scientists from the Soviet biological weapons program have illegally shared some of the program's most sensitive technologies with rogue nations and possibly terrorists. One particularly troubling report is that a former Soviet scientist may have been a conduit for the transfer to Iraq of the Russian vaccine-resistant smallpox virus strain.[56]

Despite the Biological Weapons Treaty of 1972, there are a number of countries that have or are suspected of producing biological weapons, including Iran, Iraq, North Korea, and Syria (see Table 2.1).[57]

Biological weapons may have been used between 1975 and 1983. It is alleged that the countries of Laos and Kampuchea were attacked by planes and helicopters delivering aerosols of several colors (yellow, green, and white).[58] Shortly thereafter, people and animals became ill. Somewhat later, similar clouds of aerosols were observed in Afghanistan. This phenomenon was called yellow rain, but there has been a debate about the analysis of the samples that were recovered for study. Speculation is that this material may have been the tichothecenes mycotoxin.

Two successful incidents of bioterrorism have occurred. The first was in Dalles, Oregon, from September 9 through 18 and from September 19 through October 10, 1984.[59] The salad bars of four area restaurants were contaminated with *salmonella typhmurium*, and 751 cases of salmonella gastroenteritis ensued. This outbreak of salmonellosis was caused by intentional contamination of restaurant food bars by members of the Bhagwan Shree Rajneesh commune, who were attempting to incapacitate voters in a local election.

The second incident involved weapons-grade anthrax spores that were placed in envelopes and mailed to Florida, to Washington, DC, and to New York. On October 2, 2001, Robert Stevens, a photo editor at American Media Inc., checked into a Florida hospital. He died on October 5 from inhalation anthrax.[60] On October 15, 2001, Ernesto Blanco, another American Media employee, was also diagnosed with inhalation anthrax, a rare disease in the U.S.

A memo from NBC to its employees on October 12, 2001, stated that an assistant to NBC news anchor Tom Brokaw had contracted cutaneous anthrax.[61] Anthrax arrived in an envelope addressed to Tom Brokaw at Rockefeller Plaza, and three other people who handled that envelope were found to have nasal contamination. A 7-month-old boy, the son of an ABC news producer, visited his father on September 28 and also developed cutaneous anthrax. An assistant to CBS news anchor Dan Rather tested positive for cutaneous anthrax on October 18. One New York postal

Table 2.1 Biological Weapons Programs around the World (with permission from the Monterey Institute)

Country	Program status	Possible agents	Signed biological weapons convention	Ratified biological weapons convention
Algeria	Research effort, but no evidence of production	Unknown	No	No
Canada	Former program	**Past Weaponized Agents**	04/10/72	09/18/72
	Started: 1941	Anthrax		
	Ended: 1945	**Research**		
		Brucellosis		
		Rocky Mountain spotted fever		
		Plague		
		Tularemia		
		Typhoid fever		
		Yellow fever		
		Bacillary dysentery (shiella)		
		Rinderpest		
		Botulinum toxin		
		Ricin		
China	Likely maintains an offensive program	Unknown	—	11/15/84*
Cuba	Probable research program	Unknown	04/10/72	04/21/76
Egypt	Likely maintains an offensive program	Unknown	No	No
Ethiopia	—	—	04/10/72	05/26/75
France	Former program	Past Weaponized Agents	—	09/27/84*
	Started: 1921	Potato beetle		
	Ended: 1926	**Research**		
	1927–1934 (dormant)	Anthrax		
	Started: 1935	Salmonella		
	Ended: 1940	Cholera		
	1940–1945 (German occupation)	Rinderpest		
		Botulinum toxin		
		Ricin		
Germany	Former program	Past Weaponized Agents	04/10/72	11/28/72
	Started: 1915	Glanders (WW I)		
	Ended: 1918	Anthrax (WW I)		
	1919–1939 (dormant)	**Research**		

* Countries which acceded to the treaty.

Table 2.1 (continued) Biological Weapons Programs around the World (with permission from the Monterey Institute)

Country	Program status	Possible agents	Signed biological weapons convention	Ratified biological weapons convention
	Started: 1940 Ended: 1945	Foot and mouth disease Plague Rinderpest Typhus Yellow fever Potato beetle Potato blight		
India	Research program, but no evidence of production	Unknown	01/15/73	07/15/74
Iran	Likely maintains an offensive program	Anthrax Foot and mouth disease Botulinum toxin Mycotoxins	04/10/72	08/22/73
Iraq	Previously active research and production program; probable reconstitution of program in absence of UN inspections and monitoring	Past Weaponized Agents Anthrax Botulinum toxin Ricin Aflatoxin Wheat cover smut **Research** Brucellosis Hemorrhagic conjunctivitis virus (Enterovirus 70) Rotavirus Camelpox Plague (?) Gas gangrene toxin Current Research Unknown	05/11/72	06/19/91**
Israel	Research, with possible production of agents	Unknown	No	No
Italy	—	—	04/10/72	05/30/75

TABLE 2.1 (continued) Biological Weapons Programs around the World (with permission from the Monterey Institute)

Country	Program status	Possible agents	Signed biological weapons convention	Ratified biological weapons convention
Japan	Former program	Past Weaponized Agents	04/10/72	06/08/82
	Started: 1931	Anthrax		
	Ended: 1945[a]	Plague		
		Glanders		
		Typhoid		
		Cholera		
		Dysentery		
		Paratyphoid		
		Research		
		Gas gangrene		
		Influenza		
		Tetanus		
		Tuberculosis		
		Tularemia		
		Salmonella		
		Typhus		
		Tetrodotoxin		
Libya	Research, with possible production of agents	Unknown	—	01/19/82*
Myanmar (Burma)	—	—	No	No
N. Korea	Research, with possible production of agents	Anthrax Plague Yellow fever Typhoid Cholera Tuberculosis Typhus Smallpox Botulinum toxin[b]	—	03/13/87*
Pakistan	Possible	Unknown	04/10/72	09/25/74
Russia	Research, some work beyond legitimate defense activities likely	Unknown	04/10/72	03/26/75

TABLE 2.1 (continued) Biological Weapons Programs around the World (with permission from the Monterey Institute)

Country	Program status	Possible agents	Signed biological weapons convention	Ratified biological weapons convention
Soviet Union	Former program	Past Weaponized Agents	04/10/72	03/26/75
	Started: 1926	Smallpox		
	Ended: 1992	Plague		
		Tularemia		
		Glanders		
		Venezuelan equine encephalitis		
		Anthrax		
		Q fever		
		Marburg hemorrhagic fever		
		Research		
		Ebola		
		Bolivian hemorrhagic fever		
		Argentinean hemorrhagic fever		
		Lassa fever		
		Japanese encephalitis		
		Russian spring-summer encephalitis		
		Brucellosis		
		Machupo virus		
		Yellow fever		
		Typhus		
		Melioidosis		
		Psittacosis		
		Rinderpest		
		African swine fever virus		
		Wheat stem rust		
		Rice blast		

Table 2.1 (continued) Biological Weapons Programs around the World (with permission from the Monterey Institute)

Country	Program status	Possible agents	Signed biological weapons convention	Ratified biological weapons convention
S. Africa	Former program Started: 1981 Ended: 1993	Anthrax Cholera Plague Salmonella Gas gangrene Ricin Botulinum toxin	04/10/72	11/03/75
S. Korea	—	—	04/10/72	06/25/87
Sudan	Possible research program	Unknown	No	No
Syria	Research, with possible production of agents	Anthrax Botulinum toxin Ricin	04/14/72	No
Taiwan	Possible research program	Unknown	04/10/72	02/09/73
U.K.	Former program Started: 1936 Ended: 1956	Past Weaponized Agents Anthrax Research Plague Typhoid Botulinum toxin	04/10/72	03/26/75
U.S.A.	Former program Started: 1943 Ended: 1969	Past Weaponized Agents Venezuelan equine encephalitis Q fever Tularemia Anthrax Wheat rust Rice blast **Research** Brucellosis Smallpox Eastern and western equine encephalitis Argentinean hemorrhagic fever	04/10/72	03/26/75

TABLE 2.1 (continued) Biological Weapons Programs around the World (with permission from the Monterey Institute)

Country	Program status	Possible agents	Signed biological weapons convention	Ratified biological weapons convention
		Korean hemorrhagic fever Bolivian hemorrhagic fever Lassa fever Glanders Melioidosis Plague Yellow fever Psittacosis Typhus Dengue fever Rift Valley fever Chikungunya virus Blight of potato Rinderpest Newcastle disease Fowl plague Staphylococcal enterotoxin B Botulinum toxin Ricin		
Vietnam	—	—	—	06/20/80*
Yugoslavia, Federal Republic of	None/unknown	None/unknown	04/10/72	10/25/73

[a] Milton Leitenberg, *Biological Weapons in the Twentieth Century: A Review and Analysis,* http://www.fas.org/bwc/papers/bw20th.htm, 2001. Sheldon Harris, "The Japanese biological warfare programme: an overview," in *Biological and Toxin Weapons: Research, Development and use from the Middle Ages to 1945,* Erhard Geissler and John Ellis van Courtland Mood, eds., New York, NY: Stockholm International Peace Research Institute, 1999, p. 127.

Between 1937 and 1945, Japan operated a biological weapons program in occupied Manchuria, United States Army, medical Research Institute of Infectious Diseases (USAMRIID), "Medical Defense Against Biological Warfare Agents Course: History of Biological Warfare," http://www.au.af.mu/au/awc/awcgate/usamriid/bw-hist.htm.

[b] See endnote 50; accessed on 10/07/04.

Source: Monterey Institute of International Studies; available on-line at http://cns.miis.edu/research/cbw/possess.htm. With permission. See reference 57.

worker tested positive for cutaneous anthrax on October 19, and a New York hospital worker died of inhalation anthrax on October 31.

On October 15, 2001, the office of Senate Majority Leader Tom Daschle received a letter in which anthrax spores were detected. A number of Daschle's office staff tested positive for exposure to anthrax. A similar letter sent to Senator Patrick Leahy also proved to contain anthrax on November 16, 2001. Traces of anthrax were found in the mail-handling facilities in the Capitol building. A Virginia postal worker from the Brentwood mail facility in Fairfax, VA (which processed most of the mail bound for Washington, DC), was diagnosed with inhalation anthrax on October 21, 2001. By October 22, 2001, two other postal workers employed at the Brentwood mail facility had died.

The anthrax that was used was weapons-grade and freshly made.[62] As such, the anthrax was a dry, electrostatic-free powder with particle sizes in the 1–7-μm range. This material did not clump and was small enough that it passed between the fibers of the envelopes. As the letters were mechanically processed, anthrax spores leaked from the envelopes and contaminated the postal handling facilities. Secondary contamination occurred in postal facilities in the Washington, DC, area, in Missouri, and in Indiana. A Connecticut woman died of inhalation anthrax on November 21, 2001, likely from secondary contamination. Altogether, 22 individuals developed anthrax, 11 with the inhalation form of anthrax, of whom 5 died.

2.4 CHEMICAL WEAPONS

If we have learned anything from history, it is that someone will eventually use any weapon if there is an advantage to be gained. Our colleague Dr. Dabir Viswanath (emeritus professor of chemical engineering at the University of Missouri) tells us that there is a chemical base to virtually all weapons, including WMDs. Dr. Viswanath points out that if chemicals had been widely available early in mankind's history, they probably would have been used in warfare since the inception of war.

We know, for example, that the Spartans ignited pitch and sulfur to create toxic fumes during the Peloponnesian War around 429 B.C. and during the siege of Delium in 424 B.C.

Greek fire was a secret weapon of the Eastern Roman Emperors. It was invented around 673 A.D. by a Syrian engineer named

Callinicus, a refugee from Maalbek. The formula for Greek fire is lost, so we can only speculate as to its nature. Both Arab and Greek accounts agree that it surpassed all incendiary weapons in destructive power. It has been described as a "liquid fire" that was hurled onto enemy ships from siphons and burst into flame on contact. Accounts of its use indicated that it was inextinguishable and burned even on water. The use of Greek fire in the seventh century was comparable in generating terror akin to nuclear weapons of the present day.

The Chinese employed chemicals in warfare during the Sung Dynasty (960–1279 A.D.), when they manufactured an arsenic-containing smoke for use in battles.

In Western history, the use of chemicals played a role in defeating a besieging Turkish army at the city of Belgrade in 1456 A.D. The defenders ignited rags dipped in poison to create a toxic cloud.

As discussed in the prior section on biological weapons, poisoning of water supplies was used as a military tactic in the American Civil War. The U.S. War Department issued General Order 100 on April 24, 1863, proclaiming a ban on the use of poisons of any type. The problem of chemical warfare was tackled on a global level when, on July 29, 1899, the Hague Convention II declared that "it is especially prohibited ... to employ poison or poisoned arms."

However, the Hague Convention II was disregarded when chemical weapons were used as a means to break the battlefield stalemate between opposing armies during World War I. France began this flirtation when it used tear-gas grenades in 1914. Germany retaliated with tear-gas artillery shells. On April 22, 1915, the Germans attacked the French by releasing chlorine gas at Ypres, France. This surprise attack was so successful that it caused the French line to break, but the Germans failed to take advantage because they did not anticipate the magnitude of the break. On September 25, 1915, the French used chlorine gas against German forces at the Battle of Loos. The Germans launched a projectile attack against U.S. troops with phosgene and chloropicrin shells on February 26, 1918. The U.S. formed a chemical weapons program on June 28, 1918, with the establishment of the Chemical Warfare Service.

The use of chemical weapons in war continued even after the Treaty of Versailles, with the British using adamsite against the Bolsheviks during the Russian Civil War in 1919, and the Spanish using chemical weapons against the Rif rebels in Spanish Morocco from 1922 to 1927.

The League of Nations tried to ban chemical and biological weapons again on June 17, 1925, with the Geneva Protocol for the Prohibition of the Use in War of Asphyxiating, Poisonous, or Other Gases, and of Bacteriological Methods of Warfare. The Geneva Protocol was signed but not immediately ratified by the U.S. and not signed by Japan. Despite the Geneva Protocol, Italy used mustard gas in 1936 against the Ethiopian army during its invasion of Abyssinia.

There are examples of chemical weapons being used in World War II. In 1942 the Nazis used Zyklon-B (hydrocyanic acid) in gas chambers for the mass murder of concentration camp prisoners. In December 1943, while in the port of Bari, Italy, a U.S. ship loaded with mustard gas shells was bombed by the German air force. Eighty-three U.S. troops died from the mustard gas exposure. Germany had manufactured and stockpiled a large amount of tabun and sarin nerve gases by April 1945 but avoided the use of these weapons.

During the Vietnam War, the U.S. used tear gas and four types of defoliants, including Agent Orange, from 1962 to 1970. The U.S. finally ratified the 1925 Geneva Protocol along with the Biological Weapons Convention, which it spearheaded in 1975.

Chemical weapons have been used in several Middle Eastern conflicts. During the Egyptian war with Yemen from 1963 to 1967, Egypt used phosgene and mustard gas. Iraq began using mustard gas in the Iran–Iraq War during August 1983. Iraq also initiated the first-ever use of the nerve agent, tabun, on the battlefield against Iran in 1984. From 1987 to 1988, Iraq used hydrogen cyanide and mustard gas in its Anfal campaign against the Kurds during the Halabja Massacre of 1988. During the Soviet invasion of Afghanistan, the U.S. government alleged, but was not able to substantiate, Soviet use of chemical weapons.

The international community continues to work on controlling chemical weapons. The Chemical Weapons Convention (CWC) was approved by the United Nations on September 3, 1992, and was implemented on April 29, 1997, with a ten-year period to permit disposal of chemical weapons. However, as shown in Table 2.2, there is continuing development of chemical weapons by various countries.

Table 2.2 Chemical Weapons Programs around the World (with permission from the Monterey Institute)

Country	Program status	Possible agents	Signed chemical weapons convention	Ratified chemical weapons convention
Algeria	Possible	Unknown	01/13/93	08/14/95
Canada	Former program	Mustard Phosgene Lewisite	01/13/93	09/26/95
China	Probable	Unknown	01/13/93	04/25/97
Cuba	Possible	Unknown	01/13/93	04/29/97
Egypt	Probable	Mustard Phosgene Sarin VX	No	No
Ethiopia	Probable	Unknown	01/14/93	05/13/96
France	Former program	Mustard Phosgene	01/13/93	03/02/95
Germany	Former program	Phosgene Cyanide Mustard Tabun Sarin Soman	01/13/93	08/12/94
India	Former program	Unknown	01/14/93	09/03/96
Iran	Known	Mustard Sarin Hydrogen cyanide Cyanogen chloride Phosgene	01/13/93	11/03/97
Iraq	Known Probable reconstitution of program in absence of UN inspections and monitoring	Mustard Sarin Tabun VX Agent 15	No	No
Israel	Probable	Unknown	01/13/93	No
Italy	Former program	Mustard Phosgene	01/13/93	12/08/95
Japan	Former program	Phosgene Hydrogen cyanide Mustard Lewisite Chloropicrin	01/13/93	09/15/95

* Denotes countries which accepted the treaty.

Table 2.2 (continued) Chemical Weapons Programs around the World (with permission from Monterey Institute)

Country	Program status	Possible agents	Signed chemical weapons convention	Ratified chemical weapons convention
Libya	Known	Mustard Sarin Tabun Lewisite Phosgene	No	No
Myanmar (Burma)	Probable	Unknown	01/14/93	No
N. Korea	Known	Adamsite Mustard Hydrogen cyanide Cyanogen chloride Phosgene Sarin Soman Tabun VX	No	No
Pakistan	Probable	Unknown	01/13/93	10/28/97
Russia	Known	Novichok binary nerve agents	01/13/93	11/05/97
Soviet Union	Former program	Sarin Soman Mustard Lewisite Phosgene VX analog	01/13/93	11/05/97
S. Africa	Former program	Thallium Paraoxon Mustard	01/14/93	09/13/95
S. Korea	Former program	Unknown	01/14/93	04/28/97
Sudan	Possible	Unknown	No	05/24/99*
Syria	Known	Mustard Sarin VX	No	No
Taiwan	Probable	Unknown	No	No
U.K.	Former program	Phosgene Mustard Lewisite	01/13/93	05/13/96
U.S.	Former program	Mustard Sarin Soman	01/13/93	04/25/97

Table 2.2 (continued) Chemical Weapons Programs around the World (with permission from Monterey Institute)

Country	Program status	Possible agents	Signed chemical weapons convention	Ratified chemical weapons convention
		VX Lewisite Binary nerve agents		
Vietnam	Possible	Unknown	01/13/93	No
Yugoslavia, Federal Republic of (FRY)	Former program	Sarin Mustard Tabun Soman VX Lewisite BZ	No	04/20/00

Source: Monterey Institute of International Studies; available on-line at http://cns.miis.edu/research/cbw/possess.htm. With permisison. See reference 57.

2.5 CONCLUSIONS

Nuclear, biological, and chemical weapons can be deployed as WMDs. Biological and chemical weapons have existed throughout mankind's history, and their effectiveness has improved with modern technology. Nuclear weapons were first developed in the 20th century, but their proliferation has been limited due to cost, the expertise needed to develop the technology, and the infrastructure that is required. We must be vigilant in guarding against the proliferation of all of these weapons. Because the cost of nuclear weapons is a deterrent to its proliferation, we must view current trends with concern. Our dependence on oil as an energy source is destabilizing. The U.S. spends more than $200 billion per year in foreign countries for its oil appetite, and some of these dollars end up in the hands of rogue states and terrorist groups who have a bitter hatred of the U.S. and desire to develop weapons of mass destruction. The U.S. cannot discount the possibility that it is financing its own destruction.

APPENDIX 2.1 PARTIES AND SIGNATORIES TO THE TREATY ON THE NONPROLIFERATION OF NUCLEAR WEAPONS

Country	Date of signature	Date of deposit of ratification	Date of deposit of accession (A) or succession (S)
Afghanistan	07/01/68	02/04/70	—
Albania	—	—	09/12/90(A)
Algeria	—	—	01/12/95(A)
Antigua and Barbuda	—	—	06/17/85(S)
Andorra	—	—	06/07/96(A)
Angola	—	—	10/14/96(A)
Argentina	—	—	02/10/95(A)
Armenia	—	—	07/15/93(A)
Australia	02/27/70	01/23/73	—
Austria	07/01/68	06/27/69	—
Azerbaijan	—	—	09/22/92(A)
Bahamas, The	—	—	08/11/76(S)
Bahrain	—	—	11/03/88(A)
Bangladesh	—	—	08/31/79(A)
Barbados	07/01/68	02/21/80	—
Belarus	—	—	07/22/93(A)
Belgium	08/20/68	05/02/75	—
Belize	—	—	08/09/85(S)
Benin	07/01/68	10/31/72	—
Bhutan	—	—	05/23/85(A)
Bolivia	07/01/68	05/26/70	—
Bosnia and Herzegovina	—	—	08/15/94(S)
Botswana	07/01/68	04/28/69	—
Brazil	—	—	09/18/98(A)
Brunei	—	—	03/26/85(A)
Btazzanlle and Kinshasa	—	—	10/23/78(A)
Bulgaria	07/01/68	09/05/69	—
Burkina Faso	11/25/68	03/03/70	—
Burundi	—	—	03/19/71(A)
Cambodia	—	—	06/02/72(A)
Cameroon	07/17/68	01/08/69	—
Canada	07/23/68	01/08/69	—
Cape Verde	—	—	10/24/79(A)
Central African Republic	—	—	10/25/70(A)
Chad	07/01/68	03/10/71	—
Chile	—	—	05/25/95(A)
China	—	—	03/09/92(A)
Colombia	07/01/68	04/08/86	—
Comoros	—	—	10/04/95(A)
Costa Rica	07/01/68	03/03/70	—
Cote d'Ivoire	07/01/68	03/06/73	—

Country	Date of signature	Date of deposit of ratification	Date of deposit of accession (A) or succession (S)
Croatia	—	—	06/29/92(S)
Cyprus	07/01/68	02/10/70	—
Czech Republic	—	—	01/01/93(S)
Denmark	07/01/68	01/03/69	—
Djibouti	—	—	10/16/96(A)
Dominica	—	—	08/10/84(S)
Dominican Republic	07/01/68	07/24/71	—
Ecuador	07/09/68	03/07/69	—
Egypt	07/01/68	02/26/81[a]	—
El Salvador	07/01/68	07/11/72	—
Equatorial Guinea	—	—	11/01/84(A)
Eritrea	—	—	03/03/95(A)
Estonia	—	—	01/07/92(A)
Ethiopia	09/05/68	02/05/70	—
Fiji	—	—	07/14/72(S)
Finland	07/01/68	02/05/69	—
Former Yugoslav Republic of Macedonia	—	—	04/12/95(A)
France	—	—	08/03/92(A)
Gabon	—	—	02/19/74(A)
Gambia, The	09/04/68	05/12/75	—
Georgia	—	—	03/07/94(A)
Germany, Federal Republic of	11/28/69	05/02/75[a,b]	—
Ghana	07/01/68	05/04/70	—
Greece	07/01/68	03/11/70	—
Grenada	—	—	09/02/75(S)
Guatemala	07/26/68	09/22/70	—
Guinea	—	—	04/29/85(A)
Guinea-Bissau	—	—	08/20/76(S)
Guyana	—	—	10/19/93(A)
Haiti	07/01/68	06/02/70	—
Holy See	—	—	02/25/71(A)
Honduras	07/01/68	05/16/73	—
Hungary, Republic of	07/01/68	05/27/69	—
Iceland	07/01/68	07/18/69	—
Indonesia	03/02/70	07/12/79[a]	—
Iran	07/01/68	02/02/70	—
Iraq	07/01/68	10/29/69	—
Ireland	07/01/68	07/01/68	—
Italy	01/28/69	05/02/75[a]	—
Jamaica	04/14/69	03/05/70	—
Japan	02/03/70	06/08/76[a]	—
Jordan	07/10/68	02/11/70	—
Kazakhstan	—	—	02/14/94(A)
Kenya	07/01/68	06/11/70	—

Country	Date of signature	Date of deposit of ratification	Date of deposit of accession (A) or succession (S)
Kiribati	—	—	04/18/85(S)
Korea, Democratic People's Republic of	—	—	12/12/85(A)
Korea, Republic of	07/01/68	04/23/75	—
Kuwait	08/15/68	11/17/89	—
Kyrgyzstan	—	—	07/05/94(A)
Laos	07/01/68	02/20/70	—
Latvia	—	—	01/31/92(A)
Lebanon	07/01/68	07/15/70	—
Lesotho	07/09/68	05/20/70	—
Liberia	07/01/68	03/05/70	—
Libya	07/18/68	05/26/75	—
Liechtenstein	—	—	04/20/78(A)
Lithuania	—	—	09/23/91(A)
Luxembourg	08/14/68	05/02/75	—
Madagascar	08/22/68	10/08/70	—
Malawi	—	—	02/18/86(S)
Malaysia	07/01/68	03/05/70	—
Maldive Islands	09/11/68	04/07/70	—
Mali	07/14/69	02/10/70	—
Malta	04/17/69	02/06/70	—
Marshall Islands	—	—	01/30/95(A)
Mauritania	—	—	10/26/93(A)
Mauritius	07/01/68	04/08/69	—
Mexico	07/26/68	01/21/69[a]	—
Micronesia	—	—	04/14/95(A)
Moldova	—	—	10/11/94(A)
Monaco	—	—	03/13/95(A)
Mongolia	07/01/68	05/14/69	—
Morocco	07/01/68	11/27/70	—
Mozambique	—	—	09/04/90(A)
Myanmar (Burma)	—	—	12/02/92(A)
Namibia	—	—	10/02/92(A)
Nauru	—	—	06/07/82(A)
Nepal	07/01/68	01/05/70	—
Netherlands	08/20/68	05/02/75	—
New Zealand	07/01/68	09/10/69	—
Nicaragua	07/01/68	03/06/73	—
Niger	—	—	10/09/92(A)
Nigeria	07/01/68	09/27/68	—
Norway	07/01/68	02/05/69	—
Oman	—	—	01/23/97(A)
Palau	—	—	04/12/95(A)
Panama	07/01/68	01/13/77	—
Papua New Guinea	—	—	01/13/82(A)

Country	Date of signature	Date of deposit of ratification	Date of deposit of accession (A) or succession (S)
Paraguay	07/01/68	02/04/70	—
Peru	07/01/68	03/03/70	—
Philippines	07/01/68	10/05/72	—
Poland	07/01/68	06/12/69	—
Portugal	—	—	12/15/77(A)
Qatar	—	—	04/03/89(A)
Romania	07/01/68	02/04/70	—
Russia	07/01/68	03/05/70	—
Rwanda	—	—	05/20/75(A)
St. Kitts and Nevis	—	—	03/22/93(A)
St. Lucia	—	—	12/28/79(S)
St. Vincent and the Grenadines	—	—	11/06/84(S)
San Marino	07/01/68	08/10/70	—
Sao Tome and Principe	—	—	07/20/83(A)
Saudi Arabia	—	—	10/03/88(A)
Senegal	07/01/68	12/17/70	—
Seychelles	—	—	03/12/85(A)
Sierra Leone	—	—	02/26/75(A)
Singapore	02/05/70	03/10/76	—
Slovakia	—	—	01/01/93(S)
Slovenia	—	—	04/07/92(A)
Solomon Islands	—	—	06/17/81(S)
Somalia	07/01/68	03/05/70	—
South Africa	—	—	07/10/91(A)
Spain	—	—	11/05/87(A)
Sri Lanka	07/01/68	03/05/79	—
Sudan	12/24/68	10/31/73	—
Suriname	—	—	06/30/76(S)
Swaziland	06/24/69	12/11/69	—
Sweden	08/19/68	01/09/70	—
Switzerland	11/27/69	03/09/77	—
Syrian Arab Republic	07/01/68	09/24/69	—
Taiwan	07/01/68	01/27/70	—
Tajikistan	—	—	01/17/95(A)
Tanzania	—	—	05/31/91(A)
Thailand	—	—	12/02/72(A)
Togo	07/01/68	02/26/70	—
Tonga	—	—	07/07/71(S)
Trinidad and Tobago	08/20/68	10/30/86	—
Tunisia	07/01/68	02/26/70	—
Turkey	01/28/69	04/17/80	—
Tuvalu	—	—	01/19/79(S)
Turkmenistan	—	—	09/29/94(A)
Uganda	—	—	10/20/82(A)
Ukraine	—	—	12/05/94(A)

Country	Date of signature	Date of deposit of ratification	Date of deposit of accession (A) or succession (S)
United Arab Emirates	—	—	09/26/95(A)
United Kingdom	07/01/68	11/27/68	—
United States	07/01/68	03/05/70	—
Uruguay	07/01/68	08/31/70	—
Uzbekistan	—	—	05/02/92
Vanuatu	—	—	08/26/95(A)
Venezuela	07/01/68	09/25/75	—
Vietnam, Socialist Republic of	—	—	06/14/82(A)
Western Samoa	—	—	03/17/75(A)
Yemen	11/14/68	06/01/79	—
Yugoslavia, Socialist Federal Republic of	07/10/68	03/04/70	—
Zaire	07/22/68	08/04/70	—
Zambia	—	—	05/15/91(A)
Zimbabwe	—	—	09/26/91(A)

APPENDIX 2.2 PARTIES AND SIGNATORIES OF THE BIOLOGICAL WEAPONS CONVENTION

Parties		
Afghanistan	Fiji	Mexico
Albania	Finland	Monaco
Algeria	France	Mongolia
Argentina	Gambia, The	Netherlands[d]
Armenia	Georgia	New Zealand
Australia	Germany	Nicaragua
Austria[a]	Ghana	Niger
Bahamas	Greece	Nigeria
Bahrain[a]	Grenada	Norway
Bangladesh	Guatemala	Oman
Barbados	Guinea-Bissau	Pakistan
Belarus	Honduras	Panama
Belgium	Hungary	Papua New Guinea
Belize	Iceland	Paraguay
Benin	India	Peru
Bhutan	Indonesia	Philippines
Bolivia	Iran	Poland
Bosnia Herzegovina	Iraq	Portugal
Botswana	Ireland	Qatar
Brazil	Italy	Romania
Brunei Darussalam[b]	Jamaica	Russian Federation
Bulgaria	Japan	Rwanda
Burkina Faso	Jordan	St. Kitts and Nevis
Cambodia (Kampuchea)	Kenya	St. Lucia
Canada	Korea, Democratic People's Republic of	St. Vincent and the Grenadines
Cape Verde	Korea, Republic of	San Marino
Chile	Kuwait	Sao Tome and Principe
China, People's Republic of[c]	Laos	Saudi Arabia
Colombia	Latvia	Senegal
Congo	Lebanon	Seychelles
Costa Rica	Lesotho	Sierra Leone
Croatia	Libya	Singapore
Cuba	Liechtenstein	Slovak Republic
Cyprus	Lithuania	Slovenia
Czech Republic	Luxembourg	Solomon Islands[b]
Denmark	Macedonia, former Yugoslav Republic of	South Africa
Dominica[b]	Malaysia[a]	Spain
Dominican Republic	Maldives	Sri Lanka
Ecuador	Malta	Suriname
El Salvador	Mauritius	Swaziland
Equatorial Guinea		Sweden
Estonia		Switzerland
Ethiopia		Thailand

Togo	United Kingdom[e]	Yemen
Tonga	United States	Yugoslavia, Federal Republic of
Tunisia	Uruguay	Zaire
Turkey	Uzbekistan	Zimbabwe
Turkmenistan	Vanuatu	
Uganda	Venezuela	
Ukraine	Vietnam	

Signatories

Burundi	Haiti	Myanmar (Burma)
Central African Republic	Liberia	Nepal
Cote d'Ivoire	Madagascar	Somalia
Egypt	Malawi	Syria
Gabon	Mali	Tanzania
Guyana	Morocco	United Arab Emirates[f]

[a] With reservation.
[b] Based on general declarations concerning treaty obligations applicable prior to independence.
[c] Effective January 1, 1979, the U.S. recognized the government of the People's Republic of China as the sole government of China. The authorities on Taiwan state that they will continue to abide by the provisions of the convention, and the U.S. regards them as bound by its obligations.
[d] Applicable to Netherlands Antilles and Aruba.
[e] Extended to territories under the territorial sovereignty of the U.K. Also extended to New Hebrides; continued application to Vanuatu not determined.
[f] The United Arab Emirates, which did not ratify the convention, is listed as a single country.
Source: U.S. Department of State; available on-line at http://www.state.gov/t/ac/trt/4718.htm#signatory.

REFERENCES

1. U.S. Congress Office of Technology Assessment, Technologies Underlying Weapons of Mass Destruction, OTA-BP-ISC-115; http://www.wws.princeton.edu/cgi-bin/byteserv.prl/~ota/disk1/1993/9344/9344.PDF; accessed 2/17/03.
2. Diehl, S.J. and Moltz, J.C., *Nuclear Weapons and NonProliferation*, Contemporary World Issues, Santa Barbara, CA, 2002.
3. Federation of American Scientists, Plutonium Production; http://www.fas.org/nuke/intro/nuke/plutonium.htm; accessed 2/17/03.
4. Federation of American Scientists, Uranium Production; http://www.fas.org/nuke/intro/nuke/uranium.htm; accessed 2/17/03.
5. Loyalka, S., Nuclear Weapons, in *Science and Technology of Terrorism and Counterterrorism*, Ghosh, T., Prelas, M., Viswanath, D., and Loyalka, S., eds., Marcel Dekker, New York, 2002.

6. NATO, Conventional and Nuclear Weapons — Energy Production and Atomic Physics, *NATO Handbook on Nuclear Effects*; http://www.fas.org/nuke/guide/usa/doctrine/dod/fm8-9/1ch2.htm#s2p3; accessed 2/17/03.
7. Federation of American Scientists, Nuclear Weapon Design; http://www.fas.org/nuke/intro/nuke/design.htm; accessed 1/20/02.
8. Bracchini, M.A., Manhattan Project Bomb Design, University of Texas Engineering Department; http://www.me.utexas.edu/~uer/manhattan/index.html; accessed 1/20/03.
9. Federation of American Scientists, Nuclear Effects; http://www.fas.org/nuke/intro/nuke/effects.htm; accessed 2/17/03. Nukefix, Blast Effects; http://www.nukefix.org/weapon.html; accessed 2/17/03.
10. See note 8 above.
11. Brookings Institute, Atomic Audit: The Costs and Consequences of U.S. Nuclear Weapons since 1940, Appendix D: Assessing the Costs of Other Nuclear Weapon States; http://www.brook.edu/dybdocroot/FP/PROJECTS/NUCWCOST/APPENDIXD.HTM; accessed 1/21/03.
12. Broad, W., Spies vs. Sweat: The Debate over China's Nuclear Advance, *New York Times*, Sep. 7, 1999; http://www.nytimes.com/library/world/asta/090799china-nuke.html; accessed 1/27/03.
13. PBS, The Race for the Superbomb; http://www.pbs.org/wgbh/amex/bomb/filmmore/index.html; accessed 1/29/03.
14. Envirolink Network, The Soviet Nuclear Weapons Program; http://nuketesting.enviroweb.org/hew/Russia/Sovwpnprog.html; accessed 2/10/03.
15. Envirolink Network, Britain's Nuclear Weapons; http://nuketesting.enviroweb.org/hew/Uk/index.html; accessed 2/9/03.
16. Envirolink Network, France's Nuclear Weapons; http://nuketesting.enviroweb.org/hew/France/FranceOrigin.html; accessed 2/19/03.
17. Envirolink Network, China's Nuclear Weapons; http://nuketesting.enviroweb.org/hew/China/ChinaTesting.html; accessed 2/10/03.
18. Mordechai Vanunu — the World's First Nuclear Hostage; http://www.vanunu.freeserve.co.uk/; accessed 3/10/03.
19. Vanunu, M., photos of Dimona — 1986; http://www.nonviolence.org/vanunu/photos.html; accessed 3/8/03.
20. Stevens, E., Israel's Nuclear Weapons — A Case Study, Infomanage International; http://infomanage.com/nonproliferation/najournal/israelinucs.html; accessed 3/10/03.

21. Envirolink Network, Israel's Nuclear Weapons Program; http://nuke-testing.enviroweb.org/hew/Israel/index.html; accessed 2/10/03.

22. The Nuclear Weapon Archive, A Guide to Nuclear Weapons, http://nuclearweaponarchive.org/Israel/Isrsa497.txt, accessed 10/07/04.

23. Envirolink Network, India's Nuclear Weapons Program; http://nuke-testing.enviroweb.org/hew/India/IndiaOrigin.html; accessed 2/10/03.

24. BBC, India's Nuclear Testing, BBC Special Report, May 1998; http://news.bbc.co.uk/hi/english/special_report/1998/05/98/india_nuclear_testing/; accessed 2/7/03.

25. Envirolink Network, Pakistan's Nuclear Weapons Program; http://nuketesting.enviroweb.org/hew/Pakistan/PakOrigin.html; accessed 2/10/03.

26. Monterey Institute of International Studies, Resources on India and Pakistan; http://cns.miis.edu/research/india/; accessed 2/7/03.

27. Federation of American Scientists, Nuclear Forces Guide; http://www.fas.org/nuke/guide/index.html; accessed 2/18/03.

28. CNN, Timeline: North Korea's Nuclear Weapons Development, July 17, 2003; http://www.cnn.com/2003/WORLD/asiapcf/east/02/07/nkorea.timeline.nuclear/index.html; accessed 4/18/03; and Buckley, S., Analysis: North Korea's Nuclear Progress, Dec. 13, 2002; http://news.bbc.co.uk/1/hi/world/asia-pacific/2572525.stm; accessed 2/18/02.

29. Kerr, A., Will North Korean Nukes Rouse Japan from Its "Stupor of Peace"? *Time*, Feb. 18, 2003; http://www.time.com/time/asia/covers/501030224/viewpoint.html; accessed 2/19/03.

30. Spaeth, A., North Korea's Atomic Ambitions Are Real; So, Too, Is the Prospect of a Nuclear Arms Race across Asia, *Time*, Feb. 17, 2003; http://www.time.com/time/asia/covers/501030224/story.html; accessed 2/18/03; and Pyongyang, D.M., Spoiling for a Fight? *Time*, Feb. 17, 2003; http://www.time.com/time/asia/magazine/article/0,13673,501030217-421077,00.html; accessed 2/17/03.

31. CNN, North Korea Leaves Nuclear Pact, Jan. 10, 2003; http://www.cnn.com/2003/WORLD/asiapcf/east/01/10/nkorea.treaty/index.html; accessed 2/18/03.

32. See note 27 above.

33. See note 28 above.

34. Frank, W.J., ed., Summary Report of the NTH Country Experiment, National Security Archive, Lawrence Radiation Laboratory, University of California, Livermore, Mar. 1967; http://www.gwu.edu/~nsarchiv/nsa/NC/nuchis.html#samp; accessed 2/23/03.

35. Koch, A. and Wolf, J., Iran's Nuclear Facilities: A Profile, Center for Nonproliferation Studies, 1998; http://cns.miis.edu/ pubs/reports/pdfs/ iranrpt.pdf; accessed 2/19/03.

36. BBC, Russia Backs Iran Nuclear Programme, Mar. 12, 2001; http://news.bbc.co.uk/2/hi/world/middle_east/1215606.stm; accessed 2/19/03; and Russia and Iran Sign Protocol of Intention to Expand Nuclear Power Cooperation, *Pravda*, Dec. 25, 2002; http://english.pravda.ru/diplomatic/2002/12/25/41356.html; accessed 2/19/03.

37. Calabresi, M., Iran's Nuclear Threat, *Time*, Mar. 8, 2003; http://www.time.com/time/world/article/0,8599,430649,00.html; accessed 3/9/03.

38. Gertz, B., Ukraine and Libya Forge "Strategic" Alliance, *Washington Times,* June 10, 1996, pp. A1, A10, Center for Nonproliferation Studies, CNS database, http://www.nti.org/e_research/e1_libya_nuclear.html; accessed 2/19/03.

39. Nuclear Threat Initiative, Libya Overview; http://www.nti.org/e_research/e1_libya_1.html; accessed 2/19/03.

40. CBS, U.N.: Libya Processed Plutonium, Feb. 20, 2004; http://www.cbs-news.com/stories/2004/03/12/world/main605701.shtml; accessed 3/4/04.

41. Envirolink Network, Iraq's Nuclear Weapons Program; http://nuketest-ing.enviroweb.org/hew/Iraq/IraqAtoZ.html; accessed 2/19/03.

42. International Atomic Energy Agency, Nuclear Capabilities of Iraq; http://www.iaea.org/worldatom/Press/Booklets/Iraq/iaeaplan.html; accessed 2/23/03.

43. See note 42 above.

44. Albright, D., Iraq's Programs to Make Highly Enriched Uranium and Plutonium for Nuclear Weapons Prior to the Gulf War, Institute for Science and International Security, Dec. 2002; http://www.isis-online.org/publications/iraq/iraqs_fm_history.html; accessed 2/26/03.

45. Leyne, J., Iraq Shelved Nuclear Plans, *BBC News,* Oct. 26, 2004; http://news.bbc.co.uk/2/hi/middle_east/ 3216397.stm; accessed 3/4/04.

46. Federation of American Scientists, unclassified report to Congress on the acquisition of technology relating to weapons of mass destruction and advanced conventional munitions, 1 January through 30 June 2001; http://www.fas.org/irp/threat/bian_jan_2002.htm#6; accessed 2/18/03.

47. Karon, T., The Dirty Bomb Scenario, *Time*, June 10, 2002; http://www.time.com/time/nation/article/0,8599,182637,00.html; accessed 10/07/04.

48. http://nuclearweaponarchive.org/News/WatanAlArabi.html; last accessed 10/07/04, The Nuclear Weapon Archive, A Guide to Nuclear Weapons.

49. http://www.nbcmed.org/SiteContent/HomePage/WhatsNew/MedManual/Feb01/handbook.htm; Office of the Surgeon General, Medical NBC, Biological Casualties Handbook, Fourth Edition, February 2001, U.S. Army Medical Research Institute of Infectious Diseases; accessed 10/07/04.

50. Robey, J., Bioterror through Time, *Spotlight* (Discovery Channel series); http://dsc.discovery.com/anthology/spotlight/bioterror/history/history.html; accessed 2/27/03.

51. Healy, B., M.D., A Medical Battalion, *U.S. News and World Report*, Feb. 10, 2003, p. 76.

52. See note 50 above.

53. See note 50 above.

54. Alibek, K., *Biohazard*, Random House, New York, 1999.

55. U.S. Department of State, Biological Weapons Convention, 1972; http://www.state.gov/t/ac/bw/; accessed 3/03/03.

56. Bruce, I., Smallpox Virus Sold to Iraq, Says Defector, *London Herald*, Dec. 4, 2002; http://www.intellnet.org/news/ 2002/12/04/13796-3.html; accessed 3/03/03; and Gottlieb, S., U.S. Faltering on Smallpox Protection, *Washington Times*, Dec. 9, 2002; http://www.washtimes.com/op-ed/20021209-93372580.htm; accessed 3/03/03.

57. Monterey Institute of International Studies, Chemical and Biological Weapons: Possession and Programs Past and Present; http://cns.miis.edu/research/cbw/possess.htm; accessed 3/8/03.

58. Tucker, J.B., Conflicting Evidence Revives "Yellow Rain" Controversy, Monterey Institute of International Studies, Sep. 5, 2002; http://cns.miis.edu/pubs/week/020805.htm; accessed 03/04/03.

59. Torok, T.J., Tauxe, R.V., Wise, R.P., Livengood, J.R., Sokolow, R., Mauvais, S., Birkness, K.A., Skeels, M.R., Horan, J.M., and Foster, L.R., A Large Community Outbreak of Salmonellosis Caused by Intentional Contamination of Restaurant Salad Bars, *JAMA*, 278 (5), 389–395, 1997.

60. CNN, Officials: Florida Anthrax Case "Isolated," Oct. 5, 2001; http://www.cnn.com/2001/HEALTH/10/05/florida.anthrax/; accessed 3/6/03.

61. CNN, NBC Issues Statement on Employee's Anthrax Exposure, Oct. 12, 2001; http://www.cnn.com/2001/HEALTH/conditions/10/12/ny.nbc.anthrax.memo/; accessed 3/6/03.

62. Johnston, D. and Broad, W.J., Anthrax in Mail Was Newly Made, Investigators Say, *New York Times*, June 23, 2002; http://query.nytimes.com/search/article-page.html?res=9506E7D-9113FF930A15755C0A9649C8B63; accessed 3/8/03.

3

Characteristics of Nuclear Weapons

3.1 NUCLEAR MATERIALS

The potential development and deployment of nuclear weapons by a rogue nation or terrorist group has heightened public interest since the September 11, 2001, attack on the World Trade Center. This chapter illustrates that an enormous capital investment, a high level of industrialization, and a highly educated work force are necessary for the successful development of a nuclear weapon. The processing steps for the production and refinement of nuclear materials and basic weapons design will be reviewed. Also, the production of radioisotopes and how they may be exploited in a radiological dispersion device (RDD), or dirty bomb, will be discussed.

Modern nuclear weapons (Figure 3.1) have three distinct stages: primary, secondary, and tertiary. The primary stage "triggers" the nuclear reactions in the remaining stages. The primary stage consists of fissionable material, usually uranium or plutonium. This fissionable material produces intense energy in the form of gamma rays that provide the large radial compression forces necessary to ignite thermonuclear reactions in the secondary stage. The secondary stage typically consists of fusionable material such as lithium deuteride (LiD). The tertiary stage enhances the thermonuclear reactions by greatly increasing the number of neutrons available to react with the secondary stage. The tertiary stage typically consist of depleted uranium.

The first nuclear weapons consisted of only the primary stage. Historically, these weapons were referred to as atomic bombs, "A-bombs," or fission bombs. The destructive capability of the primary

Figure 3.1 Photograph of the "Gadget," first fission weapon. (From U.S. Department of Energy, Linking Legacies Connecting the Cold War Nuclear Weapons Production Processes to Their Environmental Consequences, DOE/EM-0319, Office of Environmental Management, Washington, DC, Jan. 1997; http://legacystory.apps.en.doe.gov; accessed 8/5/04.)

stage is formidable. The weapons developed by the Manhattan Project and deployed against Japan in 1945 fall into this category.

The nuclear weapon needs to be compact enough to fit into a delivery system (missile or aircraft), as illustrated in Figure 3.2. This is a difficult task, and even if a country has the capability of building a nuclear weapon, it may not have the technology to miniaturize the weapon.

The fission weapon ignites after a prescribed amount of fissile material is quickly brought together. This prescribed amount of material results in a supercritical configuration where the self-sustaining nuclear chain reaction propagates very quickly. The amount of the prescribed nuclear material is dependent upon geometry, quality of the nuclear material, and weapon design. Nuclear engineers use the neutron multiplication factor (k), as discussed in Chapter 2, as a measure of how close a system is to being critical or of the degree of criticality. A configuration is defined as critical, or as having the capability of sustaining a nuclear reaction, when the multiplication factor is one or greater

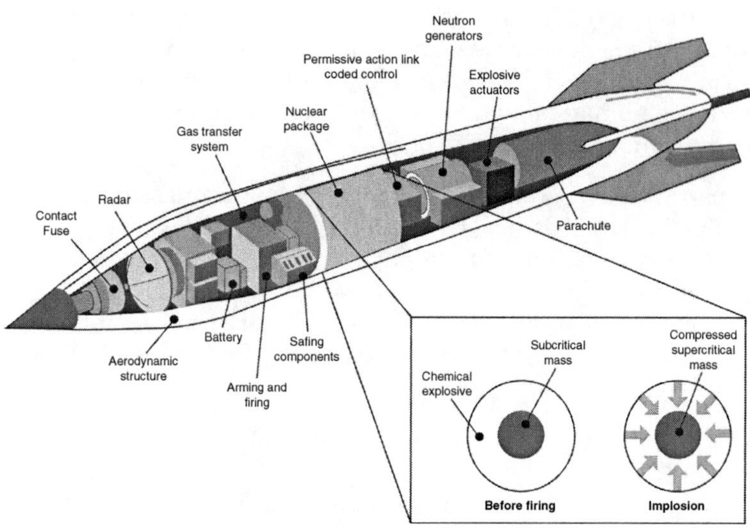

FIGURE 3.2 Components in a delivery system. (From U.S. Department of Energy, Linking Legacies Connecting the Cold War Nuclear Weapons Production Processes to Their Environmental Consequences, DOE/EM-0319, Office of Environmental Management, Washington, DC, Jan. 1997; http://legacystory.apps.en.doe.gov; accessed 8/5/04.)

($k \geq 1$). A configuration is subcritical when the multiplication factor is less than one ($k < 1$). The weapon design must be capable of quickly changing the multiplication factor from subcritical (less than one) to highly supercritical ($k > 1.5$) before structural integrity of the device is lost.

Weapon designers have found two general concepts where fissile materials can be used to construct a fission device: gun type and implosion type. These will be discussed later in the chapter.

The primary materials capable of sustaining a fission rate suitable for use in a nuclear weapon are U^{235}, Pu^{239}, and U^{233}. Other, more exotic nuclear materials can also be used in weapon design.[1] For example, in addition to uranium and plutonium, Np^{237} and Am^{241} can also be used to construct a weapon.[2] Some of the nuclear properties of Np^{237} are very similar to those of Pu^{239}.[3] Both the U.S. and Russia built up a considerable inventory of both Np^{237} and Am^{241} over the years of operating reactors. In October 2002, Los Alamos National Laboratory released details of a criticality experiment for Np^{237}.[4] The news release from Los Alamos National Laboratory states:

> A full-controlled criticality of the element neptunium was achieved in late September at Los Alamos National Laboratory's Technical Area 18 using a six kilogram nickel-clad neptunium sphere in combination with approximately 60 kilograms of enriched uranium.
>
> The experiment was conducted using the "Planet" assembly device at the Los Alamos Critical Experiments Facility or LACEF. The neptunium and enriched uranium assembly was constructed at TA-18's Critical Assembly and Storage Area-One, and mounted on the "Planet" device. The actual criticality was controlled remotely to assure the safety and security of the experiment.[5]

The criticality experiment indicated that critical assemblies of Np^{237} can be made.

Neptunium is from a class of elements called actinides. It has a half-life of over 2 million years. Np^{237} is produced in nuclear reactors from the reaction of U^{235} and U^{238} with neutrons. It is also produced from the radioactive decay of americium 241. It is not produced at very high rates by these reactions.

Americium is another controversial actinide. It is less suitable than Np^{237} for weapons because of higher radiation and heat generation rates. There are three significant isotopes of americium — Am^{241}, Am^{242m}, and Am^{243}. Americium isotopes are a by-product of plutonium production from the decay of Pu^{241}. The production rate of americium isotopes is very slow, although americium can accumulate over long time periods. Other actinides such as curium and californium may also be of concern. Other than plutonium, the other actinide isotopes have a relatively slow production rate or are too radioactive to be considered a credible proliferation threat. Neptunium and americium are not likely to be used in a newly established nuclear weapons program. A less advanced weapons program, such as that of a rogue nation or terrorist group, would focus on U^{235} and Pu^{239} as the primary fissile nuclear materials.

3.1.1 Fissile Materials

The first step in making a nuclear weapon is the production of the fissile materials. In this section we will discuss how fissile materials, uranium 235 and plutonium 239, are made.

The production of weapons-grade fissile materials involves complex technologies and extensive infrastructure, including uranium mining, processing, and isotopic enrichment; nuclear fuel production; nuclear reactors; fuel reprocessing; and plutonium separation.[6]

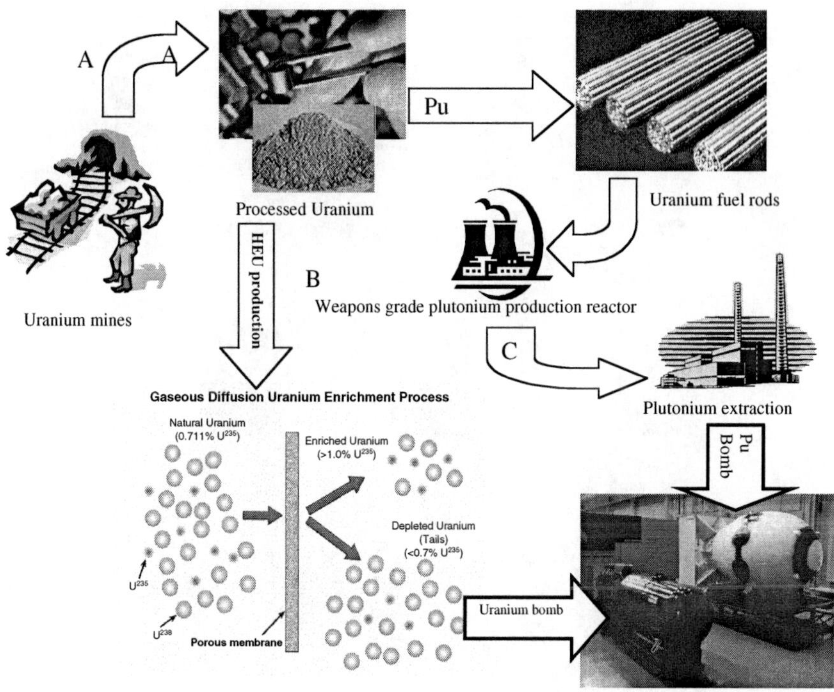

FIGURE 3.3 The nuclear fuel cycle: (A) refining the uranium ore, (B) enriching the uranium for use in a plutonium production reactor (3 to 5% enrichment) or producing highly enriched uranium (HEU > 80% enrichment), (C) reprocessing the fuel from production reactors to extract weapons-grade plutonium.

3.1.1.1 Fuel Cycles

Figure 3.3 illustrates the nuclear fuel cycle. Uranium production begins with mining. Traditional methods of ore extraction include open-pit and deep-shaft mining. Uranium ore from mining operations is transported to a mill by truck. At the mill, the uranium is chemically extracted from the ore using industrial processes similar to other mineral and metal extractions. The equipment required for uranium milling is very similar to what is used for other types of ores. The uranium ore is crushed and then processed by leaching with sulfuric acid or other alkaline agent. The leaching agent extracts the uranium, vanadium, selenium, iron, lead, and arsenic from the ore. As in other ore refining processes, about 90 to 95% of the uranium is extracted.

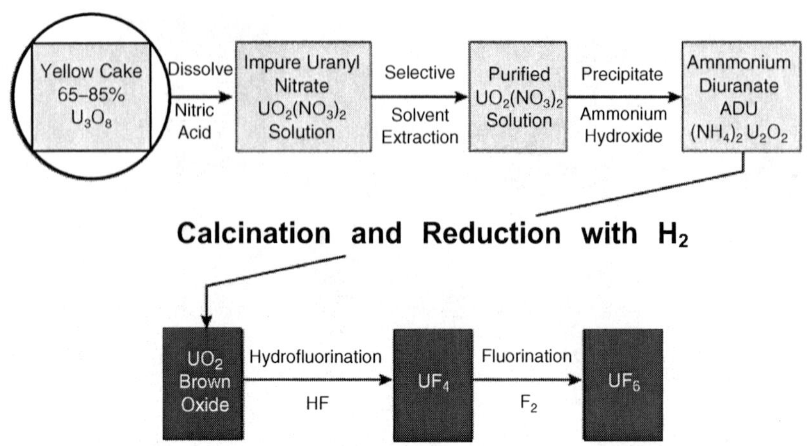

FIGURE 3.4 Conversion of yellow cake to uranium hexafluoride. (From Office of Environmental Management, Depleted Uranium Hexafluoride and Management, U.S. Department of Energy; http://web.ead.anl.gov/uranium/guide/prodhand/sld006.cfm; accessed 9/29/03.)

There are alternative methods used for low-grade uranium ore extraction such as *in situ* extraction. With this method, solutions are injected into underground deposits to dissolve the uranium. Another possible source of uranium is the dissolved uranium salts in seawater (3 to 5 parts per billion). Uranium can be extracted from seawater by using absorbing materials such as chitosan (a biological material from shellfish).[7] The uranium is extracted as U^{6+}, which can then be reacted with oxygen to form U_3O_8.

The mined uranium is extracted from ore at uranium mills. For the alternative *in situ* methods or sea extraction, it is extracted directly from the solutions or the chitosan. Regardless of the extraction process, the uranium is concentrated into "yellow cake" (U_3O_8) as a starting point for the fuel production process.

Yellow cake must be converted into uranium hexafluoride (Figure 3.4) prior to enrichment or be reduced to the metal form. The yellow cake is first dissolved in nitric acid to form an impure uranyl nitrate ($UO_2(NO_3)_2$) solution. Impurities are removed from the solution by selective solvent extraction. The processes take advantage of the transfer of uranium between organic and aqueous phases by manipulating the valence state. Tributyl phosphate is used as the organic carrier to initiate selective solvent extraction, leaving purified uranyl nitrate in an aqueous solution. The uranium valence state is changed by addition of ammonium hydroxide and ammonium diuranate ($(NH_4)_2U_2O_7$). The ammonium diuranate is reduced to uranium oxide (UO_2) with the addition of hydrogen gas. Hydrogen fluoride is then added to the uranium oxide to produce a mixture of uranium oxide and uranium tetrafluoride. Finally, fluorine gas is added to the mixture of uranium oxide and uranium tetrafluoride (UF_4) to produce uranium hexafluoride (UF_6).

Uranium in the chemical form of UF_6 is used as the feed for the enrichment process. Enrichment is defined as the process of increasing the isotopic ratio of U^{235} to U^{238}. Enrichment is required to transform natural uranium, which contains about 0.7% U^{235}, into uranium that can be used to construct nuclear reactor fuel with the 4 to 5% concentration of U^{235} that is used by most commercial power plants to produce electricity (e.g., boiling water reactor, pressurized water reactor). The only reactor that does not require enriched uranium as a fuel is the CANDU (Canadian deuterium-uranium) reactor, which uses natural uranium.

Natural uranium hexafluoride (UF_6) can be enriched by one of several processes. Current uranium enrichment facilities employ one of two technologies: gaseous diffusion or gas centrifuge. Both types of enrichment use UF_6 because it is a gas when heated. Both types of enrichment also rely on the slight mass differences between U^{235} and U^{238} to concentrate the isotopes, either through a semiporous membrane (diffusion) or by spinning at high speed (centrifuge).[8] Other potential processes, while not commercialized, can also be used to enrich uranium. These processes include laser isotope separation, electromagnetic isotope separation, and thermal diffusion. The equipment required for any of these enrichment processes is unique and requires a high degree of industrialization.

3.1.1.1.1 Gas Diffusion Technology

The U.S. is the primary user of diffusion technology. The rest of the world's nuclear programs generally use the gas centrifuge because of its superior economics, but to understand the U.S. reliance on diffusion technology, it is important to take a historical perspective. The diffusion process evolved during the Manhattan Project as the technology of choice, primarily because the centrifuge technology of that time was not sufficiently evolved to warrant the risks associated with its development. Once the diffusion plants were operational, their capacity, reliability, and longevity

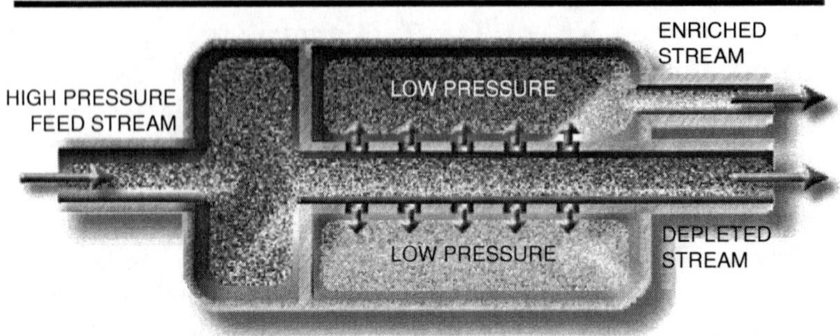

Figure 3.5 Gaseous diffusion stage of a U.S. uranium enrichment facility. (From USEC Inc., Gaseous Diffusion Enrichment Facility; http://www.usec.com/v2001_02/HTML/Aboutusec_enrichment.asp; accessed 1/3/04.)

were the reasons that the U.S. chose not to build additional enrichment capabilities using centrifuge technology.

Diffusion technology uses UF_6, a solid at room temperature, heated above 135°F, the point where it becomes gaseous. The process separates the lighter U^{235} isotopes from the heavier U^{238} by forcing the gaseous UF_6 through a series of porous membranes with microscopic openings (Figure 3.5). The lighter $^{235}UF_6$ moves through the porous membranes more easily than $^{238}UF_6$. The concentration of $^{235}UF_6$ is increased relative to $^{238}UF_6$ after passing through the porous membrane.

The equipment used in gaseous diffusion requires a high degree of industrialization. Because UF_6 is highly corrosive, the surfaces exposed to UF_6 must be manufactured from nickel or aluminum. Consequently, these materials are tracked as part of nonproliferation regimes. In addition, the facility depends upon the efficiency of the separating membrane, which must maintain very high tolerances. These membranes are typically made of nickel and aluminum oxide. Finally, the facility will consume a lot of electricity and will require a lot of cooling. The electrical infrastructure and the large amount of heat given off by the plant can be detected. Due to the complexity, cost, operational signatures, and infrastructure, proliferators are unlikely to pursue enrichment with gaseous diffusion.[9]

3.1.1.1.2 Gas Centrifuge Technology

The details of gas centrifuge technology are classified for national security reasons, and the parts not classified are protected by export control restrictions. The basic theory of a centrifuge is well known since it originates from the work of Gernot Zippe. The basic centrifuge designs used in Russian, U.S., and the European uranium separation program were heavily influenced by Dr. Zippe, who was captured during World War II by the Soviet Union and held as a prisoner of war. While a prisoner of war in 1946, he began his work on gas centrifuge technology. After being released by the Soviet Union, he collaborated with Professor Jesse W. Beams at the University of Virginia in the late 1950s on the gas centrifuge. When the U.S. classified the gas centrifuge technology in the early 1960s, Zippe returned to Europe, where he continued his gas centrifuge research.

The design of a basic centrifuge is shown in Figure 3.6. A gas centrifuge has several key features, including the rotor, the motor drive, the casing, the vacuum system, suspension systems, the UF_6 feed line, the depleted UF_6 tails line, and the enriched UF_6 line. The casing that encloses the centrifuge unit is air tight so that it can operate under a vacuum. The vacuum is necessary for two reasons: first, it helps to maintain UF_6 purity, and second, it reduces the friction on the high-speed spinning rotor, which generates centrifugal forces that act upon the UF_6 gas. The spinning rotor forces the slightly heavier U^{238} isotope to the outer wall, creating a radial separation factor between the U^{235} and U^{238} isotopes that is used to regionally enrich the UF_6. In addition to a radial separation, there is also a vertical separation that is created by complex counterflows in the centrifuge. The regional separation allows for convenient extraction points for the depleted and enriched flows. The enrichment per pass is very small, so it takes about 100 passes or stages to provide the 4 to 5% enrichment that is used by commercial power plants. In contrast, it takes about 1000 stages for a gaseous diffusion plant to achieve the same enrichment. The equipment used in the gas centrifuge technology is very specific and requires a high-level industrial base.

The capacity of a centrifuge is small. To produce enough highly enriched uranium (HEU) for a single nuclear weapon, several thousand centrifuges would have to operate for a year. Unfortunately, because the electrical consumption of a gas centrifuge is

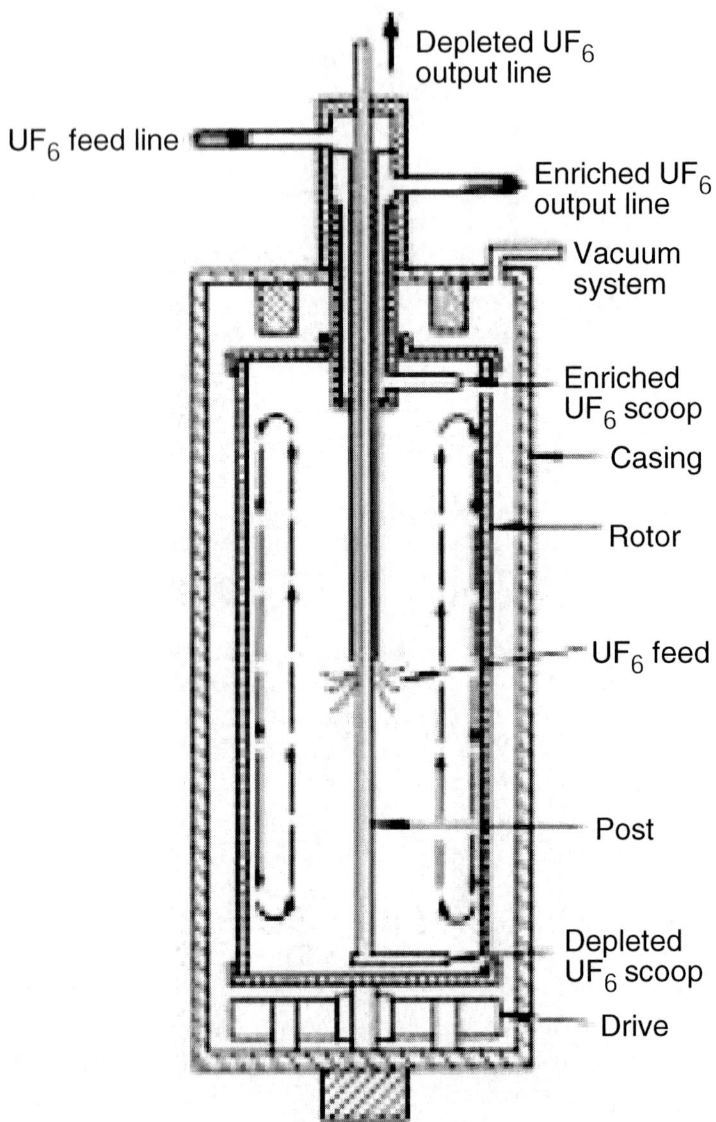

Figure 3.6 Gas centrifuge schematic. (From Green, R., Back to the Future, *Nuclear Eng. Int.*, September, 36–39, 2003; http://www.usec.com/v2001_02/Content/AboutUSEC/NEIAmericanCentrifugeArticle_09_03.pdf; accessed 1/4/04.)

moderate, it will not have easily identifiable electrical and cooling systems. Consequently, it is difficult to detect potential proliferators using gas centrifuge technology, as indicated by events in Iran late in 2003.[10] It appears that the gas centrifuge technology obtained by Iran and North Korea came from Pakistan,[11] but this is informed speculation, thus indicating that purchases from states assisting proliferators are difficult to trace.[12]

3.1.1.1.3 Laser Isotope Separation

There are two general types of laser isotope separation. One type excites atomic uranium with selected wavelengths of light and then uses the slight excitation energy difference between U^{235} and U^{238} to preferentially excite U^{235}. This is known as the atomic vapor laser isotope separation (AVLIS) process. In AVLIS, uranium metal is first vaporized under vacuum. The vapor is then illuminated with laser light tuned precisely to the wavelengths that are specifically absorbed by U^{235}. Specifically green light is generated with a diode-pumped solid-state laser that is capable of producing very short, high-intensity pulses at a high repetition rate. The green light then travels through a fiber-optic cable to pump a high-power dye laser. The dye laser emits light in three wavelengths, from red to orange, that is absorbed by U^{235}. Each of the three colored lights selectively moves the electron to higher excitation levels, resulting in the ionization of the U^{235}. The ionized uranium can be separated from the un-ionized uranium with an electric field. The enriched material is collected and condensed into metal nuggets, while the depleted material is allowed to condense on a tailing collector and removed (Figure 3.7).

The AVLIS process is energy efficient and conceptually simple, but actually building an AVLIS facility will be difficult and expensive, even for countries with a highly evolved technology and industrial base such as the U.S. Countries with limited technical resources will have to purchase the various technologies involved with AVLIS, and these types of purchases are traceable.

A second method, molecular laser isotope separation (MLIS), uses an infrared laser (e.g., carbon dioxide or carbon monoxide) to excite the rotational and vibrational levels of UF_6. (There is a slight excitation energy difference between $^{235}UF_6$ and $^{238}UF_6$.) In the original process conceived by scientists from Los Alamos National Laboratory in 1971, an infrared laser operating at around 16-μm wavelength selectively excites $^{235}UF_6$, leaving $^{238}UF_6$ in its ground state. A second laser system (e.g., an ultraviolet laser such

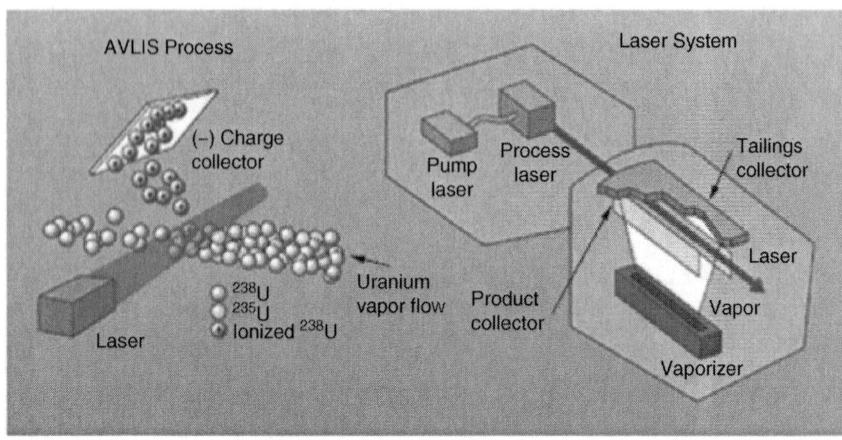

FIGURE 3.7 Laser isotope separation process for uranium enrichment. (From Lawrence Livermore National Laboratory, Laser Technology Follows in Lawrences Footsteps; http://www.llnl.gov/str/Hargrove.html; accessed 1/4/04.)

as the xenon chloride excimer laser) then dissociates the excited $^{235}UF_6$ into $^{235}UF_5$ plus a fluorine atom. The $^{235}UF_5$ has different properties that allow it to precipitate from the gas. The difficulties of combining an infrared laser and ultraviolet laser in the same system forced researchers to examine second laser systems in the infrared. Because the energy of an infrared laser is not sufficient to dissociate $^{235}UF_6$ directly, new pathways for infrared multiphoton excitation and photodissociation of polyatomic molecules had to be developed. As a result of these complexities, MLIS work in the U.S., U.K., France, and Germany has been terminated. A small MLIS program in Japan remains, and South Africa is still pursing MLIS for low-enriched uranium (LEU) production.

A novel harvesting technique that uses UF_6 and infrared lasers was developed by Dr. Jeff Eerkins in the late 1980s at Isotope Technologies. The process did not require a second laser system to photodissociate $^{235}UF_6$, instead using the different condensation rates of exited $^{235}UF_6$ and $^{238}UF_6$ to separate the isotopes. The method is known as CRISLA (condensation repression by isotope selective laser activation). Silex Corporation has adopted the CRISLA process and continues to pursue this method of isotope separation commercially.

MLIS has the advantage of low overall power consumption, and it fits in well with the present nuclear infrastructure because it can use UF_6 as the feed gas. However, it is a high-level technology that is detectable because of the special laser technologies required. The technology also requires considerable industrialization for a homegrown technology. Most countries would have to purchase the systems, and these purchases can be tracked.

Many of the same comments made with regard to MLIS apply to CRISLA, except that CRISLA uses a carbon monoxide laser that is sold for industrial purposes. It would be easier for proliferators to purchase such systems for legitimate commercial uses.

3.1.1.1.4 Electromagnetic Isotope Separation

Electromagnetic Isotope Separation (EMIS) uses a uniform magnetic field to separate charged particles of different masses. Beginning with solid uranium tetrachloride (UCl_4), the material is heated to produce UCL_4 vapor, which is then bombarded with electrons to produce U^{235} and U^{238} ions that are accelerated by an electrical potential. After acceleration, each of the ions has the same kinetic energy. The ions are then passed through a uniform magnetic field, where their trajectories are modified by the Lorentz force:

$$F = q(v \times B) \tag{3.1}$$

The heavier U^{238} ion will have a larger orbital diameter than U^{235} in the presence of the magnetic fields (Figure 3.8). This separation in orbital diameter allows correctly positioned collectors to collect the U^{235}-rich stream. This process takes only two passes to make weapons-grade uranium. The collection rate is very low, thus requiring long operational times to collect sufficient materials for a nuclear weapon. It takes a lot of energy and labor to enrich uranium with EMIS, and this process is not economically competitive with gas diffusion or a gas centrifuge. However, despite these shortcomings, EMIS was the method that Iraq pursued for its enrichment program due to its simplicity.

3.1.1.1.5 Thermal Diffusion

Thermal diffusion was one of the first isotope separation processes employed by the Manhattan Project. A thermal diffusion plant was built at Oak Ridge, TN, and operated for about 1 year to provide enriched feed material for EMIS. The plant was dismantled when the gaseous diffusion plants came on line. Gaseous diffusion is about 140 times more efficient than thermal diffusion. The thermal diffusion process is carried out across a thin liquid or gas film,

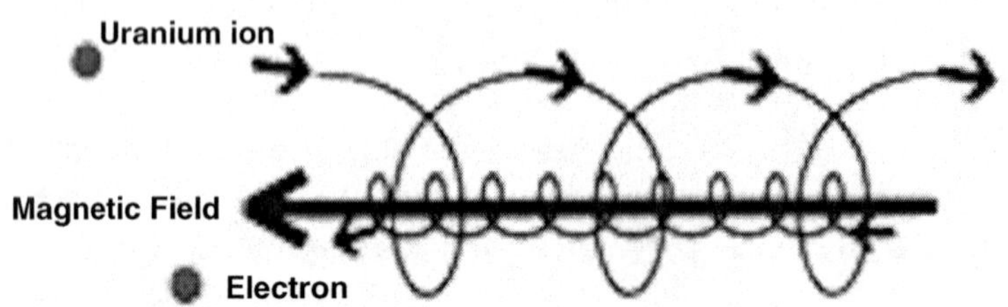

Figure 3.8 Ion motion in a magnetic field.

which is cooled on one side and heated on the other to create a large temperature gradient in the film. The convection currents flow upward on the hot surface and downward on the cold surface. The light isotope–bearing liquid or gas (U^{235}) diffuses to the hot side, and the heavy isotope–bearing liquid or gas (U^{238}) diffuses to the cold surface. Consequently, the light isotope concentrates at the top of the film, while the heavy isotope concentrates at the bottom of the film. The process is simple and has a low capital cost, but it consumes a lot of energy. The process is still used in industry as a practical way of separating light isotopes such as noble gases and carbon.

3.1.1.1.6 Plasma Separation Process

The plasma separation process (PSP) has been researched primarily in the U.S. and France. Conceptually, this process uses high magnetic fields generated with superconducting magnets combined with ion cyclotron resonance heating. Uranium is first vaporized from a solid target by bombarding it with ions. Uranium plasma is then formed by using microwave excitation, and the uranium ions are then trapped in the magnetic field created by the superconducting magnets. As in the case of EMIS, the uranium ions orbit the magnetic field lines (Figure 3.8). The ions pass through an electric field oscillating at the ion cyclotron resonance frequency for the U^{235} ions, which is higher than the ion cyclotron resonance frequency for U^{238}. This causes the U^{235} ions to gain energy, which causes the helical orbit of the U^{235} ions to increase.

The plasma then flows through a series of closely spaced parallel slats. The larger orbit of U^{235} makes it more likely to collect on the parallel slats, while the U^{238} is more likely to pass through the slats. The material deposited on the slats is enriched.

PSP technology requires a number of high-technology items, such as superconducting magnets, microwave sources, and radio frequency sources. These items are produced by highly industrialized countries and would have to be purchased by most other countries interested in developing PSP.

3.1.1.2 Plutonium Production Pathway

In addition to highly enriched uranium (HEU), plutonium can also be used as a fissile material in a nuclear weapon. Low-enriched uranium (LEU) may also be used to fuel a nuclear reactor. Neutrons produced in the reactor breed plutonium through interactions with natural uranium (Equation 3.2). In path B in Figure 3.3, HEU is produced by making numerous passes through the enrichment process until the material is enriched to weapons-grade concentrations. In path C, the enrichment required for most reactors is in the 3 to 5% range. The LEU can be used to power commercial nuclear power plants or recycled for use in plutonium production reactors.

Weapons-grade plutonium is produced by irradiation of uranium (U-238) by neutrons inside an operating nuclear reactor. A small portion of the U-238 in the fuel rods will capture a neutron and then beta decay into Pu-239 (Equation 3.2).

$$U^{238} + n \rightarrow U^{239} \rightarrow Pu^{239} + \beta + \bar{\nu} \qquad (3.2)$$

where n is a neutron, β is a beta particle, and $\bar{\nu}$ is an antineutrino.

The U.S. has built and operates 14 plutonium production reactors. These reactors — located at Hanford, WA, and Savannah River, GA — have produced about 103 metric tons (tonne, t) of plutonium between 1943 and 1985.[13]

The nine Hanford reactors were graphite-moderated with a 36-ft^3 core (Figure 3.9). Horizontal process channels ran through the graphite block to accommodate the uranium fuel and cooling-water flow channels. Each of the 2004 process channels was loaded with a 1-in.-diameter uranium metal fuel slug. These fuel slugs were clad with either aluminum or zirconium and exposed for about 90 days to neutrons produced in the reactor core. The fuel

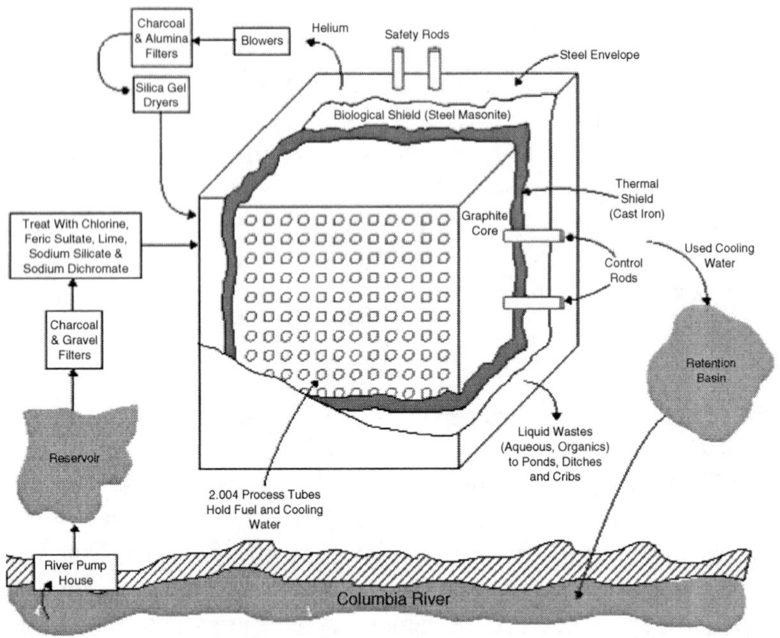

FIGURE 3.9 Simplified diagram of a plutonium production reactor. (From U.S. Department of Energy, Linking Legacies Connecting the Cold War Nuclear Weapons Production Processes to Their Environmental Consequences, DOE/EM-0319, Office of Environmental Management, Washington, DC, Jan. 1997; http://legacystory.apps.en.doe.gov; accessed 8/5/04.)

slugs were inserted into the core at the front face of the reactor and discharged through the rear face, where they were placed into large pools for cooling. According to a student calculation, about 0.25 to 0.3% of the uranium was converted to plutonium. The calculation was based on the total amount of fuel process reported in DOE/EM-0319 and plutonium inventories reported in the literature.[13] The Hanford reactor was a dual-use system for power and plutonium production.

The five Savannah River reactors were designed differently. These reactors each used a large tank of "heavy water" in which highly enriched fuel and separate depleted-uranium targets were submerged. The depleted-uranium targets were exposed to neutrons produced in the reactor. Similarly to the Hanford reactors, only a small fraction of the uranium was converted into plutonium.

In Russia, plutonium was initially produced by reactors similar in design to the Hanford reactors. Russia continued with

FIGURE 3.10 RBMK reactor design. (From Argon National Laboratory, Soviet Nuclear Power Plant Design; http://www.insc.anl.gov/rbmk/reactor/reactor.html; accessed 1/8/04.)

graphite-moderated reactors with a dual-use system for power production and plutonium production. The Reactor Bolshoy Moshchnosty Kanalny (RBMK) or channel reactor uses a large graphite block (about 21 ft high) to moderate the core. There are about 1600 vertical tubes of about 3.5-in. diameter that circulate pressurized cooling water (Figure 3.10).[14] Like the CANDU reactor,[15] the RBMK can be refueled on-line, which is a valuable feature for a plutonium production reactor. It is important to limit the time that the uranium is exposed to neutrons in order to limit the buildup of Pu^{240} and Pu^{241}. Like the Hanford reactors, which irradiate the uranium for about 90 days for weapons-grade plutonium production, other types of weapons-grade plutonium production reactors would require similar irradiation times, and on-line refueling is an important feature to limit downtime.

The CANDU reactor uses heavy water (D_2O, deuterium oxide) as the moderator and natural uranium as the fuel (Figure 3.11).[16] It also has the capability of being refueled on-line.

The resources required for the construction and operation of a nuclear reactor are clearly beyond the capability of most countries. As stated in Chapter 2, Iraq spent about $20 billion on its nuclear

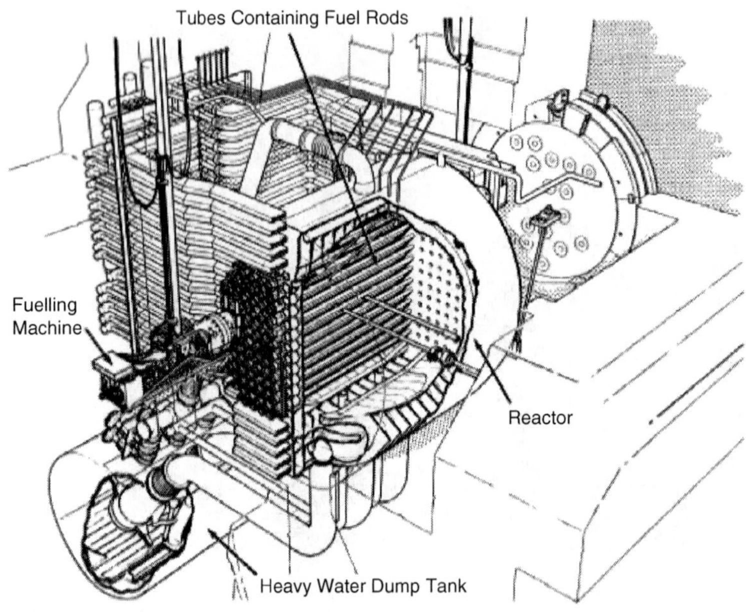

Figure 3.11 Cutaway of a CANDU Reactor. (From CANDU Cut Away, CANTEACH selected images; http://canteach.candu.org/imagelib/00000-General/NPD_Reactor_Cutaway.pdf; accessed 5/20/04. With permission.)

program with no tangible results. A would-be nuclear power would need a source of Pu^{239} or HEU to begin the process of manufacturing a weapon. There are still concerns about the security of the nuclear stockpile in the former Soviet Union. Redirection of plutonium from U.S. or foreign stockpiles or recovery from spent reactor fuel is a possible threat, but of low probability.

3.1.1.2.1 Redirection from Existing Stockpiles

The security of nuclear stockpiles is an important issue to those countries that possess nuclear weapons capability. The U.S., for example, maintains plutonium stockpiles in well-guarded vaults located in secure government reservations. This plutonium is in the form of pits (softball-size nuclear weapon core, shown as the nuclear package in Figure 3.2), metallic "buttons" (Figure 3.12), or various in-process scraps or waste solutions. These supplies are under the surveillance of the International Atomic Energy Commission, which has safeguards in place to restrict redirection of

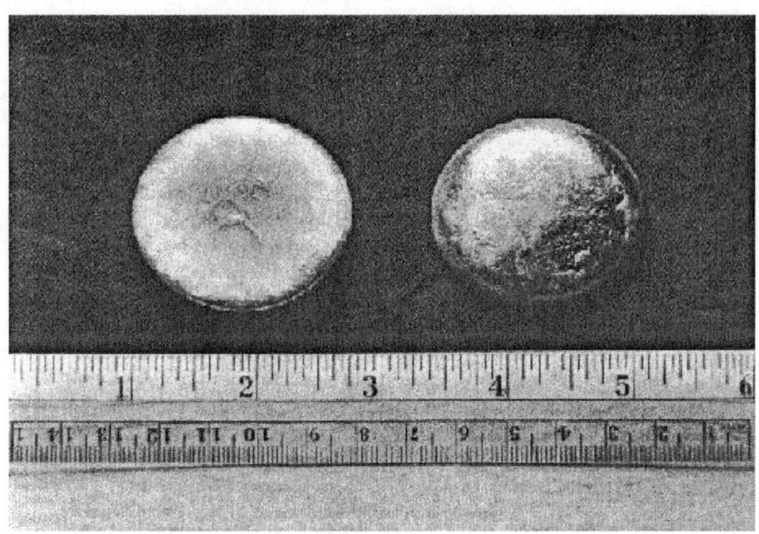

FIGURE 3.12 Plutonium "buttons." (From U.S. Department of Energy, Linking Legacies Connecting the Cold War Nuclear Weapons Production Processes to Their Environmental Consequences, DOE/EM-0319, Office of Environmental Management, Washington, DC, Jan. 1997; http://legacystory.apps.em.doe.gov; accessed 8/5/04.)

the material. In addition to reprocessed plutonium stockpiles, the Department of Energy (DOE) also maintains over 2200 t of plutonium-laden spent reactor fuel at various locations. The majority of this spent fuel is stored at Hanford, WA, Savannah River, GA, and Idaho Falls, ID. This spent fuel is typically stored in open pools at moderately secured facilities. While safeguarded, the spent nuclear fuel is less secure than the stockpiled plutonium.

In 2002 DOE stored more than 12,000 plutonium pits at the Pantex Plant, TX. DOE designated 7,000 to 8,000 of these pits as "surplus." An additional 8,000 to 10,000 pits are maintained in the nation's nuclear weapons arsenal (Table 3.1). In addition, DOE has asserted that 12.0 t of plutonium has been "lost" or sent abroad.[17]

3.1.1.2.2 Plutonium Inventory

In addition to the production reactors, the U.S. also generated 0.6 Mt plutonium from government-owned nonproduction reactors, 1.7 t plutonium from commercial nuclear reactors (generated from the West Valley, NY, reprocessing plant), and obtained 5.7 t plutonium from foreign sources.[19] The active plutonium inventory

TABLE 3.1 U.S. Plutonium Stockpile[18]

Category	Weapons grade (t)	Fuel grade (t)	Reactor grade (t)	Total (t)
Pits	66.1	0	0	66.1
Irradiated fuel	0.6	6.6	0.3	7.5
Buttons/waste non-pit	18.4	7.6	0	26.0
Total	85.1	14.2	0.3	99.6

held by DOE and the Department of Defense (DoD) is in the form of nuclear weapons triggers and plutonium pits, contained within irradiated nuclear fuel, or in an in-process form.

Much of the data from the Russian program is classified, but it is estimated that it produced about 150 Mt of plutonium, and that amount is growing by about 1.5 Mt/yr due to the operation of the RMBK reactors.[20]

3.1.1.2.3 Isotopic Considerations in Weapons-Grade Plutonium

Weapons-grade plutonium primarily consists of the Pu^{239} isotope. Plutonium is produced from the neutron capture of uranium in a nuclear reactor. In addition to Pu^{239}, several other plutonium isotopes form in the reactor fuel. The amount of a second isotope, Pu^{240}, is the key variable for determining the usefulness of the plutonium in weapons applications. Plutonium 240 has a high spontaneous fission rate that can lead to the pre-initiation of a weapon. As the isotopic ratio of Pu^{240} to Pu^{239} increases, the total amount of plutonium also needs to be increased to ensure a high enough k_{eff} value upon implosion. Early weapons, such as the Fat Man dropped on Hiroshima, had Pu^{240} content as low as 1.5%. Table 3.2 shows the average plutonium isotopic make up of weapons-grade plutonium provided from the Hanford and Savannah River reactor facilities.[21] The Pu^{240} content is determined by the amount of time the uranium fuel is exposed in the reactor and the neutron energy levels. Both Pu^{239} and Pu^{240} are produced at constant rates. However, the Pu^{239} acts as a reactor fuel and "burns out" more quickly than the Pu^{240}. As a general rule, the longer the fuel is kept in the operating reactor, the greater the amount of total plutonium produced. However, longer exposures times also result in higher ratios of Pu^{240} to Pu^{239}. Plutonium producers must optimize the fuel exposure and reactor power levels to maximize

TABLE 3.2 Weapons-Grade Plutonium: Isotopic Composition (%)

	Hanford	Savannah River
Plutonium 238	<0.05	<0.05
Plutonium 239	93.17	92.99
Plutonium 240	6.28	6.13
Plutonium 241	0.54	0.86
Plutonium 242	<0.05	<0.05

Source: U.S. Department of Energy, Linking Legacies Connecting the Cold War Nuclear Weapons Production Processes to Their Environmental Consequences, DOE/EM-0319, Office of Environmental Management, Washington, DC, Jan. 1997; http://legacystory.apps.em.doe.gov; accessed 8/5/04.

total plutonium conversion while minimizing the ratio of Pu^{240}. As one might suspect from Table 3.2, the isotopic content varies by the production reactor design. This difference in isotopic content is a useful tool in identifying where the plutonium was produced.

Spent commercial electric power reactor fuel is another potential source of plutonium. As a general rule, spent power reactor fuel has too high a Pu-240 ratio to be useful for weapons development. For weapons use, the plutonium needs to contain greater than 80% Pu^{239}. As U^{235} is exposed in a reactor core, Pu^{240} also builds up. The fuel in a commercial PWR (pressurized water reactor) or BWR (boiling water reactor) power plant is designed to stay in the core; for a long time. PWR and BWR refueling is time consuming, thus, PWRs and BWRs are not suitable for short fuel burn-up times. However, as indicated in Table 3.3 and Figure 3.13, a PWR during the initial stages of fuel burn-up does produce weapons-grade plutonium. A commercial fuel assembly collects about 20,000 megawatt days per metric ton of metal fuel (MWD/MTM) exposure during a typical 18-month fuel cycle. For weapons use, an acceptable Pu-239/Pu-240 ratio exists for commercial fuel exposed to less than 12,000 MWD/MTM, or about nine months of power operations.

The challenges in handling the fuel are substantial whether the source of spent nuclear fuel is commercial or defense. Spent fuel is extremely radioactive and requires special shielding and cooling considerations. The high radiation fields require specialized facilities that make detection of these activities possible.

Table 3.3 Plutonium Isotopic Composition in Commercial Reactor Fuel (%)

Exposure (MW·d/t fuel)	Pu-239	Pu-240	Pu-241	Pu-242	Total Pu	Pu-239 (% of total Pu)
0	0	0	0	0	0	0
1,000	0.437	0.006	0.000	0.000	0.44	98.6
2,000	0.909	0.028	0.002	0.000	0.94	96.8
4,000	1.731	0.101	0.018	0.000	1.85	93.6
8,000	2.999	0.316	0.103	0.005	3.42	87.6
12,000	3.899	0.572	0.246	0.018	4.74	82.3
20,000	4.957	1.110	0.616	0.083	6.77	73.3
34,000	5.475	1.967	1.213	0.341	9.00	60.9
44,000	5.846	2.458	1.626	0.627	10.56	55.4
56,000	5.426	2.875	1.784	1.042	11.13	48.8
60,000	5.263	2.964	1.799	1.192	11.22	46.9

Note: For weapons use, an acceptable Pu-239/Pu-240 ratio exists for commercial fuel exposed to less than 12,000 MWD/MTM or less than nine months of power operations.

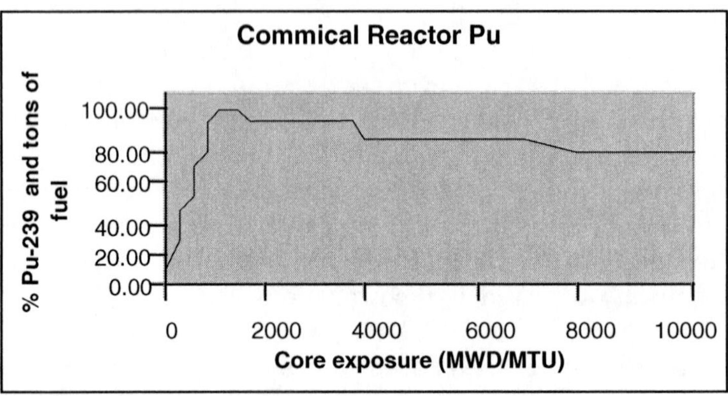

Figure 3.13 Pu^{239} production in commercial power reactors.

3.1.1.2.4 *Extraction of Plutonium from Spent Fuel*

The U.S. operated eight chemical separation plants that were used to extract the plutonium from spent reactor fuel. The U.S. used three different chemical-industrial processes for these separation operations:

- Bismuth phosphate
- REDOX (reduction and oxidation)
- PUREX process

A rogue country would employ one of these methods for clandestine weapons development. Irradiated fuel contains hundreds of different radioactive isotopes, collectively called fission products. The spent fuel is about 97% uranium, about 3% fission products, and 0.3% plutonium. These fission products and the remaining uranium fuel matrix must be chemically separated before the plutonium can be applied for weapons use. These three processes will be reviewed to highlight the complexity and resources needed.

3.1.1.2.4.1 Bismuth Phosphate Process. During the early 1940s the metallurgical laboratory at the University of Chicago[22] evaluated several chemical separation processes for use in the Manhattan Project. The project concluded that the bismuth phosphate process was best suited for the first separation facilities. The Manhattan District built three large bismuth phosphate plants at Hanford. The plants were called T, B, and U and were nicknamed "canyons" or "Queen Marys" because of their enormous size. The end product was plutonium nitrate solution. The process was based on plutonium's coprecipitation with bismuth phosphate while in the +4 valence state but not in the +6 valence state.

The process began by removing the aluminum reactor fuel cladding by submerging the spent-fuel elements in a boiling sodium hydroxide solution. The bare uranium metal (which contained a small amount of fission products and plutonium) was subsequently dissolved in concentrated aqueous nitric acid solution. The plutonium was separated and concentrated by using many precipitation cycles and redissolution using bismuth phosphate. The end product was a plutonium nitric solution that was further decontaminated and concentrated from about 330 gallons down to 8 gallons using a lanthanum fluoride carrier. The concentrate was transformed into a wet plutonium nitrate paste that was calcified and further reduced to plutonium metal. Some of the concentrated plutonium nitrate was precipitated out of the solution as plutonium peroxide by the addition of hydrogen peroxides, sulfates, and ammonium nitrate. The plutonium peroxide was filtered, dried, dissolved in nitric acid, and boiled down into a thick wet paste. In both cases, the end product was plutonium metal. This metal was cast into hockey-puck-size ingots (Figure 3.12) called "buttons." This step is not insignificant because of problems with plutonium metallurgy, an issue that is discussed later in this chapter.

The physical facilities for the separation process were by necessity large to accommodate the necessary radiation shielding. The main process buildings (canyons) were over 800 ft long, 102 ft high, and 85 ft wide. Each facility incorporated 6-ft-thick concrete walls to shield workers from radioactivity. Each plant was divided into 20 process cells with removable 8-ft-thick shield covers or plugs. The canyons had overhead cranes and manipulators that allowed the equipment to be remotely manipulated. Any direct exposure to the plant process equipment was hazardous and could result in a fatal radiation exposure in less than a minute. Each canyon had shielded operating galleries that ran the length of the buildings for electrical and control equipment, pipes, and operators. A closed-circuit television system and optical instruments allowed workers to see inside the canyons to remotely manipulate the equipment. Each facility had a ventilation system to draw in air from the occupied areas to the contaminated areas before it exhausted through filters and a tall stack. With the bismuth phosphate process, 1 t of uranium fuel produced about 2.5 kg of plutonium product. Each metric ton of fuel processed also generated approximately 10,000 gal of liquid waste that resulted in a discharge of about 1.5 Mgal of wastewater into the ground each day.

It is clear that even a small-scale separation plant based on the bismuth phosphate process (Figure 3.14) would be difficult to conceal from surveillance satellites or air samples gathered by intelligence networks.

3.1.1.2.4.2 Reduction and Oxidation (REDOX) Process. The bismuth phosphate process had inefficiencies and only recovered the plutonium leaving the uranium and other useful actinides in the waste steam. Prompted by a uranium shortage in the late 1940s, the U.S. developed the REDOX fuel separation processes that recovered the uranium. The U.S. began operation of the first REDOX plant at Hanford in 1952. REDOX was the first countercurrent, continuous-flow solvent-extraction process used for recovery of plutonium. REDOX produced plutonium, uranium, and neptunium from the irradiated reactor fuel. These products were separated from fission products by a nonsoluble interface between organic hexone, normal paraffin solvents, and aqueous nitrite solution. The REDOX process began by dissolving the cladding and irradiated fuel in nitric acid. The resulting solution was neutralized and passed through long solvent-extraction columns, where an organic solvent was added. The uranium, plutonium, and neptunium transferred across to the organic solvent leaving the fission products in the aqueous phase. The uranium, plutonium, and neptunium were then each separately reduced chemically and recovered back into the aqueous phase. The uranium, plutonium,

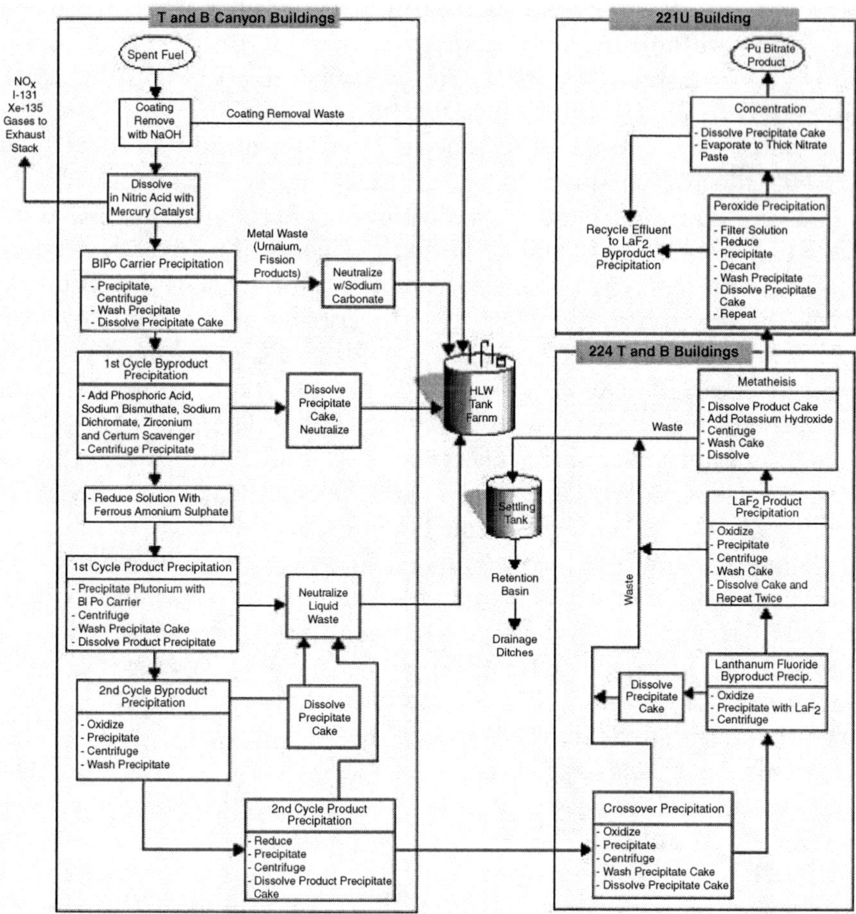

FIGURE 3.14 Bismuth phosphate process. (From U.S. Department of Energy, Linking Legacies Connecting the Cold War Nuclear Weapons Production Processes to Their Environmental Consequences, DOE/EM-0319, Office of Environmental Management, Washington, DC, Jan. 1997; http://legacystory.apps.em.doe.gov; accessed 8/5/04.)

and neptunium were separated from each other by manipulation of the valance states of the products with chromates and pH.

The REDOX plant, although large and heavily shielded, was not nearly the size of the canyon-shaped buildings that housed the bismuth phosphate plants. The REDOX plant was designed to process up to 3 t of fuel per day. The U.S. had increased the plant's capacity to 12 t per day by 1958.[23] Part of the capacity increase was due to the construction of the 233-S Plutonium Concentration

Building, where criticality-safe equipment accomplished the third and final plutonium concentration step. Plutonium nitrate solutions were reduced to metallic plutonium and uranylnitrate hexahydrate. The later product solution from REDOX was calcified back to uranium metal and recycled for fuel manufacturing. The REDOX plant continued operation until its retirement in 1967.

It is clear that even a small-scale separation plant based on the REDOX process would be difficult to conceal from surveillance satellites or from atmospheric samples gathered by intelligence networks or from its associated infrastructure.

3.1.1.2.4.3 PUREX Process. The PUREX process was first used at the Savannah River site to recover plutonium from the five Savannah River reactors. The PUREX process was subsequently adopted at Hanford (Figure 3.15) and at the Idaho Chemical Processing Plant due to its many advantages over REDOX. For example, REDOX relied on hexone chemistry. Hexone has a flash point of 69°F, which required all the process equipment to be operated in an inert atmosphere. The PUREX process provided increased efficiency and reduced operating costs compared with the REDOX process. PUREX, developed by Knolls Atomic Power Laboratory in the early 1950s, was first demonstrated at the Separations Process Research Unit in Schenectady, NY.[24] The first large-scale chemical-separation operation at the Savannah River site began in November 1954. The Hanford PUREX plant was started up in July 1955.

PUREX recovered plutonium, uranium, and neptunium in separate cycles by countercurrent solvent extraction with tributylphosphate used as the organic solvent. The process began with the irradiated fuel immersed in a bath of boiling sodium hydroxide, which perforated the zirconium fuel cladding. The fuel elements were then mechanically reduced in size and dissolved in nitric acid. Like the REDOX process, the acid solution was neutralized and the organic solvent was introduced. The uranium, plutonium, and neptunium were transferred between the organic and aqueous phases by manipulation of the valance states. The PUREX process used smaller countercurrent, continuous-flow, "pulsed" solvent-extraction columns.

The desired products of plutonium, uranium, and neptunium were concentrated together in an organic solvent (normally paraffin) and then purified by chemical scrubbing with dilute nitric acid. Two further cycles of solvent extraction and scrubbing separated, concentrated, and purified the aqueous solutions of plutonium, uranyl,

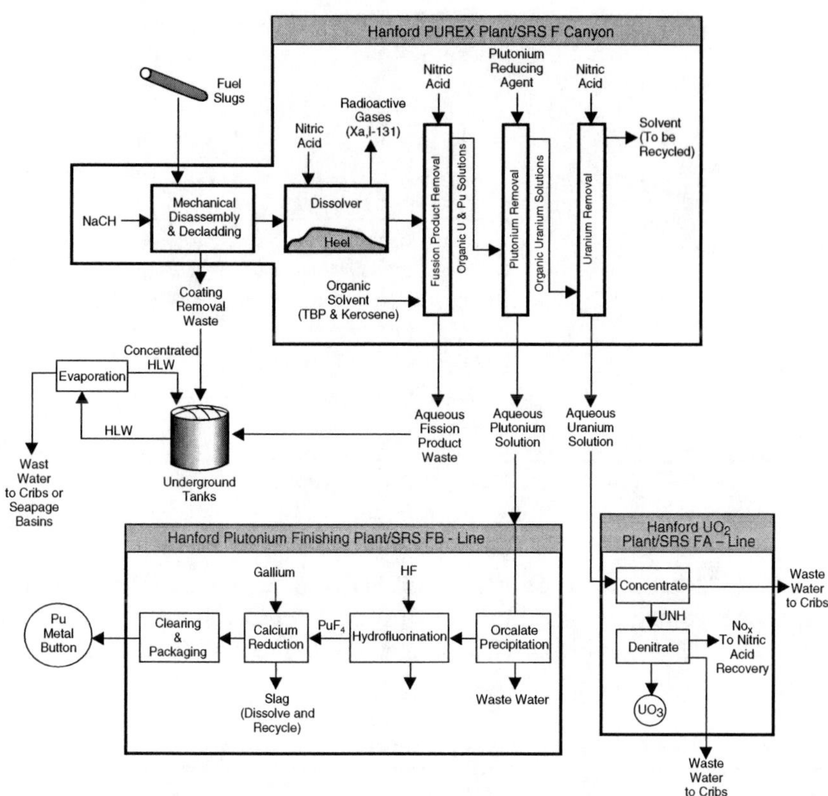

Figure 3.15 PUREX process. (From U.S. Department of Energy, Linking Legacies Connecting the Cold War Nuclear Weapons Production Processes to Their Environmental Consequences, DOE/EM-0319, Office of Environmental Management, Washington, DC, Jan. 1997; http://legacystory.apps.em.doe.gov; accessed 8/5/04.)

and neptunium nitrates. The plutonium nitrate solutions were solidified to an oxide powder or metal and machined into weapons components at the plant in Rocky Flats, CO.

Like REDOX, it would be very difficult to conceal a PUREX plant given spy satellites, infrastructure, and intelligence.

3.1.1.2.5 Plutonium Metallurgy

Plutonium is inherently chemically unstable. Plutonium metal can spontaneously change density by as much as 25%, be as brittle as glass, or be as malleable as aluminum (Figure 3.16). Plutonium expands when it solidifies, similar to freezing water,[25] is highly reactive in air, and damages materials on contact. All of these

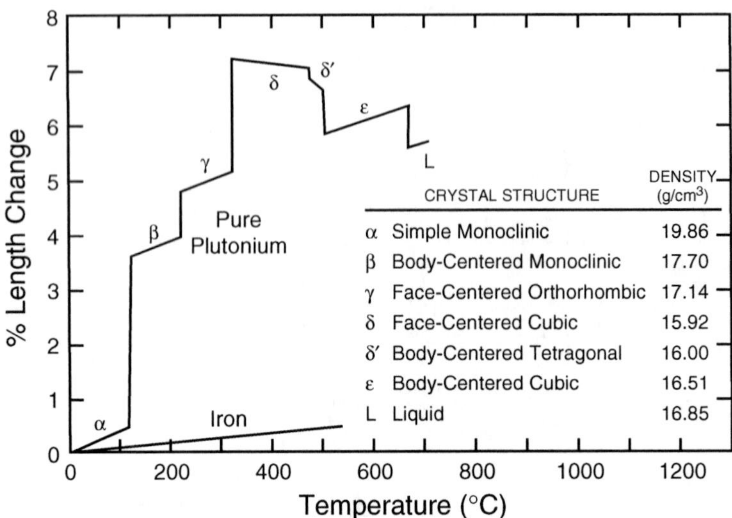

FIGURE 3.16 Plutonium phase chart. (From Lawrence Livermore National Laboratory, operated by the University of California for the U.S. Department of Energy; http://www.llnl.gov/str/JanFeb04/Wong.html.)

TABLE 3.4 Physical Properties of Plutonium

Density	15.9 to 19.9 g/cm^3, depending on metal phase; loose PuO_2 powder has a density of about 2 g/cm^3; sintered pellets have a density of 10.3 to 11.0 g/cm^3
Melting point (pure metal)	640°C
Boiling point (pure metal)	3327°C
Oxidation rate	Slow in dry air; rapid under moist conditions or when heated; may result in low spontaneous ignition temperature
Action of acids and bases	Dissolves readily in concentrated hydrochloric, hydriodic, and perchloric acids; partially soluble in concentrated sulfuric and nitric acids or sodium hydroxide solutions

Source: Lawrence Livermore National Laboratory, operated by the University of California for the U.S. Department of Energy, Jan. 6, 2004; http://www.llnl.gov/str/JanFeb04/Wong.html; accessed 10/03/04.

characteristics make plutonium difficult to handle, store, or transport. Table 3.4 lists the physical properties of plutonium.[26]

Most of the plutonium produced in the U.S. from the separation plants was shipped to Rocky Flats, CO, and machined into warhead pits. The plutonium was usually in the form of a metal,

Figure 3.17 Plutonium-handling glove box. (From U.S. Department of Energy, Linking Legacies Connecting the Cold War Nuclear Weapons Production Processes to Their Environmental Consequences, DOE/EM-0319, Office of Environmental Management, Washington, DC, Jan. 1997; http://legacystory.apps.em.doe.gov; accessed 8/5/04.)

but liquids and powder were also produced. Plutonium is extremely dangerous to workers, even in small quantities. The chief hazards are internal personnel contamination by inhalation or injection, pyrophoricity, and inadvertent criticality. Because of the hazards, plutonium metallurgy required workers to use glove boxes equipped with safety ventilation systems (Figure 3.17), inert atmospheres, and criticality control measures.

Plutonium presents a significant respiratory health hazard for workers. The radiological inhalation limits for nuclear workers are based on a unit called the derived air constant (DAC). A DAC is a unit radiation of dose equivalent to 2.5 mrem internal exposure from a radioactive substance. The DAC is based on the U.S. annual allowable internal dose regulatory limits from internal deposition received by a worker exposed to an airborne radioactive source. The annual allowable limit is 5000 mrem commuted effective dose. A worker exposed to 1 DAC/h during a 40-h work week over a year would receive the annual allowable limit. For plutonium, 1 DAC = 3×10^{-12} Curic per milliliter (in air).[27] This DAC value corresponds to about 4.3×10^{-12} g/ml (air). This is at or below the detection limit for most handheld radiation instruments. U.S. plutonium separation facilities typically deal with airborne contamination levels on the order of millions of DACs. Current technology has not provided the personal protective measures for individuals to enter into areas that contain airborne radiation levels of 1 million DAC. Plutonium machining facilities generate even higher levels of contamination.

3.1.1.2.6 Properties: Metal, Oxides, and Oxidation

Plutonium metal reacts with oxygen at room temperature to form plutonium oxide. Plutonium oxidizes very quickly, with rates varying as a function of temperature, surface area, oxygen concentration, moisture concentration, extent of alloying, and thickness of surface-protective oxides. Moisture has the largest effect on the oxidation rate and significantly impacts processing (Figure 3.18) and storage of plutonium metals and oxides. Several plutonium oxides can be formed directly from metal or decomposition of plutonium compounds. Plutonium oxide (Figure 3.19) is pyrophoric in air and rapidly forms plutonium dioxide and heat. The dioxide is not reactive in air but heats slowly with water vapor at elevated temperatures.

3.1.1.2.7 Plutonium Hydride

Hydrogen generation during plutonium processing presents a significant flammability hazard. Hydride forms during corrosion of plutonium metal by the hydrogen contained in water, organic materials, and other sources. The hydride rapidly oxidizes by dry air at room temperature to produce PuO and hydrogen. The quality of the hydride produced depends on the rate of hydrogen formation and on the magnitude of the hydrogen-containing source. The reactivity of plutonium hydride in air is a function of particle size, presence or absence of a protective oxide layer, and the hydrogen/plutonium ratio. Plutonium hydride is also pyrophoric in air at room temperature. As a result, plutonium hydride must be handled and stored in a very dry and oxygen-free (inert) environment.

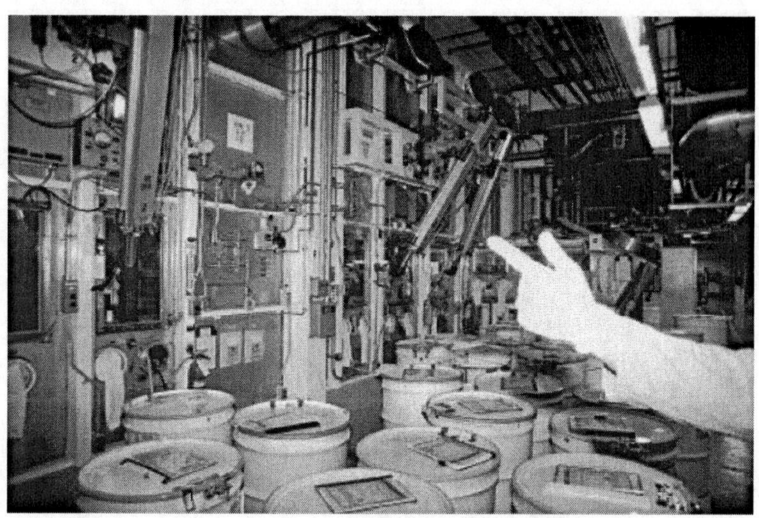

FIGURE 3.18 Plutonium processing facility. (From U.S. Department of Energy, Linking Legacies Connecting the Cold War Nuclear Weapons Production Processes to Their Environmental Consequences, DOE/EM-0319, Office of Environmental Management, Washington, DC, Jan. 1997; http://legacystory.apps.em.doe.gov; accessed 8/5/04.)

3.1.1.2.8 Carbides and Nitride

Plutonium carbides, oxycarbides, and nitride are very reactive and potentially pyrophoric. Carbides, oxycarbides, and nitride materials must not be exposed to air or oxygen-containing atmospheres (greater than 4%). These compounds will also readily react with moisture and form gaseous methane, acetylene, and ammonia. PuO reacts with nitrogen at elevated temperatures to form plutonium nitride (PuN).

3.1.1.2.9 Plutonium Reactions Involving Water

Water vapor will accelerate the oxidation of plutonium, with the hydrogen reacting directly with the metal. The oxidation rate increases about a factor of ten in humid air (at room temperatures). Again, plutonium metal must be handled in a very dry atmosphere. In the U.S., plutonium is typically handled in glove-box enclosures that are inerted with nitrogen or argon. Rapid oxidation is avoided when the oxygen concentration is maintained below 4%. Rapid metal oxidation occurs when moisture levels increase to 1.3% (or about

Figure 3.19 Plutonium oxide. (From U.S. Department of Energy, Linking Legacies Connecting the Cold War Nuclear Weapons Production Processes to Their Environmental Consequences, DOE/EM-0319, Office of Environmental Management, Washington, DC, Jan. 1997; http://legacystory.apps.em.doe.gov; accessed 8/5/04.)

50% relative humidity).[28] Plutonium dioxide can adsorb up to 8% of its weight as water on the surface. The quantity adsorbed is a direct function of the surface area of the oxide. The principal hazard associated with adsorbed water is pressurization of sealed oxide containers through evaporation of water, radiolysis, or direct reaction with the oxide to form a higher oxidation level and hydrogen gas.

Plutonium metallurgy operations are highly sophisticated and require a great deal of technology and a highly educated work force. Figure 3.20 illustrates typical metallurgy operations used at the Hanford Plutonium Finishing Plant to produce stock plutonium "buttons" to be later machined into pits.

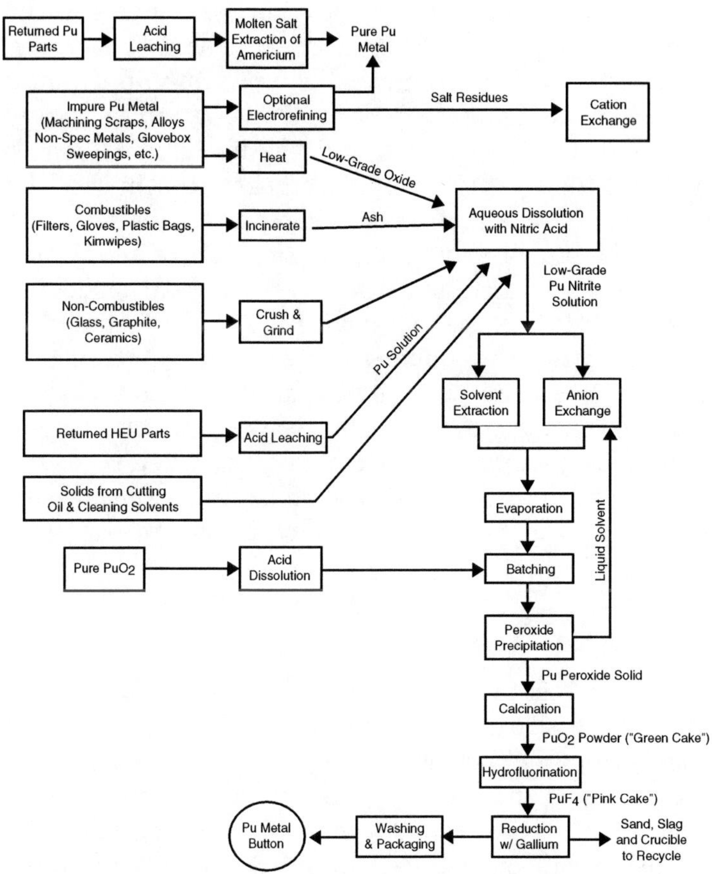

Figure 3.20 Plutonium metallurgy operations. (From U.S. Department of Energy, Linking Legacies Connecting the Cold War Nuclear Weapons Production Processes to Their Environmental Consequences, DOE/EM-0319, Office of Environmental Management, Washington, DC, Jan. 1997; http://legacystory.apps.em.doe.gov; accessed 8/5/04.)

3.1.1.2.10 Spontaneous Combustibility and Pyrophoricity of Plutonium Compounds

Plutonium can also spontaneously combust from the slow buildup of heat (spontaneous heating) and may instantly ignite when exposed to air (pyrophoricity). Some of the most serious fires that have occurred within U.S. facilities were caused by the ignition of finely divided plutonium particles.[29] When heated to ignition temperature, plutonium reacts at an accelerated oxidation rate, which sustains continued oxidation. The combustion temperature is a function of the heat dissipation rate to the surroundings and the surface area of oxidizing metal. Plutonium fires at U.S. facilities usually exceeded the melting temperature of plutonium metal (640°C) and resulted in the material consolidating into a molten configuration. Fine metal, turnings, and casting skulls tend to ignite readily and achieve a high enough temperature that results in melting until the reactive surface area is reduced. The resulting oxide layer limits the burning and the oxidation rate of plutonium. Plutonium combustion is similar to that of a charcoal briquette. Plutonium metal ignition temperature depends on the factors that affect the oxidation rate. Finely divided plutonium metal, such as metal powder of fine machine turnings, ignites near 150°C. This temperature may be easily reached if a coexisting pyrophoric material such as a hydride spontaneously ignites at room temperature. Bulk or massive plutonium characterized as having a specific surface area less than 10 cm/g requires temperatures in excess of 400°C to ignite.

3.1.1.2.11 Storage and Handling

Plutonium should be stored as pure metal or in its dioxide form in a dry, inert, or slightly oxidizing atmosphere (Figure 3.21). The formation of oxide from metal is accompanied by a large expansion in volume (up to 70%) that may bulge or breach the primary container. Case studies show that mechanical wedging resulting from this expansion can even breach a second metal container, resulting in localized release of contaminants and possible exposure of personnel.[30] Oxidation of the metal and subsequent container rupture can be prevented by hermetically sealing. The U.S. typically used commercial cans for this purpose. Plutonium radioactively decays, producing alpha particles and helium molecules. Over the long term, the helium pressure builds, and the sealed containers become pressurized and may bulge or fail.

3.1.1.2.12 Criticality Hazards for Plutonium

Prevention of inadvertent criticality is always a key consideration when handling plutonium or plutonium-based solutions. An inadvertent criticality would result in very intense pulses of radiation potentially lethal to personnel in the immediate area. The initial pulse may be followed by a series of subsequent pulses that lead to a continuous stream of radiation and power output. Personnel handing the plutonium would not be able to avoid exposure to the

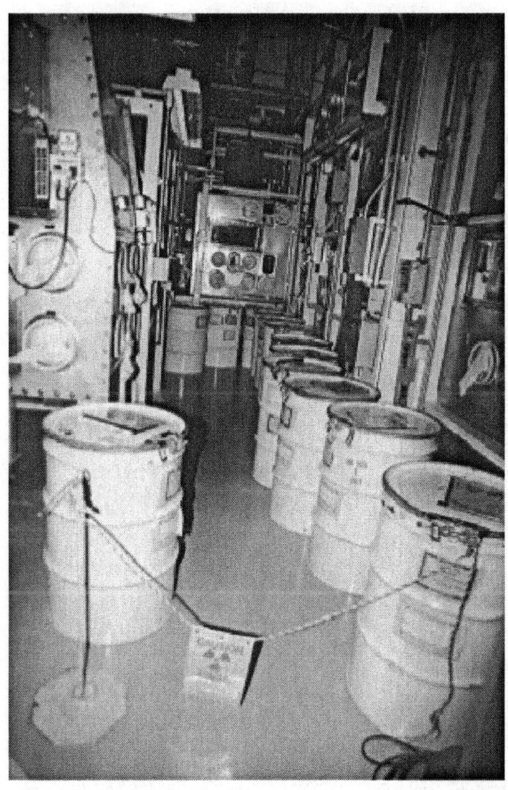

FIGURE 3.21 Typical plutonium containment. (From U.S. Department of Energy, Linking Legacies Connecting the Cold War Nuclear Weapons Production Processes to Their Environmental Consequences, DOE/EM-0319, Office of Environmental Management, Washington, DC, Jan. 1997; http://legacystory.apps.em.doe.gov; accessed 8/5/04.)

initial pulse of radiation. The pulse is generally less than a second in length and is difficult to anticipate.

The fission process accompanying an inadvertent criticality would emit a large gamma ray flux. The gamma emissions would produce a continuous energy spectrum between 10 keV to about 10 MeV. An average of 8.1 photons per fission, at 7.25 MeV, would be emitted during the first 50 nsec. An additional 0.98-MeV photons would be emitted during the remainder of the first second. Short-lived fission products contribute another 0.3 MeV/fission of gamma radiation during the first second,[31] resulting in very high doses.

The potential for an inadvertent criticality with plutonium is strongly influenced by several physical parameters. For example, a configuration consisting of eight 3-kg plutonium metal cylinders, in a $2 \times 2 \times 2$ array, submerged in water, would exceed a minimum critical mass.[32] Parameters affecting inadvertent criticality include:

- Material mass (fissionable and other materials; 640 kg is the minimum critical mass for Pu^{239})
- Material density (solid) or concentration (liquid processing)
- Container volume and shape
- Composition of nonfissionable materials (absorbers and moderators)
- Container design or surrounding conditions (presence of neutron reflectors)
- System geometry
- Environmental conditions (temperature)

The U.S. instituted stringent administrative and engineering controls to minimize the probability of inadvertent criticality at government and civilian facilities. These controls include extensive criticality-prevention modeling and double-contingency requirements when handling or storing any fissile materials. Double contingency requires at least two controls to maintain the material in a subcritical configuration.

3.1.1.2.13 Uses in Weapons

Fission weapons can be categorized as two basic design concepts:[33] gun type and implosion type.

3.1.1.2.13.1 Gun Type, Using HEU. The gun-type weapon design can use only HEU. The gun-type design is based on the concept of quickly forcing together two subcritical masses of HEU to form a critical mass (Figure 3.22). The two masses of HEU are brought together in a linear device that resembles the barrel of a large gun. The gun-type design is the simplest way of producing a nuclear weapon. Little Boy was the first gun-type device. The scientists who designed it were so confident that it would work that they never tested it before Little Boy was air-dropped on August 6, 1945, at Hiroshima, Japan. Little Boy used about 62 kg of HEU, weighed approximately 4000 kg, and had an explosive yield equal to 15 kt of TNT. Pakistan began its nuclear program with the production of HEU using gas-centrifuge separation and the gun-type design. Pakistan, as we now know, sold this technology to Lybia, Iran, North Korea, and possibly others.[34]

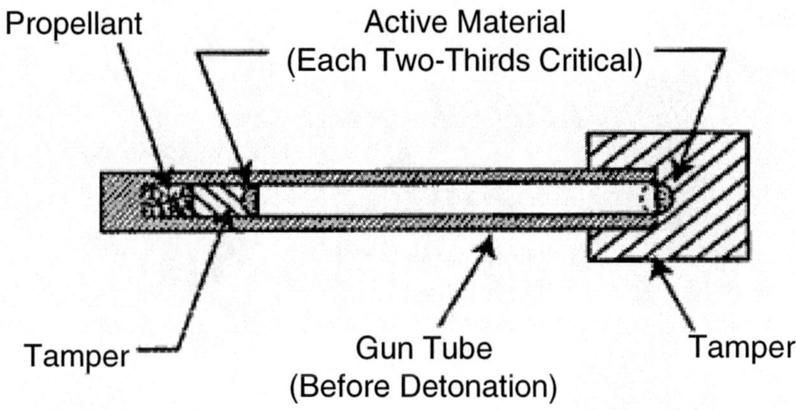

FIGURE 3.22 Diagram of a gun-type nuclear device.[54]

3.1.1.2.13.2 Implosion Type, Using Plutonium or HEU. The implosion weapon is based on the concept that a symmetrical compression of a hollow sphere of plutonium will form a supercritical mass (Figure 3.23). The weapon uses conventional high explosives to compress the sphere. The implosion quickly reduces the sphere diameter by half while increasing the plutonium metal density by a factor of eight. The Fat Man weapon was an implosion device used at Nagasaki in 1945 with a 21- to 23-kt yield. Fat Man was 12 ft long with a 60-in. diameter and weighed about 10,300 lb. Fat Man used about 6.2 kg of plutonium. The implosion concept is used in modern nuclear weapon design to trigger the more powerful fusion reaction. Implosion weapons are far more difficult to build than gun-type weapons, but they are more efficient. The Iraq nuclear program sought to build an implosion bomb using HEU. North Korea, on the other hand, chose to go the route of Pu^{239}, which required a nuclear reactor and separation facilities.

3.1.1.2.13.3 Weapon Components. Research, development, and testing have been an essential part of the U.S. nuclear weapons complex as well as for other countries with a nuclear weapons program. Two national laboratories — Laurence Livermore National Laboratory in Livermore, CA, and Los Alamos National Laboratory in Los Alamos, NM — devoted billions of dollars to develop and refine nuclear weapons. A third national laboratory

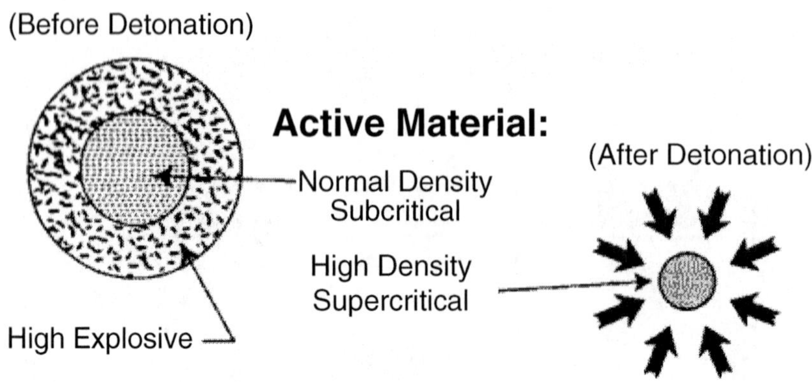

FIGURE 3.23 Diagram of an implosion-type nuclear device.[54]

in Sandia, NM, worked on the electronic mechanisms for nuclear warheads as well as designs for coupling the warheads to bombs and missiles. While simplified basic weapon design information is within the public domain (Figure 3.2), the rogue state would need sophisticated engineering capability to properly manufacture weapon components. To illustrate this point, the major components of an implosion device — the initiator, active material, tamper, and explosive lenses — are examined.

Initiator. An implosion device requires a neutron initiator to begin the chain reaction. The Fat Man initiator consisted of a shape-charged cone machined into a beryllium shell. The explosive facilitated a shock wave to mix the beryllium and polonium components. The Trinity device initiator design[35,36] was patterned after a hollow beryllium ball with wedgelike grooves machined in the internal surface, with the axes of all grooves parallel to each other. This initiator used gold and nickel plating integrated into layers to generate neutrons to start the chain reaction. The collapsing grooves mixed the beryllium and polonium to generate the initial neutrons.

Active Material. The active material used in the first implosion devices was delta-phase plutonium metal with a specific weight of 15.8 g/cm^3. The plutonium was manufactured into a hollow ball consisting of two halves. The two halves, like the initiator balls, were pressed in an atmosphere of nickel-carbonyl

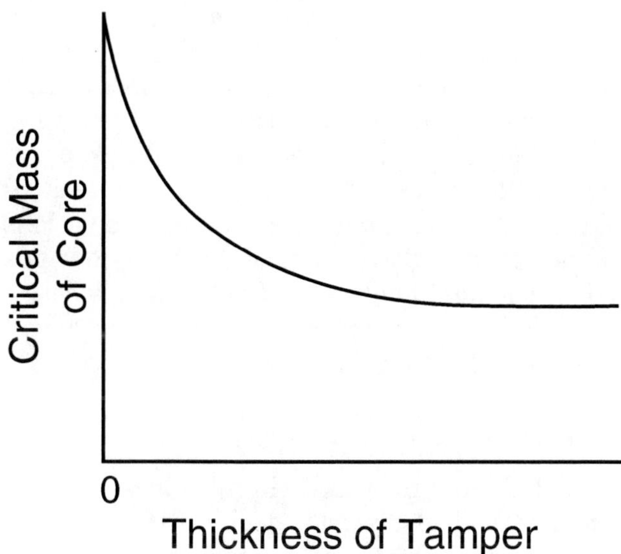

Figure 3.24 Required tamper as a function of active material.

to prevent reactions with oxygen. The external diameter of the ball was between 80 and 90 mm. The weight, including the initiator, ranged from 7.3 to 10 kg. A 0.1-mm-thick corrugated gold gasket was located between the halves of the sphere. The gasket prevented penetration of high-speed gas jets, which might prematurely activate the initiator. The sphere included a 25-mm-diameter opening to allow insertion of the initiator into the center of the weapon. This opening was closed with a plutonium plug prior to detonation. The active material was clad with aluminum.

Tamper. Early implosion devices used a natural uranium tamper shell to surround the core (Figure 3.24). The tamper served as a neutron reflector and an inertial restraint to explosive disassembly. The tamper external surface was covered with a layer of boron, which absorbed the thermal neutrons that were spontaneously emitted. This reduced the probability of predetonation.

Explosive Lenses. Design of the explosive lenses was one of the most challenging engineering problems encountered during development of early implosion devices. The lenses had to systemically reduce the diameter of the active material by half while increasing the plutonium metal density by a factor of eight. The first device used 32 blocks of high explosives, wrapped with a layer of aluminum. The internal surface of the explosive blocks facing the center was spherical and had a diameter about equal to the external diameter of the aluminum layer. Special slots in the external surfaces of the blocks allowed for the insertion of 20 hexagonal lenses and 12 pentagonal lenses. A 1/16-in. felt lining separated the lenses from the aluminum cladding. The high-explosive lens used in the Fat Man weapon weighed a total of 2 t. Early designs also had to accommodate the heat load generated from radioactive decay of active material. The plutonium pit was an intrinsic heat source, producing about an 18-W heat load.

3.1.1.2.14 Chemical Separation Waste Management

Chemical separation and plutonium processing produces a large amount of radioactive waste. These wastes include the cladding wastes produced by the removal of the coating from irradiated fuel elements and the high-level wastes containing the fission products separated from the uranium and plutonium. Miscellaneous low-level and transuranic waste streams come from plutonium-concentration and finishing processes, uranium solidification, floor drains, laboratory analysis, and other activities. Any clandestine weapon production would produce similar amounts of radioactive wastes.

The bismuth phosphate process wastes included coating-removal waste, first- and second-cycle decontamination wastes, and cell drainage waste. The first three waste types were neutralized with sodium hydroxide and stored in sixteen 500,000-gallon underground tanks. Each tank was made of reinforced concrete lined with a quarter inch of steel plate. Twelve of the tanks were 75 ft in diameter, and four were 20 ft across. The fourth waste stream was discharged into the ground. Wastes from the final plutonium perfection process (224 buildings) were stored in a 20-ft-diameter settling tank, then combined with used cooling water and discharged to retention basins and drainage ditches.

Radioactive air emissions from chemical separation were also a continuing problem at U.S. production facilities. Xenon and iodine gases were released from the fuel matrix when the slugs dissolved. The presence of these gases in air samples is an indicator that a country has embarked on reprocessing. Beginning in the fall of 1947, emissions of radioactive particulates and mists from the stacks appeared. Workers installed scrubbers and sand and fiberglass filters to reduce these emissions. Iodine emissions continued to be a problem, although they were lessened by an increase in fuel cooling times to between 90 and 125 days. The U.S. installed silver iodide reactors in 1950 to scrub most of the iodine from the stack gases. Mercury, silver, potassium, and sodium added to the dissolver also reduced the generation of iodine gas by keeping the material dissolved in the waste.

Clandestine development of a Pu^{239} implosion weapon is beyond the resource capability of most rogue countries without outside assistance. Furthermore, it is almost impossible to hide the waste steams generated from plutonium production.

3.1.2 Peaceful Uses

Even though weapons have the most notoriety of all the applications of nuclear science, nuclear technology's most significant impact on mankind has been and will continue to be for peaceful purposes. Since its discovery, radiation has been used for the treatment of cancer and for medical diagnostics. Nuclear technology has saved countless lives. Nuclear science plays a critical role in research, and nuclear reactors provide an energy source that does not contribute to greenhouse gas emissions.

It is unfortunate that most people associate nuclear science and technology with weapons. Many myths about the technology have evolved from this perception. One such myth is that there are enough nuclear weapons to destroy the world many times over. This assertion when examined in detail does not stand up. What exactly does it take to destroy a world? A large asteroid, commonly referred to as a nemesis asteroid, is hypothesized to have caused the extinction of the dinosaurs 65 million years ago. Most people would agree that this event was a world destroyer. The impact of this asteroid had an explosive energy 1000 times larger than the world's entire nuclear arsenal.[37] About 600 smaller asteroids with an equivalent explosive energy of about that of the world's nuclear arsenal have struck the earth.[38] The smaller asteroid strikes were destructive, but not world destroyers. Their impacts were thousands of times less destructive than the asteroid that is believed by many to have caused the mass extinction 65 million years ago. Explosive energies approaching that of a nemesis asteroid have also been attributed to super volcanoes,[39] but there have been many smaller volcanic events with explosive energies on the order of the world's nuclear arsenal since the last mass extinction. One final comparison that is contemporary is that in 10 to 20 min, a hurricane will release more energy than all the world's nuclear weapons combined.

Prior to the Three Mile Island (TMI) accident on March 28, 1979,[40] the movie *The China Syndrome* was released. The premise of *The China Syndrome* was that a nuclear power plant core meltdown would lead to the fuel forming a liquid critical mass that would melt through the floor of the reactor containment building and then would continue to burn through the earth, where the mass would react with water, causing the material to vent into the atmosphere. The speculation of nuclear critics was that millions of people would die in a reactor meltdown. These critics called *The China Syndrome* prophetic after TMI. That the "China syndrome" was physically impossible was secondary to publicity. In actuality, TMI suffered a partial core meltdown. The containment system worked as designed. There were no fatalities due to the TMI accident. The most significant impact was economic, in that the Metropolitan Edison Company, the owner of the plant, and its investors lost quite a bit of money.

On April 26, 1986, the Chernobyl No. 4 reactor suffered a meltdown in the Ukraine. Chernobyl 4 was an RMBK reactor with no containment. The graphite moderator caught fire and burned for nine days releasing about 12×10^{18} Bq of radioactivity into the atmosphere. There were initial reports of a devastated landscape with hordes of dead and injured people. When we ask students in our courses how many died in the Chernobyl 4 accident, they give answers in the thousands to millions. The real answer is 30. These were mainly the firefighters who sacrificed themselves to put out the fire.[41] We have learned a lot from Chernobyl. For example, radioactive material precipitates out of the plume much more rapidly than anyone had realized. There was no "China syndrome." In contrast, an examination of the consequences of other types of industrial accidents, offers a different perspective on relative risks. On December 3, 1984, gas leaked from a tank of methyl isocyanate at a pesticide plant in Bhopal, India, owned and operated by Union Carbide India, Ltd. About 3800 persons died, 40 persons experienced permanent total disability, and 2680 persons experienced permanent partial disability.[42] There are several Bhopal-type pesticide plants near large U.S. cities.

The inability to safely store nuclear waste is a myth that has been perpetuated by critics of nuclear technology for some time. This myth too can easily be deflated. Natural fossil nuclear fission reactors were discovered in the present day Gabon Republic in equatorial Africa.[43] These reactors are located at the Oklo uranium deposit located in the southeastern corner of the Gabon Republic and another deposit at Bangombe, about 35 km southeast of the Oklo mine. Two billion years ago, the relative abundance of U^{235} as compared with U^{238} was greater than 3%. In order for fission to occur, the following is needed: enriched uranium, a low concentration of neutron absorbers, an abundance of neutron-moderating material (e.g., water), and a sufficient core size to limit neutron leakage losses. The uranium ore in the Oklo and Bangombe mines was in a river bed and thus had water, contained enriched uranium, had a low concentration of neutron absorbers, and was present in very large amounts, thus meeting the criteria for criticality. The reactors became critical 2 billion years ago and continued to operate for approximately 1 million years. The total amount of energy produced by these reactors is greater than the energy cumulatively generated by nuclear man-made power reactors since their inception. If the nuclear waste had transported out of the ore of a fissile reactor as fast as nuclear critics believe, then we never would have discovered the fossil nuclear reactors after 2 billion years. In other words, the ore body was a sufficient barrier to trap the nuclear waste, even though it was exposed to water. The proposed nuclear waste storage technology is far superior to a uranium ore body.[44] The U.S. proposes to store its high-level nuclear waste at Yucca Mountain, NV. The plan is to combine the natural barriers in Yucca Mountain with man-made barriers that will work together to provide a comprehensive protection system. First of all, Yucca Mountain is located in an arid region that has been stable over a long time period. The mountain consists of alternating layers of volcanic rock above and below the level of the repository. The rocks above the repository contain few fractures, thus blocking the moisture pathway. In the repository itself, water is trapped in the small fractures in the surrounding rock, thus eliminating standing water. The waste containers are designed to have multiple barriers. Each has a titanium drip shield and a waste container with a special metal called Alloy 22 as an outer barrier. Inside the container, the waste is in solid form and is doubly encapsulated. Both Alloy 22 and titanium are corrosion-resistant. Corrosion is expected to penetrate only about 0.08 in. in 10,000 years.

There are numerous other myths about nuclear science and technology that would take a separate book to address and dispel.

The psychological impact that nuclear weapons has on nuclear science is far-reaching. For example, nuclear magnetic resonance imaging was an enormous medical breakthrough about 20 years ago, but the word *nuclear* scared patients, and the instrument was renamed magnetic resonance imaging (MRI). When nuclear weapons are viewed rationally, the threat that they pose can be evaluated without psychological issues. More importantly, the science involved in nuclear technologies can be viewed in an unencumbered light. It is the authors' hope that the issues involving nuclear technology can be analyzed for the risks that they actually pose and not the perceptions that have been ingrained in the national psyche.

3.2 RADIOACTIVE MATERIALS

Radioactive materials can be either naturally occurring or man-made (e.g., fission products, neutron activation). Materials are made up of atoms, and the atoms have a positively charged nucleus with orbiting electrons. In nuclear science we focus on the nucleus, which is made up of protons and neutrons. We identify the radioactive nucleus by the number of neutrons (N) and the number of protons (Z) in its nucleus. The number of protons in the nucleus governs the chemical properties of the material. The number of neutrons in the nucleus governs the nuclear properties of the material. In Figure 3.25, all known isotopes are shown graphically plotted with the number of neutrons (N) presented on the x-axis and the number of protons (Z) is on the y-axis. The stable isotopes are shown as black squares, the beta emitters as the shaded squares, the beta-plus emitters as light shadows, and the alpha emitters are of higher mass. Figure 3.25 tells you how the number of neutrons impacts the nuclear properties. All radioactive isotopes decay to become stable isotopes (black squares). If an isotope has more neutrons than its stable form, it will emit beta radiation to become stable. One of the most common types of decay is beta emission (squares below the stable elements), where a neutron in the nucleus is converted into a proton, and an electron (beta particle) and antineutrino are emitted. If a nucleus has more protons than its stable form, it will emit beta-plus (positron) radiation. The most common type of decay is beta-plus decay (squares above the stable isotopes), where a proton in the nucleus is converted into a neutron, and a positron (beta plus) and neutrino are emitted. An alpha particle, a helium nucleus, is typically emitted by a heavy isotope.

Another feature that is not evident in Figure 3.25 is that the further an isotope is from the stable isotopes, the faster is the

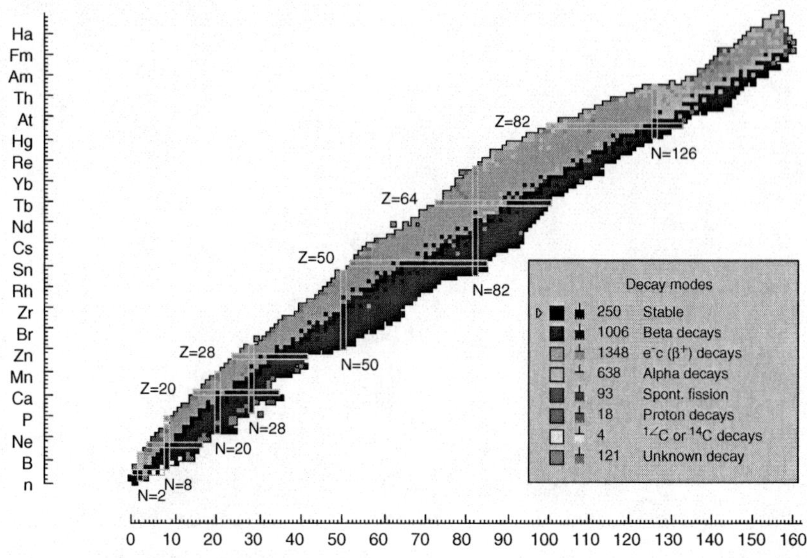

FIGURE 3.25 Graphic representation of all the known isotopes.

radioactive emission process. The rate of decay is described by the isotopes' half-life. (The half-life is the time it takes a given number of radioactive atoms to decay to half the original number of radioactive atoms.) The decay of radioactive elements is a statistical process. This process can be modeled by a differential equation called the rate equation. Rate equations are used in many fields such as biological science to study population and in energy resources. The rate equation written out is shown below:

$$\frac{dN}{dt} = -kN \tag{3.3}$$

where N is the number of radioactive atoms, t is time, and k is a decay constant.

The solution to this equation predicts how the number of radioactive atoms changes with time. As shown below, the change is dominated by an exponential with an argument that is dependent on k and t.

$$N(t) = N(0)e^{-kt} \tag{3.4}$$

A critical parameter called the half-life can be found by solving for the time at which half of the radioactive atoms decay:

$$\frac{N\left(t_{1/2}\right)}{N\left(0\right)} = 0.5 = e^{-kt_{1/2}} \quad (3.5)$$

$$-kt_{1/2} = \ln\left(0.5\right) \quad (3.6)$$

$$k = \frac{0.693}{t_{1/2}} \quad (3.7)$$

Typically, in nuclear science, the decay rate of nuclei is described by a half-life. From the half-life, you can calculate the decay constant (k) as shown above. This number is important because the decay constant is used to calculate the activity of the radioactive material. Activity A is defined in Equation 3.8 as the decays per second and is the product of the decay constant (k) times the number of radioactive nuclei (N).

$$\text{A} = kN \text{ decays/sec} \quad (3.8)$$

The Curie (named for Madame Marie Curie) is a unit defined as 30 billion decays per second. Sources of radioactive materials are typically defined by their activity. For example, a micro-Curie beta source will emit 30,000 beta particles per second.

The energy of the radiation is also important information. Because radiation is made up of single particles with a low mass, the energy will be a small number even for a very energetic particle. The unit of energy that is used for radiation is an electron volt (eV). Kinetic energy is defined as

$$E = \frac{1}{2}mv^2 \quad (3.9)$$

where E is kinetic energy, m is mass in kilograms of the particle, and v is the particle velocity in meters per second.

If an electron has a velocity near the speed of light, say 20 million m/sec, and a mass of 9.11×10^{-31} kg, its energy is

$$E = 1.822 \times 10^{-17}\,\text{J} \quad (3.10)$$

The definition of a joule (J) is the amount of energy needed to raise the temperature of 1 cm³ of water by 1°C. This is an energetic electron, and the electron volt helps scientists to gauge just how energetic it is. The electron volt is 1.6×10^{-19} J. Thus the electron used in the above example has an energy of 114 eV. In general, radiation has energies ranging from 1 keV (1,000 eV) to 1 MeV (1,000,000 eV).

3.2.1 Sources of Radioactivity

3.2.1.1 Beta Emitters

A beta emitter is an unstable nucleus with more neutrons than the stable isotope counterpart. A good example illustrating this principle is hydrogen. Normally, the hydrogen nucleus is made up of a single proton. Another stable form of hydrogen is deuterium, which has a nucleus with one proton and one neutron. Tritium, an unstable form of hydrogen, has a nucleus made up of a proton and two neutrons. Tritium decays by beta emission, with a half-life of 12.36 years, to the more stable helium.

$$ {}^{3}_{1}\mathrm{T}_{2} \rightarrow {}^{3}_{2}\mathrm{He}_{1} + \beta + \bar{\nu} + 18\,\mathrm{keV} \tag{3.11} $$

where T is tritium, He is helium, β is a beta particle, and $\bar{\nu}$ is an antineutrino.

3.2.1.2 Alpha Emitters

An alpha emitter is typically a heavy nucleus that emits an alpha particle (helium nucleus) as its decay product. An example of an alpha emitter is polonium 210.

$$ {}^{210}_{84}\mathrm{Po}_{126} \rightarrow {}^{4}_{2}\mathrm{He}_{2} + {}^{206}_{82}\mathrm{Pb}_{124} + 5.4\,\mathrm{MeV} \tag{3.12} $$

3.2.1.3 Gamma Emitters

A gamma ray emitter is an excited nucleus that emits a gamma ray (energetic electromagnetic wave) as the nucleus proceeds to a lower energy level. An example is the decay of cobalt 60 to nickel 60, which emits both beta and gamma radiation.

$$ {}^{60}_{27}\mathrm{Co}_{33} \rightarrow {}^{60}_{28}\mathrm{Ni}_{32} + \beta + \bar{\nu} + \gamma \tag{3.13} $$

The details of cobalt 60 decay can be seen in Figure 3.26.

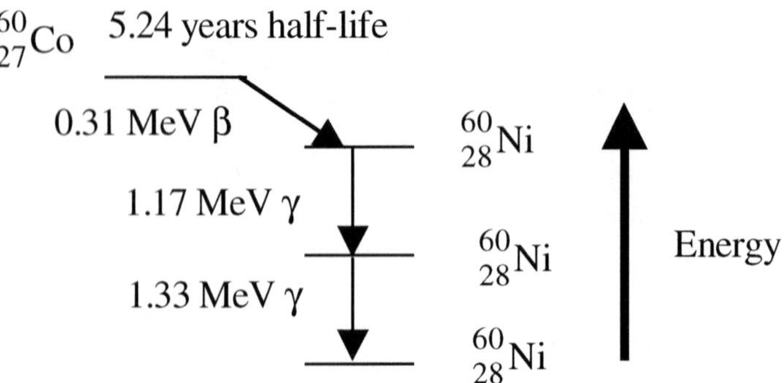

FIGURE 3.26 Decay scheme for cobalt-60.

3.2.1.4 Spontaneous Fission

Spontaneous fission occurs with man-made heavy isotopes such as californium 252. Plutonium was transformed to plutonium 242, plutonium 244, americium, curium, and californium 252 as part of a DOE project to promote the applications of radioisotopes for industry, medicine, and nuclear and radiation research. Californium 252 was produced in the Savannah River reactors and in the Oak Ridge National Laboratory (ORNL) high-flux isotope reactor.

$$^{252}_{98}Cf_{154} \rightarrow \text{light fragment} + \text{heavy fragment} + \text{neutrons} + \text{gamma rays} \tag{3.14}$$

where Cf is californium.

3.2.2 Production

The market for isotopes worldwide is very large, encompassing medical, industrial, and scientific applications. There are a number of production facilities engaged in isotope production, as seen in Table 3.5.

The proliferation concern with isotopes is their use in dirty bombs.

3.2.3 Medical Applications

The largest endeavor in nuclear science is in medical applications. Specifically, the use of radioisotopes in diagnostics and treatment

TABLE 3.5 Isotope Production Information

Reactors	Number
Research reactors	75[a]
Fast neutron reactors	2
Nuclear power plants	≈10
Accelerators	188
Cyclotrons: medical isotopes	48
Cyclotrons: Positron Emmission Tomography (PET)	130
Nondedicated accelerators	10
Isotope separation	
Separation facilities	21
Stable isotope production facilities	9
Producing countries of the world	50
Western Europe	17
Eastern Europe and Russia/Kazakhstan	8
North America	3
Asia and Middle East	12
Rest of the world	10

[a] Six are high-flux reactors.
Source: Nuclear Energy Institute, Beneficial Uses and Production of Isotopes; http://www.nei.org/doc.asp?catnum=3&catid=191; accessed 1/11/04.

of disease is a high growth area. Medical isotopes are used in 30 million procedures each year. These procedures include nuclear imaging, assay, and therapy.

3.2.3.1 Diagnostics

Diagnostic radiopharmaceuticals currently dominate the medical isotope arena. Diagnostic nuclear medicine begins with the administration of very small amounts of radioactive substances that are distributed in the body based on the product's physical and chemical properties. The radiopharmaceutical usefulness of the substance depends upon its affinity for certain organs or sites within the body. The radioactive materials emit radiation, and the site can be imaged with detectors or cameras focused on the radiation. The raw data from the detector or camera are analyzed with software.

There are 17 different elemental groups of radiopharmaceutical compounds approved for diagnostic procedures by the Food

Table 3.6 Applications in Nuclear Imaging

Gamma imaging
  8,200 departments use gamma cameras
  17,000 gamma cameras are used for
    Lungs: embolisms, breathing difficulties
    Bones: tumors, infection
    Thyroid: hyper/hypothyroidism
    Kidney: renal fixation
    Brain: embolisms, blood flow, tumors
    Liver and pancreas: cirrhosis, necrosis
    Abdomen: tumors
    Blood: leukocytes
    Heart: myocardial infarction
Positron imaging (PET)
  150 PET centers
  200 PET cameras are used for
    Bone density measurements

Source: Nuclear Energy Institute, Beneficial Uses and Production of Isotopes; http://www.nei.org/doc.asp?catnum=3&catid= 191; accessed 1/11/04.

and Drug Administration (FDA). From these 17 groups, there are 51 different compounds for specific diagnostic applications that have been developed. About 117 radiopharmaceuticals based on these 51 compounds have been approved for use. For example, technetium has 53 radiopharmaceuticals approved for use.

Nuclear medicine imaging procedures are used to identify abnormalities very early in the progression of a disease. Early detection for many of these diseases can lead to successful early treatment. Radiopharmaceuticals have dramatically improved patient care worldwide. The legitimate supply of these radiopharmaceuticals, particularly technetium products, is critical to advances in health care. On the other hand, the production of radioisotopes does draw concern from those concerned with potential misuse of the technology. Table 3.6 lists the applications in nuclear imaging.

3.2.3.2 Assay and Therapy

Because 50% of all prostate, breast, and lung cancer patients eventually develop bone cancer, it is critical to treat bone cancer and manage pain. Radiopharmaceuticals have been employed for bone cancer for both purposes. Five radiopharmaceuticals are either in general use or in clinical trials:

1. Phosphorus-32 was introduced in the early 1940s.
2. Strontium-89 has been approved by the FDA for general use and is most commonly used.
3. Rhenium-186 is currently in phase II and phase III trials.
4. Samarium-153 is currently in phase II and phase III clinical trials.
5. Tin-117m is in phase I clinical trials.

There is tremendous growth potential in therapeutic isotopes:

- Many clinical trials have shown good results with therapeutic isotopes. These isotopes treat cancer and could lead to an eventual cure because individual cells can be targeted.
- The FDA approved strontium-89 for use in 1995, and iodine-131 and rhenium-186 are nearing approval.
- Alpha emitters are gaining attention with the clinical use of bismuth-213.
- Phosphorous-32 has been effective in destroying malignant tumors caused by pancreatic cancer.

Many industry experts expect the demand for therapeutic isotopes to grow rapidly and eventually to surpass the demand for diagnostic isotopes. This will certainly lead to an increase in demand for isotopes, which could also increase opportunities for misuse. Table 3.7 lists various medical uses of isotopes.

A significant number of isotopes have applications in medicine (Table 3.8), and this list will grow as the field matures.

3.2.4 Commercial Applications

Isotopes have found numerous applications in industry, including measurement, analysis, security, smoke detection, sterilization, and lighting (Table 3.9).

As previously described, californium 252 is an excellent spontaneous fission neutron source. Neutron sources are used for oil-well logging, industrial radiography, reactor start-up, nuclear physics research, and medical applications.

3.2.5 Research

Isotopes such as carbon 14, carbon 13, nitrogen 15, oxygen 18, and deuterium (H-2) can be used in biochemical molecules as a means of tracing conversion processes. They have found uses in many areas in chemical and materials research. Table 3.10 lists applications of isotopes in research.

Table 3.7 Assay and Therapeutic Uses of Isotopes

Assay
- Radioimmunoassay
- Assay in microbiology, hematology, biochemistry, molecular biology, and immunology
- Detecting tumor markers or hormones
- Measure levels of steroids, growth factors, and presence of *Helicobacter pylori*

Therapy
- Radiotherapy with radiopharmaceuticals for hyperthyroidism, synovitis, and cancers
- Radiotherapy with sealed sources
  - Cobalt therapy
  - Primary application is destroying cancer cells
    - 1,500 units
    - 1,300 centers
  - Gamma knives (85) used in treatment of brain tumors
  - Brachytherapy
  - Primary application is implantation of radioactive seeds in tumors
    - 3,000 oncology centers
    - ≈50,000 procedures each year
  - Irradiation of blood for transfusion
  - Irradiation of blood for transfusions in organ transplant patients
    - 1,000 irradiators
  - Endovascular radiotherapy
  - Radioactive stents to prevent vessel collapse

Source: Nuclear Energy Institute, Beneficial Uses and Production of Isotopes; http://www.nei.org/doc.asp?catnum=3&catid= 191; accessed 1/11/04.

3.3 DIRTY BOMBS

Dirty bombs are made with chemical explosives wrapped with radioactive materials.[45] The goal of the dirty bomb is to spread radioactive materials over a wide area.[46] The idea of dirty bombs is not new. For example, Adolph Hitler's Third Reich had an interest in using a dirty bomb on the U.S. after it entered the war. As part of this effort, a rocket plane was being researched as a delivery system.

The dirty bomb is more of a psychological weapon than a WMD. First of all, radiation is most lethal when it is concentrated. Prior to the exploding of the device, the radiation will be concentrated. After the explosion, it will be widely dispersed. Second, if the material is dispersed, highly sensitive nuclear sensors can detect very small amounts of radioactive material. The cleanup process is much less complex when the hot spots can be found.

Table 3.8 Isotope Applications in Medicine

Isotope	Half-Life	Applications
Actinium 225	10.0 d	Cancer treatment
Actinium 227	21.8 yr	Cancer treatment
Americium 241	432 yr	Osteoporosis and heart imaging
Arsenic 72	26.0 h	SPECT (single photon emission computed tomography) or PET
Arsenic 74	17.8 d	Biomedical applications
Astatine 211	7.21 h	Cancer treatment
Beryllium 7	53.2 d	Berylliosis studies
Bismuth 212	1.10 h	Cancer treatment and cellular dosimetry
Bismuth 213	45.6 months	Cancer treatment
Boron 11	Stable	Melanoma and brain tumor
Bromine 75	98 months	SPECT or PET
Bromine 77	57 h	Labeling
Cadmium 109	462 d	Cancer detection and pediatric imaging
Californium 252	2.64 yr	Cervical, skin, brain cancer
Carbon 11	20.3 months	Radiotracer in PET
Carbon 14	5730 yr	Radiolabeling
Cerium 139	138 d	Calibration
Cerium 141	32.5 d	Gastrointestinal diagnosis and myocardial blood flow
Cesium 130	29.2 months	Localizing agent
Cesium 131	9.69 d	Radiotherapy
Cesium 137	30.2 yr	Irradiators, PET, and tumor treatment
Chromium 51	27.7 d	Labeling and dosimetry
Cobalt 55	17.5 h	SPECT or PET
Cobalt 57	272 d	Calibration
Cobalt 60	5.27 yr	Teletherapy and disinfection of surgical equipment and medicines
Copper 61	3.35 h	SPECT or PET
Copper 62	4.7 months	Tracer
Copper 64	12.7 h	PET, SPECT, and treatment of colorectal cancer
Copper 67	61.9 h	Cancer treatment/diagnostics, radioimmunotherapy, SPECT, or PET
Dysprosium 165	2.33 h	Rheumatoid arthritis treatment
Europium 152	13.4 yr	Medical
Europium 155	4.73 yr	Osteoporosis
Fluorine 18	110 months	Radiotracer and PET
Gadolinium 153	242 d	SPECT
Gallium 64	2.63 months	Pulmonary diseases ending in fibrosis of lungs
Gallium 67	78.3 h	Hodgkins/non-Hodgkins lymphoma
Gallium 68	68.1 months	PET and detection of pancreatic cancer

Table 3.8 (continued) Isotope Applications in Medicine

Isotope	Half-Life	Applications
Germanium 68	271 d	PET
Gold 198	2.69 d	Ovarian, prostate, and brain cancer
Hydrogen 3	12.3 yr	Labeling and PET
Indium 111	2.81 d	Detection, labeling, and imaging
Indium 115m	4.49 h	Label
Iodine 122	3.6 months	Brain blood flow
Iodine 123	13.1 h	Brain, thyroid, kidney, and myocardial imaging and neurological disease (Alzheimer's)
Iodine 124	4.17 d	Radiotracer and PET
Iodine 125	59.9 d	Osteoporosis detection and diagnostic imaging
Iodine 131	8.04 d	Treatment and imaging
Iodine 132	2.28 h	Diagnostics
Iridium 191m	6 sec	Cardiovascular
Iridium 192	73.8 d	Prostate, brain, breast, and gynecological cancers
Iron 55	2.73 yr	Heat source
Iron 59	44.5 d	Medical
Krypton 81m	13.3 sec	Imaging
Lead 203	2.16 d	SPECT and PET
Lead 212	10.6 h	Label
Lutetium 177	6.68 d	Heart disease treatment and cancer therapy
Manganese 51	46.2 months	Localizing agent
Manganese 52	5.59 d	PET
Molybdenum 99	65.9 h	Parent for Tc-99m generator
Niobium 95	35 d	PET
Nitrogen 13	9.97 months	PET
Osmium 191	15.4 d	Ir-191m generator
Osmium 194	6.00 yr	Cancer treatment
Oxygen 15	122 sec	PET and SPECT
Palladium 103	17 d	Prostate cancer
Palladium 109	13.4 h	Radiotherapeutic agent
Phosphorus 32	14.3 d	Diagnosis/treatment
Phosphorus 33	25 d	Label
Plutonium 238	2.3 yr	Pacemaker
Radium 223	11.4 d	Cancer treatment
Radium 226	1.60e 3 yr	Production of Ac-227, Th-228, Th-229
Rhenium 186	3.9 d	Cancer treatment
Rhenium 188	17 h	Cancer treatment
Rhodium 105	35.4 h	Label
Rubidium 82	1.27 months	PET
Ruthenium 97	2.89 d	SPECT, PET, and gamma-camera imaging

TABLE 3.8 (continued) Isotope Applications in Medicine

Isotope	Half-Life	Applications
Ruthenium 103	39 d	PET and microspheres
Samarium 145	340 d	Cancer treatment
Samarium 153	2.00 d	Cancer treatment
Scandium 46	84 d	PET
Scandium 47	3.34 d	Cancer treatment
Selenium 72	8.4 d	Brain imaging
Selenium 75	120 d	Radiotracer
Silicon 28	Stable	Radiation therapy
Strontium 85	65.0 d	Detection
Strontium 89	50 d	Bone cancer pain
Strontium 90	29.1 yr	Generator system
Sulfur 35	87.2 d	Labeling
Tantalum 178	9.3 months	Imaging of heart and blood vessels
Tantalum 179	1.8 yr	X-ray fluorescence source
Tantalum 182	115 d	Bladder cancer treatment
Technetium 96	4.3 d	Research
Technetium 99m	6.01 h	Imaging
Terbium 149	4.13 h	Cancer treatment
Thallium 201	73.1 h	Imaging
Thorium 228	720 d	Cancer treatment
Thorium 229	7300 yr	Grandparent for alpha emitter Bi-213
Thulium 170	129 d	Lymphoma treatment
Thulium 171	1.9 yr	Medical
Tin 117m	13.6 d	Bone cancer pain relief
Tungsten 188	69.4 d	Cancer treatment
Xenon 127	36.4 d	Neuroimaging
Xenon 133	5.25 d	Lung imaging, SPECT imaging of brain
Ytterbium 169	32 d	Gastrointestinal diagnosis
Yttrium 88	107 d	Cancer tumor therapy
Yttrium 90	64 h	Internal radiation therapy of liver cancer
Yttrium 91	58.5 d	Cancer treatment
Zinc 62	9.22 h	Cerebral blood flow
Zinc 65	244 d	Medical
Zirconium 95	64.0 d	Medical

Source: Nuclear Energy Institute, Beneficial Uses and Production of Isotopes; http://www.nei.org/doc.asp?catnum=3&catid= 191; accessed 1/11/04.

The effect of uncontrolled release of radioisotopes is illustrated by three events. In 1987 at Goiânia, Brazil, a scavenger in a scrap yard pried open a container that had come from an abandoned cancer treatment center. The container had 20 g of radioactive

Table 3.9 Commercial Applications for Isotopes

Control
Physical measurement gauges
  Density, level, weight, thickness, mass per unit area
  Sheet-making for metals, paper, plastics, rubber, printed circuits, precious-metal coatings, or electrical contacts
Analytical instrumentation
  Sulfur
  Raw mineral materials
  Pollution measurements
  Air particulates
Security instrumentation
  Neutron-gamma reaction monitors used to detect explosives or drugs
  Lighting airport runways and emergency exits using tritium for lighting
Laboratory or portable devices
  Fluorescence analyzers for ores
  Humidity/density meters for agronomy and civil engineering
  Oil well-logging for measuring oxygen and nitrogen content of oil
  Smoke detectors
  Irradiation (about 180 gamma irradiators currently operating in the world)
  Sterilization: medical supplies and consumer products
  Food irradiation
  Plastic curing
  Tracers
  Examines efficiency of chemical reactions
  Measures mass transfer
  Examines behavior of pollutants
  Nondestructive testing
  Gamma radiography

Source: Nuclear Energy Institute, Beneficial Uses and Production of Isotopes; http://www.nei.org/doc.asp?catnum=3&catid= 191; accessed 1/11/04.

cesium 137 in it. The powder glowed and delighted people living nearby. The canister was taken from home to home so that people could see the wonderful and strange powder. One six-year-old girl, Leide das Neves Ferreira, "rubbed the powder on her body so that she glowed and sparkled." Four people died from radiation sickness and over 200 people were exposed. In the cleanup operation, many of the buildings that had been contaminated with cesium 137 were leveled.[47]

In November 1995, Chechen rebels buried a reported 13.5 kg of cesium (Cs^{137}) in Moscow's Ismailovsky Park.[48] The Chechen rebels then contacted a local television station to publicize that they had buried the material and where it was buried. Neither the rebels nor the source of the Cs^{137} was identified.[49]

TABLE 3.10 Applications of Isotopes in Research

Biomedical
Biological research
Molecular biology
Toxicological research
Agrochemical research
Materials research
Mossbauer spectroscopy
Tracers for determining hardness and wear resistance

Source: Nuclear Energy Institute, Beneficial Uses and Production of Isotopes; http://www.nei.org/doc.asp?catnum=3&catid=191; accessed 1/11/04.

The U.S. has also had a recent case of missing radioactive isotopes. On March 4, 1998, 19 tubes containing Cs^{137} were reported missing at the Moses Cone Health System, Inc., in Greensboro, NC. The total activity of the material missing from the facility was 604 mCi.[50] As will be discussed in the following sections, another factor that determines the relative danger of radioactivity is the activity of the material.

3.4 BIOLOGICAL EFFECTS OF RADIATION

Exposing a human to radiation exposes the body's cells to the energy contained in that radiation. The energy is deposited in the cells, causing damage to the molecules that make up the cells. How that energy deposits in the cell depends upon the type of radiation. There are charged particles such as beta and alpha particles; there is electromagnetic radiation such as gamma rays; and there are neutrally charged particles such as neutrons.[51]

3.4.1 Effects of Alpha Particles

As discussed in prior sections, alpha particles are a helium atom stripped of its electrons. Thus, an alpha particle has a charge. As the alpha particle moves through atoms or molecules, it interacts by ionizing them. This process causes the alpha particles to lose their energy before they travel very far. Alpha particles stop very rapidly. The distance they travel in a gas such as air is 1 to 2 in., and the distance they travel in a solid such as skin is about 50 μm, or about the thickness of the dead layer of skin cells on the body.

Alpha particles are not an external radiation hazard because they are stopped in the dead layer of skin. If inhaled or ingested, they can cause damage to cells near where they lodge internally. Due to the fact that they stop quickly, they do more damage than beta particles.

3.4.2 Effects of Beta Particles

Beta particles are electrons and, as such, have a charge (half that of an alpha particle). They are less massive than atoms or molecules, and they give up energy to nearby atoms and molecules, causing ionization. The amount of energy given up per encounter is less than that given up by an alpha particle; nonetheless, they do stop relatively quickly. For example, they travel about 3 m in air or about 1 mm in human tissue.

Beta particles have limited penetration in human tissue, resulting in damage limited to within a millimeter or so from the point deposited. This is called a "shallow" radiation dose. Inhaled or ingested, beta emitters can cause damage to cells within a millimeter or so of the area in which they deposit.

3.4.3 Effects of Gamma Rays

Gamma rays and X rays are electromagnetic radiation or photons. They have no charge or mass and interact with the electrons in atoms or molecules through the electromagnetic field component of the photon. Gamma and X rays penetrate deeply into matter due to the low probability of interaction. Because they interact with electrons, the more electrons that the material contains, the higher is the interaction probability and the quicker the electromagnetic radiation loses its energy.

Gamma and X rays can penetrate the human body and will deposit some of their energies as they penetrate the body. They are best shielded with dense materials such as lead. Due to the high penetrating power of gamma/X-ray radiation, they can cause radiation exposure to the whole body rather than to a small area of tissue near the source (like alphas or betas). Gamma/X rays deliver a dose of radiation to tissue whether the source is inside or outside the body. Gamma radiation is an external hazard.

3.4.4 Effects of Neutrons

Neutrons are particles that are ejected from the nuclei of atoms. They have no electrical charge and do not interact directly with electric fields. Interactions occur when a neutron collides with the nucleus of an atom. Five types of interactions that can occur are[52]

1. Elastic scattering: billiard ball–type collisions, where energy and momentum are conserved
2. Inelastic scattering: the nucleus absorbs some of the kinetic energy of the neutron
3. Charged particle–producing reactions: a neutron is captured, and the resulting unstable nucleus releases a charged particle (e.g., the interaction of boron-10 with a neutron for lithium and an alpha particle, $^{10}B(n,Li)\alpha$ reaction)
4. Radioactive capture: a neutron is captured, and the resulting unstable nucleus emits a gamma ray
5. Neutron multiplying reactions: a neutron is captured, and the resulting unstable nucleus emits neutrons and other products (e.g., fission reaction)

The quality factor is a means of measuring the level of damage that radiation causes in biological systems. In Table 3.11, the properties of the various radiation types that we discussed are summarized along with the quality factor. Note that an alpha particle has a quality factor of 20, while a beta particle has a quality factor of 1. This roughly indicates that an alpha particle will create about 20 times greater cell damage than a beta particle.

TABLE 3.11 Summary of Various Types of Radiation and Characteristics

Type	Alpha	Beta	Gamma	Neutron
Penetrating power	Very small	Small	Very large	Very large
Hazard	Internal	Internal, external	External	External
Shielding material	Paper	Plastic, aluminum	Lead, steel, concrete	Water, concrete, steel (for high-energy neutron)
Quality factor	20	1	1	2–10

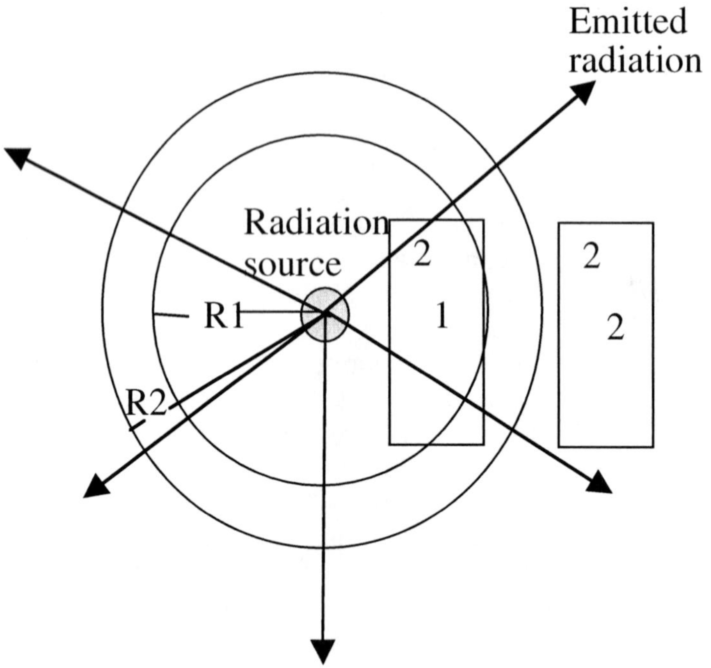

FIGURE 3.27 The effect of distance on radiation.

3.4.5 Calculation of Dose

Dose is a means of providing a measurement that relates to the damage that radiation causes the cells of a living organism. Radiation, meaning alpha, beta, gamma, and neutron emissions, is emitted from a source of material that is solid, liquid, or gas (Figure 3.27).

Because it is the individual particles or rays that cause the damage to the cells when they strike the human body, the number of particles or rays hitting the body is the critical parameter for cell damage. In Figure 3.27, the source is surrounded by spherical shells: one closer (with radius R1) than the other (with radius R2). Two boxes of the same size are shown in the figure. Box 1, being the closest, is intersected by two rays, and box 2, being the furthest away, is not intersected by any rays. This illustrates the point that distance from a source reduces the risk of being hit by a ray. This illustration helps us to understand that distance is an effective shield from radiation. Looking at the spherical surfaces, we can see the effect of shielding from a simple mathematical calculation. The area of a sphere is

$$A = 4\pi R^2 \tag{3.15}$$

where π is a constant ≈3.14 and R is the radius of the sphere.

If the radiation source gives off a constant number of particles or rays per second and they travel in random directions, we can calculate the average number of particles or rays that intersect either of the spherical shells per unit area. For example, if the sources gives off 10,000 particles or rays per second, and R1 is 1 m and R2 is 10 m, then the average number of particles or rays intersecting the spherical shells per unit area per second is

$$\text{Shell 1} = \frac{10{,}000}{4\pi(1\,\text{m})^2} \cong 800\,\frac{\text{particles}}{\text{m}^2 \cdot \text{sec}} \tag{3.16}$$

$$\text{Shell 2} = \frac{10{,}000}{4\pi(10\,\text{m})^2} \cong 8\,\frac{\text{particles}}{\text{m}^2 \cdot \text{sec}} \tag{3.17}$$

Thus, an object with a surface area of 1 m^2 located at shell 1 would have 800 particles striking it per second, while a similarly sized object located at shell 2 would have only eight particles striking it per second. Thus, one could assume that the average damage done would be 100 times less at shell 2 than at shell 1.

Ionizing radiation creates ion pairs (an ion and electron) when it interacts with a given medium. The total number of ion pairs produced is dependent upon the energy that the radiation deposits in the medium. If the medium is air and Q is the total charge liberated as X-ray or gamma-ray photons interact with a small volume, v, having a mass, m, then the radiation exposure, X, at the point of interest is

$$X = \frac{Q}{m} \tag{3.18}$$

where Q is the number of ion pairs in the small volume and m is the mass in kilograms of the air.

The unit *roentgen* (R) is used to describe the charge accumulation (in coulombs) per kilogram of air.

$$\text{R} = 2.58 \times 10^{-4}\,\text{C/kg air} \tag{3.19}$$

The roentgen is used only for X-ray or gamma-ray photons with energies of less than 3 MeV (million electron volts).

In order to develop a unit of radiation measurement that could be applied more generally to all radiation, including charged particles and neutrons, the concept of radiation absorbed dose (rad) was introduced. The rad is defined as the absorption of 0.01 J of energy per kilogram of material.

$$\text{rad} = 1 \times 10^{-2}\ \text{J/kg} \quad (3.20)$$

The absorbed dose, D, can be expressed in the unit rad, as shown in the relationship in Equation 3.21

$$D = \frac{E/m}{10^{-2}\,\text{J/kg}\cdot\text{rad}} \quad (3.21)$$

where E is the energy absorbed in joules, m is mass of material in kilograms, and the denominator in Equation 3.21 is a conversion factor.

Using this equation for absorbed dose, we can calculate a number of important relationships. Suppose that 1 g of tissue absorbs a dose of 5000 rad. With this information, we can calculate the amount of energy absorbed by the tissue by rearranging Equation 3.21.

$$\begin{aligned} E &= 10^{-2}(\text{J/kg}\cdot\text{rad})D(\text{rad})m(\text{kg}) \\ &= 0.01 \times 5000 \times 0.1 = 5\ \text{J} \end{aligned} \quad (3.22)$$

The roentgen and rad can be compared when the medium is air

$$D_{\text{air}}(\text{rad}) = 0.869X(\text{R}) \quad (3.23)$$

where D is the dose in rad and X is the dose in roentgen.

There is a conversion factor that converts roentgen to dose in media other than air.

$$D_{\text{medium}}(\text{rad}) = fX \quad (3.24)$$

where f is the conversion factor for a medium (0.869 for air).

The dose equivalent (DE) is a concept that has to do with the amount of damage that the type of radiation does to a cell. The quality factor (QF) is a means of making a comparison between the various types of radiation. The dose equivalent, defined by the unit rem, is related to the product of dose and quality factor, as seen in Equation 3.25.

$$DE(\text{rem}) = D(\text{rad}) \times QF \tag{3.25}$$

Understanding the definition of the units rad and rem is an important step in being able to discuss the biological effects of ionizing radiation. When ionizing radiation interacts with a living cell, it can ionize molecules, and depending on its penetration power, molecules can be affected near the surface of the cell or throughout the cell volume. Different molecules in the cell can be impacted, including the most important part of the cell, the chromosomes, which contain genetic information. The cell has mechanisms that can repair damaged molecules, including the chromosome, if the damage is not too bad. Even under normal conditions, cell damage and chromosome damage occurs constantly. In most cases, the cell is able to repair the damage and operate normally. Sometimes the cell repairs itself and operates abnormally, which may be an underlying cause of cancers. A cell could also be so damaged that it is unable to repair itself and it dies.

Cells in the body have specializations, and as would be expected, radiation has different effects on different cells. Fast-growing cells are particularly susceptible to the effects of radiation. An example would be bone marrow cells that produce blood. Radiation doses can be acute (a dose of 10 rad or greater to the whole body over a short period of time, meaning a few days at most) or chronic (meaning a small constant dose over a long period of time).

Acute doses of radiation may result in effects that are readily observable and cause identifiable symptoms (acute radiation syndrome). For example, the onset of radiation sickness symptoms can be observed for acute whole-body doses greater than 100 rad. Acute whole-body doses greater than 450 rad is the point where 50% of the general population will die within 60 days without medical treatment. This is known as the LD_{50} (lethal dose for 50% of sampled population).

Doses below 100 rads to the thyroid gland can cause benign tumors. In acute radiation exposure, the bone marrow syndrome begins at doses above 100 rad. The bone marrow, spleen, and lymphatic cells are damaged, and the victim's blood count drops. The victim may experience internal bleeding, fatigue, weakened immune system, and fever. In the range of 125 to 200 rad, exposure to the ovaries will result in the loss or suppression of menstruation in 50% of women. With doses of 200 to 300 rad, skin will redden and hair may start to fall out due to hair follicle damage. A 600-rad exposure to the ovaries or testicles can result in sterilization.

When the dose exceeds 1000 rad, the cells in the gastrointestinal tract (stomach and intestines) are damaged (gastrointestinal tract syndrome). The victim will exhibit symptoms including nausea, vomiting, diarrhea, dehydration, electrolyte imbalance, digestion problems, and bleeding ulcers in addition to the symptoms of the bone marrow syndrome.

When the dose exceeds 5000 rad, the cells of the central nervous system are damaged (central nervous system syndrome). Nerve cells do not reproduce. When this occurs, the victim will have a loss of coordination, confusion, coma, convulsions, and shock as well as the symptoms of syndromes that occur at lower doses.

All humans are exposed to chronic doses of radiation from either background radiation or from man-made sources. Naturally occurring radiation comes from cosmic radiation, sources from the earth, and sources in the human body. Cosmic radiation comes from the sun and stars and consists of positively charged particles and gamma radiation. The average cosmic radiation dose at sea level is approximately 0.026 rem per year. At higher elevations, this dose will increase due to the reduction in distance the radiation has to travel through the earth's atmosphere, which helps to shield the radiation. Most of the radiation from the earth comes from the natural uranium, thorium, and radium in the soil. Depending on where a person lives and the type of home lived in, this number can vary. On average, a person living in the U.S. will receive 0.200 rem of radiation per year, with a dose to the lungs of about 2 rem per year. Lastly, our bodies contain naturally produced radionuclides such as potassium 40. The average dose from the radiation in our bodies is about 0.040 rem per year.

Man-made radiation comes from medical sources, products that we use, residual fallout from weapons testing, and industrial sources. Medical sources such as X rays on average produce a dose of 0.014 rem per year. Consumer products such as television sets, old watches that use radium for luminescence, smoke detectors, and lantern mantles produce an average dose of 0.01 rem per year. Fallout from weapons tests that occurred in the 1950s and 1960s gives a dose of about 0.002 rem per year. Industrial sources of radiation impact only those who work in the industries where these sources are used.

TABLE 3.12 Estimated Days of Life Expectancy Lost due to Various Risk Factors

Risk Factor	Estimated Loss of Life Expectancy (days)
Smoking 20 cigarettes per day	2370 (6.5 years)
Overweight by 20%	985 (2.7 years)
Mining and quarrying	328
Construction	302
Agriculture	277
Government	55
Manufacturing	43
Radiation exposure	
340 mrem/yr for 30 years	49
100 mrem/yr for 70 years	34

Source: National Academy of Science, Board of Radiation Effects Research; http://nrc51/xpedio/groups/dels/documents/webpage/002437.doc; accessed 1/14/04.

The average chronic dose for the general population is ≈0.36 rem per year. The risks associated with such low doses of radiation are debatable. But generally, the scientific community overestimates the risk by using a linear extrapolation model by extrapolating from the well-known risks associated with several hundred rem when developing tables of comparative risk such as those shown in Table 3.12. The linear model was intended to be conservative because the number of fatalities it predicted was so low. Scientists, being conservative by nature, always assume the worst possible case when they do not fully understand a phenomenon that might impact health. Linear extrapolation, albeit unrealistic, was developed in the 1950s and was meant to be the worst-case estimate for the effects of radiation at low doses. We know much more now. There is evidence that low doses of radiation actually have beneficial effects, such as stimulating the immune system.[53] However, many scientists and critics misuse the linear extrapolation model to embellish their own misperceptions of the negative effects of low radiation doses.

3.5 EFFECTS OF A NUCLEAR EXPLOSIVE

Nuclear explosions have both immediate and delayed effects. When a nuclear blast occurs near the surface of the earth, it digs a crater provided that the fireball radius is greater than the height of the

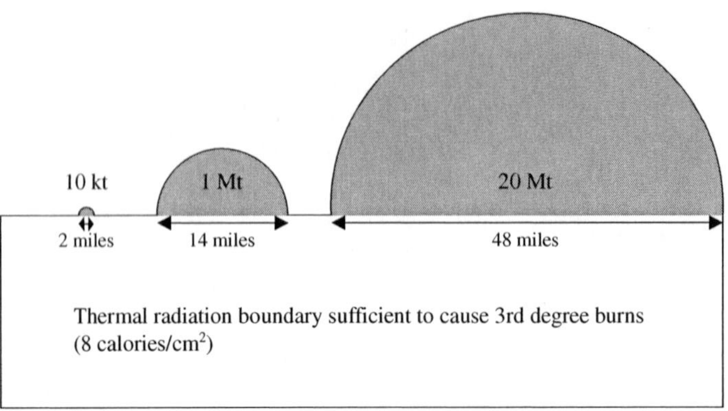

Figure 3.28 Thermal blast effects from 10-kt, 1-Mt, and 20-Mt nuclear explosions.

blast. Some of the debris from the crater will deposit at the rim, and the rest will be carried into the atmosphere and deposit as fallout. If the blast height is greater than the fireball radius, a crater will not be formed. The immediate effects include the blast effects, the thermal radiation effects, and the prompt effects from nuclear radiation.[54] The blast damage is caused by static overpressure that can crush an object. In addition, high winds create a dynamic pressure that can knock down structures. Due to the large amount of energy released in a nuclear explosion, a fireball, or a core at high temperature, radiates energy much like a hot object on the stove. This effect is called thermal radiation. Figure 3.28 shows the thermal energy release for different nuclear explosions. The figure uses a boundary of 8 calories/cm^2, which is the approximate limit that causes third-degree burns. The release of ionizing radiation from a nuclear explosion can also account for immediate effects (Table 3.13).

The effects from a nuclear explosion can impact a large area. Table 3.14 shows the distances where a thermal radiation field of 8 cal/cm^2 (sufficient to cause third-degree burns), a blast overpressure of 4.6 psi (sufficient to collapse buildings), and a radiation dose of 500 rem (sufficient for LD_{50}) occur for different nuclear yields.

3.5.1 Specific Effects

3.5.1.1 Thermal

The nuclear blast creates a fireball. Photons ranging from the ultraviolet to the far infrared are released. The speed of these

TABLE 3.13 Immediate Effects of Energy Release from a Nuclear Explosion[54]

	Low Yield (<100 kt)	High Yield (>1 Mt)
Thermal radiation	35%	45%
Blast wave	60%	50%
Ionizing radiation (80% gamma, 20% neutrons)	5%	5%

TABLE 3.14 Nuclear Blast Distance Resulting in Thermal Exposure of 8 cal/cm^2, a Blast Overpressure of 4.6 psi (at the Optimum Burst Height), and a Radiation Dose of 500 rem[54]

Yield (kt)	Thermal Effects (miles)	Blast Effects (miles)	Radiation Effects (miles)
1	0.4	0.5	0.5
5	0.8	0.8	0.7
7.5	1.0	0.9	0.8
10	1.1	1.0	0.8
20	1.5	1.2	0.9
100	2.8	2.1	1.3
500	5.5	3.6	1.7
1,000	7.2	4.5	1.9
2,000	9.6	5.6	2.2
10,000	18.6	9.6	3.0
20,000	24.8	12.1	3.4

electromagnetic waves is equivalent to the speed of light. Thus, this effect will be the first experienced. The visible light will produce flash blindness, much like looking into the flash of a camera, in people who are looking at the explosion. This effect can last for several minutes. For a 1-Mt explosion, flash blindness can occur at up to 13 miles on a clear day or 53 miles on a clear night. A permanent retinal burn will occur if the flash is focused through the lens of the eye, as might occur with someone driving toward the blast.

For a 1-Mt explosion, first-degree burns (equivalent to a bad sunburn) occur at distances up to 9 miles; second-degree burns (causing damage of the epidural skin layer leading to blisters) occur at distances up to 8 miles; and third-degree burns (which destroy the three layers of skin) occur at distances up to 7 miles. If the human body has over 24% third-degree burns or over 30% second-degree burns, a fatality will probably result without medical intervention. Given that the U.S. has facilities to treat maybe 2,000 severe-burn victims, it is very likely that prompt medical attention will not be available as a nuclear blast can produce more than 10,000 burn victims. The effects of thermal radiation depend upon the weather conditions. For example, an extensive amount of moisture or a high concentration of particles (smog) will absorb thermal radiation.

Thermal radiation can ignite fires. The production of fires is highly dependent upon the types of materials that are being exposed. Large fires can cause massive human casualties. For example, the Tokyo firebombing in 1945 killed 124,000 civilians, and the Dresden firebombing in 1945 killed 135,000 civilians. Two types of fires can occur, based on the amount of kindling materials. If the available kindling is above ≈5 lb/ft^2, then a firestorm can occur (e.g., Tokyo, Hamburg, and Hiroshima in World War II). A firestorm has violent inrushing winds that create very high temperatures, but the fire does not radially spread outward. Firestorms are likely to kill a high proportion of people trapped in them due to heat and asphyxiation. The second type of fire is a conflagration, in which the fire spreads along a front (e.g., the Great Chicago Fire on October 9, 1871[55] and the San Francisco Earthquake on April 18, 1906[56]). A conflagration spreads slowly enough so that people in its path can move unless they are trapped or incapacitated.

3.5.1.2 Shock Wave

A blast can kill people by direct pressure. The human body can withstand up to 30 psi of direct overpressure, but death can also occur by indirect methods (Table 3.15). For example, the high winds associated with an overpressure of 2 to 3 psi are strong enough to blow people out of an office building. Overpressures of ≈10 psi will collapse most factories and commercial buildings, and overpressures of ≈5 psi can collapse most lightly constructed residential buildings. It is not surprising that most deaths result from the collapse of occupied buildings, from people being blown into objects, or from buildings or smaller objects being blown onto or into people. The effects are not easily predictable.

TABLE 3.15 Blast Effects of a 1-Mt Explosion 8000 ft Above the Earth's Surface[54]

Distance from Ground Zero		Peak Overpressure	Peak Wind Velocity	
(mi)	(km)	(psi)	(mph)	Typical Blast Effects
0.8	1.3	20	470	Reinforced concrete structures are leveled
3.0	4.8	10	290	Most factories and commercial buildings are collapsed; small wood-frame and brick residences destroyed and distributed as debris
4.4	7.0	5	160	Lightly constructed commercial buildings and typical residences are destroyed; heavier construction is severely damaged
5.9	9.5	3	95	Walls of typical steel-frame buildings are blown away; severe damage to residences; winds sufficient to kill people in the open
11.6	18.6	1	35	Damage to structures; people endangered by flying glass and debris

3.5.1.3 Radiation

Nuclear weapons produce ionizing radiation, and as we have seen in prior discussions, these types of radiation impact biological organisms in two ways. The first is through direct effects, and the second is through long-term effects. Nuclear radiation can be intense over a limited range. As seen in Table 3.14, the lethal distance of direct radiation is less than the lethal distance from the blast and thermal radiation effects. Fallout radiation, which comes from the materials dug out of the crater and debris from the bomb, is in the form of particles that are made radioactive by the effects of the explosion. These particles are distributed at varying distances from the blast.

A dose of approximately 600 rem within a six- to seven-day time period has a 90% chance of creating a fatality without medical attention. A dose of 450 rem, as discussed previously, is the LD_{50} dose where 50% of the population would die without medical treatment and the other half would be sick but would recover. Statistically, a dose of 300 rem might have a 10% death rate, and lower doses would pose a decreasing risk. A dose of 200 rem would cause nausea and lower resistance to other diseases. Doses below 100 rem will not cause any noticeable short-term effects, but they will do long-term damage.

The long-term effects of smaller does are measured statistically. For example, a short-term exposure to 50 rem has no noticeable short-term effects, but in a large exposed population, about 0.4 to 2.5% of those exposed would be expected to contract some form of cancer in their lifetimes.

3.5.1.4 Electromagnetic Pulse

An electromagnetic pulse (EMP) occurs when the gamma rays from a nuclear burst are absorbed by the air and ground. The electric field strength in an EMP is very large (thousands of volts) and is capable of burning out most modern electrical devices. The area of impact is about that of the thermal radiation. If the burst is a high airburst, then the impact could be much larger.

3.5.1.5 Fallout

The fallout from an airburst poses some long-term health hazards, but these are trivial compared with the other consequences of a nuclear attack.[54] In perspective, we can examine the data from the nuclear explosions at Hiroshima and Nagasaki, which take into account the direct effects of a 15- and 20-kiloton blast (Table 3.16).

3.5.2 Uses for a State

Nuclear weapons have been used as a deterrent with the exception of the U.S. deployment against the Japanese cites of Hiroshima and Nagasaki. The U.S. justified the deployment on the assumption that the total number of human causalities could be reduced. Japan was a defeated country but vowed to fight to the last man if the U.S. invaded. With the U.S. military superiority, the casualties resulting from an invasion of the Japanese mainland were estimated to be in the millions. And most importantly, only the U.S. possessed nuclear weapons at that time.

TABLE 3.16 Data for Nuclear Blast Effects at Hiroshima and Nagasaki[54]

Zone (mile radius)	Population	Population Density of Zone (square miles)	Killed	Injured
		Hiroshima		
0–0.6	31,200	25,800	26,700	3,000
0.6–1.6	144,800	22,700	39,600	53,000
1.6–3.1	80,300	3,500	1,700	20,000
Totals	256,300	8,500	68,000	76,000
		Nagasaki		
0–0.6	30,900	25,500	27,300	1,900
0.6–1.6	27,700	4,400	9,500	8,100
1.6–3.1	115,200	5,100	1,300	11,000
Totals	173,800	5,800	38,000	21,000

What would have changed if the Japanese possessed nuclear weapons as well? Clearly an invasion would have been foolhardy. The U.S. could not have afforded an invasion nor the Japanese a nuclear attack on their mainland. Both sides most likely would have sought a diplomatic solution to end hostilities.

This same dilemma has played out in modern times. The U.S. and USSR were engaged in a cold war from 1949 to 1991. Both sides recognized early on the dangers of a nuclear exchange and resorted to bilateral treaties to minimize the risk of a nuclear confrontation.

India and Pakistan both declared themselves as nuclear-weapon states in 1998, and since then, they have had several close calls over the disputed Kashmir region. But the key word is *close.* It is hard to see how even a radical government could possibly risk a nuclear war. The consequences are too severe.

We have seen the regimes of Iraq, Libya, Iran, and North Korea pursue the development of nuclear weapons. To varying degrees, the international community has been able to use political and economic pressures to control the development of nuclear weapons in these countries.

International pressure has been effective when there is cooperation among the key nations in Europe, Asia, and the Americas.

Problems ensued in 2003 when the administration of President George W. Bush invaded Iraq and deposed the regime of Saddam Hussein without UN or NATO cooperation. Soon thereafter, the nuclear programs in North Korea and Iran began accelerating their development of nuclear weapons. There is wide agreement that the primary goal of the acceleration was to deter a potential invasion. If a nation possessed nuclear weapons, the cost of invasion would be too high to contemplate. The U.S. invasion of Iraq was not deterred by the chemical and biological weapons that the Bush administration claimed Iraq had.[57] Clearly, the military value of chemical and biological weapons was not a sufficient deterrent. At the time of writing this text, the prewar appraisal of Iraq's chemical and biological weapons program appears to have been grossly overestimated. The U.S. occupation government in Iraq has searched for weapons of mass destruction and has not been able to uncover any, despite a considerable effort.

Nuclear weapons are an effective invasion deterrent. The weapons are more predictable and can be used on troop concentration with a high degree of effectiveness. For example, Russia has shifted its strategic military policy to include the use of tactical nuclear weapons as a deterrent to protect its large borders rather than relying on conventional forces entirely.[58] Thus, it is not surprising that the governments of Iran and North Korea have accelerated their nuclear programs given President Bush's characterization of Iraq, Iran, and North Korea as an "evil axis."[59] It is unlikely that these moves go beyond deterrent aspirations given the Bush Doctrine[60] — a significant change in U.S. policy that includes preemptive strikes — that is at the heart of the justification for the invasion of Iraq.

With a competent delivery system such as ballistic missiles, long-range bombers, and nuclear submarines, the role of nuclear weapons change slightly. Nuclear weapons in this case can threaten the assets of a distant country, change the balance of power, and change strategies. North Korea has engaged in long-range missile development, and this has been of concern to the U.S. and its allies. However, to engage the U.S. and its allies in strategic nuclear warfare would be foolhardy. North Korea has used its technology to gain political leverage and to generate cash.

3.5.3 Uses in Terrorism

The difficulty of obtaining nuclear materials makes this an almost impossible option for terrorist groups. For all practical purposes, a terrorism organization will not be able to develop its own nuclear weapon. The scenario that is of concern is that a state-sponsored or state-assisted terrorist organization might obtain a weapon from a rogue state with nuclear weapons. Another scenario of concern is that a terrorist might purchase a nuclear weapon through the black market. This threat was of most concern when the USSR collapsed in 1991.[61]

If a nuclear weapon falls into the hands of terrorists, then a whole spectrum of problems arise. First of all, the terrorists need not invest in sophisticated delivery systems, but they could smuggle the weapon to the target. If the weapon is detonated, then how would the culprit be identified?

In our view, the free world would unite and cooperate with more resolve than it did after September 11, 2001, to track down and punish the culprits. If the weapons were taken by theft, there should be no doubt that the world would find out who took the weapon, to whom it was sold, and who was responsible. If the weapon were obtained from a rogue state, the details would be uncovered. There are very few countries that have the capabilities of producing weapons-grade plutonium or highly enriched uranium. Investigators would have the advantage of focusing on a limited number of sources to track down the culprits. Additionally, the isotopes from a nuclear explosion can be collected and analyzed. Weapons-grade plutonium can be traced to the reactor where it was produced by isotopic ratios.

No matter how the weapon was transferred and who was involved, the guilty would be found and punished. Terrorist groups understand this and would be foolish to risk using nuclear weapons if they could more effectively use other weapons of mass destruction without the risks.

3.6 EFFECTS OF A DIRTY BOMB

A dirty bomb is a chemical explosive wrapped with radioactive material. The force of the explosion disperses the radioactive material. As discussed previously in this chapter, radioactivity is deadly if it is concentrated. The dirty bomb goes counter to using radioactivity most effectively as a weapon in that its most concentrated state is before the explosion. Also, it takes a high degree of sophistication and knowledge to effectively aerosolize the radioactive particles that are created by an explosion. A well-aerosolized material can be inhaled and deposited in the lungs if conditions are optimum. However, getting the right conditions is unlikely. Even if everything worked well, the number of people who inhaled the particles would not be large, and the amount of material inhaled would not be lethal. Finally, even small amounts of radioactivity can be detected with nuclear sensors. The sensors will be useful in two ways:

1. Detection of a dirty bomb smuggled before detonation
2. Assisting the cleanup of postexplosion, minimizing the damaging effects

The dirty bomb's biggest impact, if it can manage to escape detection, is psychological. People have an irrational fear of radiation that has been cultivated by the antinuclear movement, and this fear is the most effective weapon a terrorist can exploit.

3.6.1 Uses for a State

States have considered dirty bombs, an example being Adolph Hitler's looking at dirty bombs as a payload for the Nazi rocket plane bomber project. But the effects of a dirty bomb do not warrant their use for military purposes. There are a multitude of more effective weapons.

A rogue state might provide terrorist groups with materials to make a dirty bomb. However, the rogue state would risk a great deal if discovered. It is unlikely that a rogue state would take that risk, considering the consequences.

3.6.2 Uses in Terrorism

Terrorist groups have considered a dirty bomb, as we know from reports of al Qaeda operations.[62] The first problem they have is obtaining radioactive materials, and the second problem is to escape detection. If the bomb is assembled, the radiation is in its most concentrated form before detonation. This means that the source of radiation will most probably be at its most lethal. If it is not shielded, the person delivering it will die before it can be delivered. Additionally, it will be easily detected. Terrorist are not fools; they tend to choose methods of attack that have the best chance of success. A dirty bomb would be a very poor risk when there are better options.[63]

There has been speculation that attacks could be launched on our infrastructure, such as nuclear power plants and nuclear waste transportation. Nuclear reactors are one of the most hardened targets in the world against ground assult.[64] A recent analysis indicates that the containment of a nuclear power plant can withstand the impact of larger modern commercial aircraft.

Attacking nuclear fuel shipments has been examined as a threat, but it is difficult for a number of reasons, including the difficulty of finding the shipment schedule and the technology used to transport the materials.[65] There are easier targets for terrorists to choose from.

Terrorists are practitioners of the low-hanging-fruit theorem: they prefer methods of attack that have a high probability of working. High-risk attacks using dirty bombs or attacking hardened targets such as nuclear power plants or nuclear waste shipments are not the best options when lower-risk attacks with weapons of mass destruction are available, as will be discussed in Chapters 4 and 5.

3.7 CONCLUSIONS

Nuclear weapons are very complex and will most likely continue to find future uses as a deterrent. Dirty bombs have value only as a psychological weapon due to public fear.

APPENDIX 3.1 SEPARATION TECHNOLOGIES

There are four main uranium separation technologies that have been used on a large scale. These include the gas centrifuge, thermal diffusion, electromagnetic diffusion, and gaseous diffusion (Figure A3.1).

Gaseous diffusion plants make up the main production capability of the U.S. These are very large plants (Figure A3.2 and Figure A3.3). The K-25 Gaseous Diffusion Plant at Oak Ridge Tennessee require a number of stages to separate uranium isotopes. Figure A3.5 shows the uranium metal reduction plant in Fernold, OH.

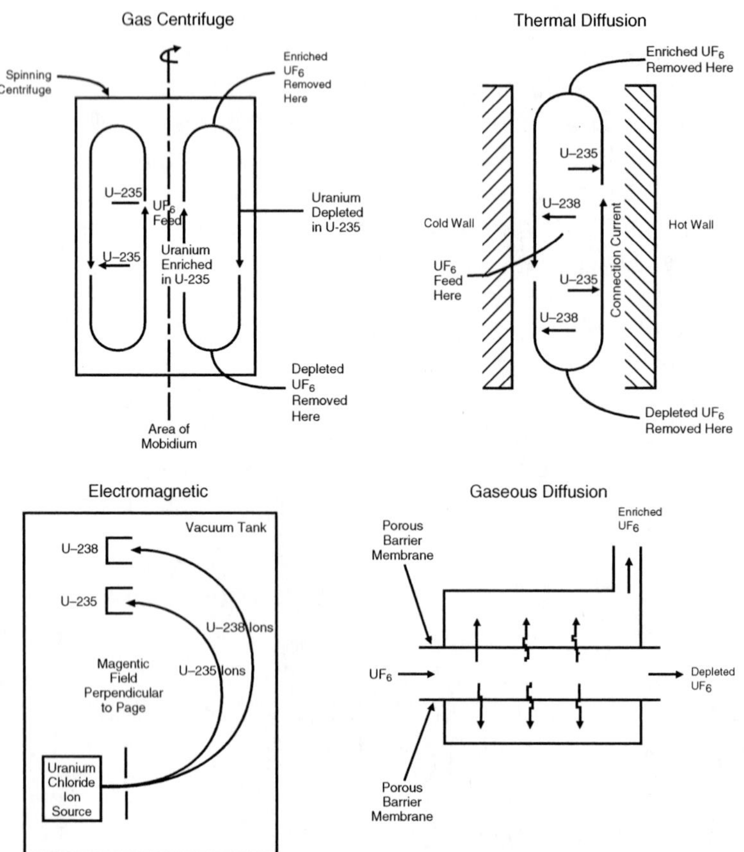

Figure A3.1 Diagrams of the gas centrifuge, thermal diffusion, electromagnetic diffusion, and gaseous diffusion separation technologies.

Figure A3.2 The Portsmith Gaseous Diffusion Plant in Piketon, OH. (From U.S. Department of Energy, Linking Legacies Connecting the Cold War Nuclear Weapons Production Processes to Their Environmental Consequences, DOE/EM-0319, Office of Environmental Management, Washington, DC, Jan. 1997; http://legacystory.apps.em.doe.gov; accessed 8/5/04.)

Figure A3.3 The K-25 Gaseous Diffusion Plant at Oak Ridge, TN. (From U.S. Department of Energy, Linking Legacies Connecting the Cold War Nuclear Weapons Production Processes to Their Environmental Consequences, DOE/EM-0319, Office of Environmental Management, Washington, DC, Jan. 1997; http://legacystory.apps.em.doe.gov; accessed 8/5/04.)

Figure A3.4 Gaseous diffusion stage of a U.S. enrichment facility. (From U.S. Department of Energy, Linking Legacies Connecting the Cold War Nuclear Weapons Production Processes to Their Environmental Consequences, DOE/EM-0319, Office of Environmental Management, Washington, DC, Jan. 1997; http://legacystory.apps.em.doe.gov; accessed 8/5/04.)

Figure A3.5 Uranium metal reduction plant, Fernold, OH. (From U.S. Department of Energy, Linking Legacies Connecting the Cold War Nuclear Weapons Production Processes to Their Environmental Consequences, DOE/EM-0319, Office of Environmental Management, Washington, DC, Jan. 1997; http://legacystory.apps.em.doe.gov; accessed 8/5/04.)

REFERENCES

1. Institute for Science and International Security, Key Nuclear Explosive Materials; http://www.isis-online.org/; accessed 3/9/03.
2. O'Neill, K., The *Nuclear Terrorist Threat*, Institute for Science and International Security, Aug. 1997; http://www.isis-online.org/publications/terrorism/nightmare.html.
3. Rothstein, L., Explosive secrets, *Bull. Atomic Scientists*, 55 (2), 1999; http://www.bullatomsci.org/issues/1999/ma99/ma99rothstein.html; accessed 3/9/03.
4. Acronym Institute, Los Alamos Experiment Achieves Neptunium Criticality, Nov. 15, 2002; http://www.acronym. org.uk/dd/dd68/68nr09.htm; accessed 3/11/03.
5. Los Alamos National Laboratory, Neptunium Criticality Achieved, News Release, Oct. 17, 2002; http://www.lanl.gov/worldview/news/releases/archive/02-118.shtml; accessed 3/11/03.
6. Smyth, H.D., *Atomic Energy for Military Purposes*, Princeton University Press, NJ, 1945; http://nuclearweaponarchive.org/Smyth/; accessed 1/15/04.
7. Hasan, S., Ghosh, T.K., Prelas, M.A., and Ross, L., Jr., Adsorption of uranium on chitosan coated perlite beads, in *Transactions of 2002 ANS Winter Meeting*; http://www2.ans.org/pubs/transactions/indices/pdfs/2002_Winter_Meeting/23.pdf; accessed 10/07/03.
8. Federation of American Scientists, Uranium Production; http://www.fas.org/nuke/intro/nuke/uranium.htm; accessed 1/5/04.
9. Sanger, D.E. and Broad, W.J., From Rogue Nuclear Programs, Web of Trails Leads to Pakistan, *New York Times*, Jan. 4, 2004; http://www.nytimes.com/2004/01/04/international/04NUKE.html?ex=1388552400&en=ed99ff9ccb671e3d&ei=5007&partner=USERLAND; accessed 1/18/04.
10. CNN, IAEA: Iran Secretly Made Nuclear Material, Nov. 12, 2003; http://www.cnn.com/2003/US/11/11/Iran.nuclear/index.html; accessed 1/5/04.
11. See note 10 above.
12. CNN, Pakistan Probes Iran Link, Dec. 23, 2003; http://www.cnn.com/2003/WORLD/asiapcf/south/12/23/pakistan.nuclear/index.html; accessed 1/4/04.
13. Anon., Plutonium: The First 50 Years, United States Plutonium Production, Acquisition, and Utilization from 1944 through 1994, DOE/EM-0319, Linking Legacies, January 1997; http://www.osti.gov/html/osti/opennet/document/pu50yrs/pu50y.html.

14. Nuclear Tourist, RBMK Reactor; http://www.nucleartourist.com/type/rbmk.htm; accessed 1/8/04.

15. Garland, W.J., How and Why Is CANDU Designed the Way It Is? http://canteach.candu.org/library/20000101.pdf; accessed 1/8/04.

16. See note 15 above.

17. Office of Scientific and Technical Information, Plutonium: The First 50 Years: United States Plutonium Production, Acquisition, and Utilization from 1944 through 1994; http://www.osti.gov/html/osti/opennet/document/pu50yrs/pu50y.html.

18. U.S. Department of Energy, Closing the Circle on the Splitting of the Atom: The Environmental Legacy of Nuclear Weapons Production in the United States and What the Department of Energy Is Doing about It, Jan. 1996; http://legacystory.apps.em. doe.gov; accessed 8/5/04.

19. See note 13 above.

20. Greenpeace International, Expanding the Threat of Russian Weapons-Grade Plutonium — "The Western Option," briefing paper, Oct. 2002; http://www.greenpeace.org/multimedia/download/1/44755/0/russian_doc_oct_10th_5.45_version.doc; accessed 1/8/03.

21. U.S. Department of Energy, Feed Materials Planning Basis for Surplus Weapons: Usable Plutonium Disposition, Office of Fissile Materials Disposition, Washington, DC, 1997.

22. See note 13 above.

23. Basis of Interim Operation (BIO) for the Surveillance and Maintenance of the REDOX Complex, Bechtel Hanford Incorporated (BHI), Hanford Environmental Restoration Project, Richmond, WA, 1997.

24. See note 13 above.

25. U.S. Department of Energy, Assessment of Plutonium Storage Issues at Department of Energy Facilities, DOE/DP-123T, U.S. DOE, Washington, DC, 1994.

26. Lawrence Livermore National Laboratory, operated by the University of California for the U.S. Department of Energy, Jan. 6, 2004; http://www.llnl.gov/str/JanFeb04/Wong.html; last accessed 10/03/04.

27. Nuclear Regulatory Commission, Title 10 CFR Part 20; http://www.nrc.gov/reading-rm/doc-collections/cfr/part020/; accessed 1/8/04.

28. Tanksi, J.A., A Model for the Initiation and Growth of Metal Hydride Corrosion, LA-UR-00-5496, presented at 23rd DOE Aging, Compatibility, and Stockpile Stewardship Conference, U.S. Department of Energy, Washington, DC, 2000.

29. U.S. Department of Energy, DOE Handbook Primer on Spontaneous Heating and Pyrophoricity, DOE-HDBK-1081-94, U.S. Department of Energy, Washington, DC, 1994.
30. U.S. Department of Energy, *Analysis of Experimental Data*, Vol. 1 of *Airborne Release Fractions/Rates and Respirable Fractions for Non-reactor Nuclear Facilities*, DOE handbook, DOE-HDBK-3010-94, U.S. Department of Energy, Washington, DC, 1994.
31. Schaeffer, N.M., ed., *Reactor Shielding for Nuclear Engineers*, TID-25951, U.S. Atomic Energy Commission, Office of Information Services, Washington, DC, 1973.
32. See note 13 above.
33. Federation of American Scientists, Nuclear Weapon Design; http://www.fas.org/nuke/intro/nuke/design.htm; accessed 1/10/04.
34. See note 9 above.
35. Federation of American Scientists; http://www.fas. org/main/home.jsp; last accessed 10/03/04.
36. Rhodes, R., *Dark Sun: The Making of the Hydrogen Bomb*, Simon and Schuster, New York, 1995.
37. Refuting Oxygen Starvation as a Major Contributing Cause in the Extinction of the Dinosaurs; http://www.maddad.org/coll700.htm; accessed 10/08/04.
38. University of Santa Cruz, Massive Tsunami Sweeps Atlantic Coast in Asteroid Impact: Scenario for March 16, 2880, press release; http://www.ucsc.edu/news_events/press_releases/text.asp?pid=355; accessed 1/10/04.
39. Yellowstone Volcano: Is "the Beast" Building to a Violent Tantrum? *National Geographic,* Aug. 30, 2001; http://news.nationalgeographic.com/news/2001/08/0828_wireyellow-stone.html.
40. PBS, Meltdown at Three Mile Island; http://www.pbs.org/wgbh/amex/three/index.html; accessed 1/09/04.
41. World Nuclear Association, Chernobyl Accident, August 2004; http://www.world-nuclear.org/info/chernobyl/inf07.htm; accessed 1/9/04.
42. Dow Chemical, Bhopal; http://www.bhopal.com/; accessed 1/10/04.
43. Natural Fossil Fission Reactors; http://www.curtin.edu.au/curtin/centre/waisrc/OKLO/index.shtml; accessed 1/10/04.
44. U.S. Department of Energy, Yucca Mountain Project; http://www.ocrwm.doe.gov/ymp/about/index.shtml; accessed 1/10/04.
45. PBS, Dirty Bomb, *Nova*; http://www.pbs.org/wgbh/nova/dirtybomb/; accessed 1/12/04.

46. Levi, M.A. and Kelly, H.C., Weapons of Mass Disruption, *Scientific Am.*, 78–81, 2002.

47. Neifert, A., Case Study: Accidental Leakage of Cesium-137 in Goiania, Brazil, in 1987; http://www.nbc-med.org/SiteContent/MedRef/OnlineRef/CaseStudies/csgoiania.html; accessed 1/12/04.

48. Oppenheimer, A., A Sickening Episode: Nuclear Looting in Iraq and the Global Threat from Radiological Weapons, *Disarmament Diplomacy*, 73, 2003; http://www.acronym.org.UK/Dd/Dd73/73op03.htm; accessed 10/08/04.

49. Times Online, Briefing: Al-Qaeda and "Dirty Bombs," Apr. 23, 2002; http://www.nci.org/02/04f/24-10.ht; accessed 1/12/04.

50. Nuclear Regulatory Commission, Report to Congress on Abnormal Occurrences for Fiscal Year 1998, Mar. 15, 1999; http://www.nrc.gov/reading-rm/doc-collections/commission/secys/1999/secy1999-079/1999-079scy.html#ATTACHMENT%20; accessed 1/12/04.

51. Nuclear Regulatory Commission, Fact Sheet on Biological Effects of Radiation; http://www.nrc.gov/reading-rm/doc-collections/fact-sheets/bio-effects-radiation.htm; accessed 1/12/04.

52. Prelas, M.A., Romero, J.B., and Person, E.F., A Critical Review of Fusion Systems for Radiolytic Conversion of Inorganics to Gaseous Fuels, *Nuclear Technology / Fusion*, 2 (2), 143–164 1982; http://prelas.nuclear.missouri.edu/ne315/Lecture/Radiation%20Energy%20Conversion.pdf; accessed 1/13/04.

53. Luckey, T.D., *Hormesis with Ionizing Radiation,* CRC Press, Boca Raton, FL, 1980; Mortazavi, S.M.J., An Introduction to Radiation Hormesis; http://www.angelfire.com/mo/radioadaptive/; accessed 1/19/04; Cameron, J.R., The good news about low level radiation exposure, *Health Physics Society Newsletter*, February, 9–11, 1992; Feinendegen, L.E., Bond, V.P., and Sondhaus, C.A., Can low level radiation protect against cancer? *Physics Society*, 27, 4–6, 1998; Smith P.G. and Doll R., Mortality from all causes among British radiologists, *Br. J. Radiol.*, 54, 187–194, 1981.

54. The Effects of Nuclear War, NTIS order no. PB-296946, May 1979; http://www.wws.princeton.edu/~ota/disk3/1979/7906_n.html; accessed 1/18/04; Glasstone, S. and Dolan, P.J., Science & Global Security, *Effects of Nuclear Weapons*, 3rd ed., U.S. Department of Defense and Energy Research and Development Administration; http://www.princeton.edu/~globsec/publications/effects/effects.shtml; accessed 1/18/04; Sublette, C., Effects of Nuclear Explosions, May 15, 1997; http://nuclearweaponarchive.org/Nwfaq/Nfaq5.html; accessed 1/18/04.

55. Chicago Historical Society, The Great Chicago Fire: Web Memory; http://www.chicagohs.org/fire; accessed 1/18/04.

56. San Francisco Virtual Museum, The Great 1906 Earthquake and Fire; http://www.sfmuseum.org/1906/06.htm; accessed 1/18/04.

57. ABC News, Making a Case, Powell Presents Tapes, Satellite Photos to Show Iraq Is Deceiving U.N., Feb. 5, 2003; http://abcnews.go.com/sections/world/DailyNews/iraq030205_powell.htm; accessed 1/18/04.

58. Luongo, K. and Davis, I., Bush-Putin Summit Fails to Bury the Cold War, May 22, 2002; http://www.basicint.org/pubs/Notes/2002bush-putin.htm; accessed 1/18/04.

59. Ford, P., "Evil Axis" and Others Talk Back, *Christian Science Monitor*, Jan. 31, 2002; http://www.csmonitor.com/2002/0131/p01s04-wome.html; accessed 1/18/04.

60. Donnelly, T., The Underpinnings of the Bush Doctrine, Jan. 31, 2003, AEI Online (Washington); http://www.aei.org/publications/pubID.15845/pub_detail.asp; accessed 1/18/04.

61. Prelas, M.A., Soviet High Tech Bonanza, *Christian Science Monitor*, Feb. 3, 1992; http://www.csmonitor.com/cgi-bin/getasciiarchive?tape/92/feb/day03/03181; accessed 1/18/04.

62. Karon, T., The "Dirty Bomb" Scenario, *Time*, June 10, 2002; http://www.time.com/time/nation/article/0,8599,182637,00.html; accessed 1/18/04.

63. Ferguson, C.D., Study Details Steps to Reduce Dirty Bomb Threat, Monterey Institute of International Studies, Jan. 16, 2003; http://www.cns.miis.edu/pubs/week/030113.htm; accessed 1/18/04.

64. Nuclear Energy Institute, CSIS "Silent Vector" Energy Terrorism Exercise Finds Nuclear Power Plants "Best Defended Targets," Oct. 21, 2002; http://www.nei.org/doc.asp?catnum=3&catid=959; accessed 1/18/04; Nuclear Energy Institute, *Washington Post* Panel of Independent Experts Gives A–/B+ to Security at Nuclear Plants, Second Highest Grade in Survey, Sep. 10, 2002; http://www.nei.org/doc.asp?catnum=3&catid=941; accessed 1/18/04; Nuclear Energy Institute, Public Health Risk Low in Unlikely Event of Terrorism at Nuclear Plant, EPRI Study Finds, Aug. 2004; http://www.nei.org/index.asp?catnum=3&catid=1024; accessed 1/18/04; Nuclear Energy Institute, Deterring Terrorism: Aircraft Crash Impact Analyses Demonstrate Nuclear Power Plant's Structure Strength, Dec. 2002; http://www.nei.org/documents/ EPRINuclearPlantStructural Study200212.pdf; accessed 1/18/04.

65. Nuclear Energy Institute, An American Success Story: The Safe Shipment of Used Nuclear Fuel; http://www.nei.org/documents/SafeShipBrochure?.pdf; accessed 1/18/04.

4

Characteristics of Biological Weapons

4.1 BIOLOGICAL AGENTS

Biological agents are defined as living organisms or toxins derived from biological organisms that can adversely affect people, animals, plants, and strategic materials (e.g., an agent that might attack rubber or gasket materials).[1] Throughout history, the balance between infectious disease and humankind has been tenuous. Disease has killed more humans than war. World War II was the first major conflict where more combatants died from directly inflicted wounds rather than from disease or infection. One of humankind's greatest achievements during the 20th century was medical science advancements that shifted the delicate balance between microbe and man in favor of humankind. Our understanding of the microbe has led to significant discoveries in antibiotics, vaccines, and treatments. These discoveries also have a direct impact on the use of microbes in warfare. As discussed in Chapter 2, 20th-century science has successfully transformed certain biological agents into weapons of mass destruction (WMDs).

The world pharmaceutical market is enormous, representing estimated total sales of more than $500 billion in 2004. The industry growth rate tops 8%, with the bulk of the sales in North America (Figure 4.1). With the growing economies of China and India, there are also promising prospects for future growth in Asia. With the growth of the pharmaceutical industry, there is also a large amount of equipment and expertise widely distributed around the world. Much of this technology is transferable to destructive purposes. The proliferation of biotechnology was inevitable. For the

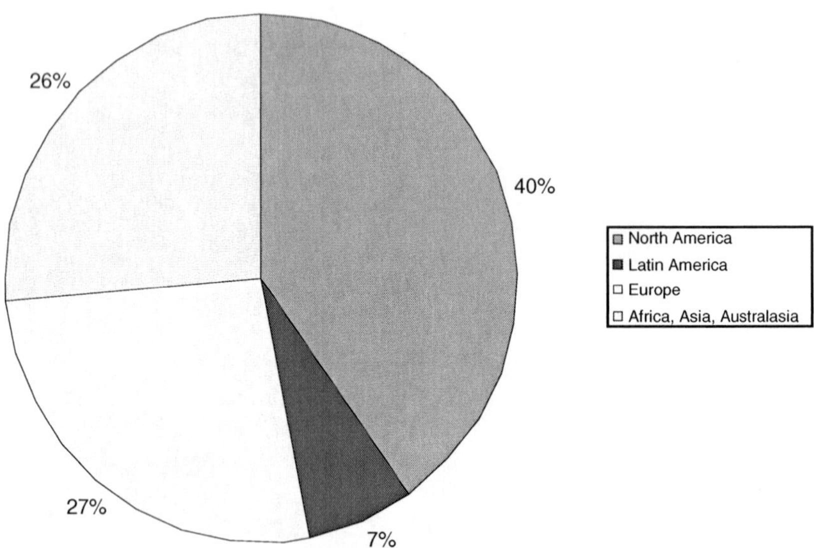

FIGURE 4.1 Pharmaceutical markets worldwide.

most part, this type of proliferation is for the benefit of humankind. However, the knowledge can be misused for the production of weapons of mass destruction. It is for this reason that the authors view bioweapons as the greatest proliferation risk for the development of weapons of mass destruction.

The Centers for Disease Control (CDC) has categorized biological agents that can be weaponized by their relative level of risk (Table 4.1). Category A biological agents are the highest priority; category B agents are the second highest priority; and category C agents are the third highest priority, which includes emerging pathogens.

Over the last five decades, science has been successful in perfecting weaponization of biological agents. What makes biological weapons (BWs) a proliferation risk is that the agents are relatively easy to obtain. The most lethal agents are naturally occurring viruses and bacteria that are obtainable from a variety of sources, including soil, water, animals, clinical specimens, or clinical and research laboratories.

Table 4.1 CDC Categories for Biological Agents

CDC Categories for Biological Agents	Definition
Category A diseases/agents	The U.S. public health system and primary health-care providers must be prepared to address various biological agents, including pathogens that are rarely seen in the U.S.; high-priority agents include organisms that pose a risk to national security because they: • Can be easily disseminated or transmitted from person to person • Result in high mortality rates and have the potential for major public health impact • Might cause public panic and social disruption • Require special action for public health preparedness
Category B diseases/agents	The second-highest-priority agents include those that: • Are moderately easy to disseminate • Result in moderate morbidity rates and low mortality rates and require specific enhancements of CDC's diagnostic capacity and enhanced disease surveillance
Category C diseases/agents	The third-highest-priority agents include emerging pathogens that could be engineered for mass dissemination in the future because of: • Availability • Ease of production and dissemination and potential for high morbidity, high mortality rates, and major health impact

Source: Centers for Disease Control, Bioterrorism Agents/Diseases, CDC, Atlanta; http://www.bt.cdc.gov/agent/agentlist-category.asp#; accessed 1/27/04.

The greatest threat of biological warfare derives from the successful modification of organisms through the use of recombinant genetic engineering. A first-generation genetically modified virus or bacteria may be enhanced by a natural agent modified for antibiotic resistance, toxin production, or a greater ability to evade human immune defenses.

In many cases the methods of weaponizing biological agents are relatively inexpensive and easy to implement. These technologies take advantage of existing equipment used to produce antibiotics, vaccines, and other industrial and food products. Because of the importance of all of these legitimate industries, the technology is readily available and is commonly used. The dual use of these technologies makes production of BW agents easy to conceal.

Biological agents are delivered by unconventional means. Due to the sensitivity of biological agents to heat, conventional explosive munitions make ineffective delivery systems. Explosions are not an efficient way of generating aerosol particles because only a small fraction of the particles generated have a size suitable for deposition in the lower respiratory tract. Explosive munitions are only 1 to 2% efficient in generating particles of the proper size.

The most effective means of delivering a biological agent is through inhalation. Biological particles must be aerosolized, with a size distribution of 1 to 5 μm, to enter the lungs. Particles larger than 5 μm will settle on environmental surfaces, or will be deposited in the upper respiratory tract. These larger particles will eventually be eliminated by mucociliary clearance. Particles smaller than 1 μm will flow through the respiratory tract as a person exhales.

There are a number of ways to produce particles in the 1- to 5-μm range. For example, commercial agricultural and industrial sprayers and aerosol generators are capable of generating particles with a fraction of particles being of optimal size. More efficient methods have been developed for generating a higher fraction of particles of the optimum size. Application of military science to the problem of dispersing a biological agent has led to the development of point-source bomblets. These bomblets are used in munitions. The military has also developed specialized sprayers that produce a stream of particles used as a line source that are dispersed from airplanes or cruise missiles.

Biological agents can also be used to contaminate food or water systems/supplies. Because heat adversely affects many pathogens and toxins, agents would have to be used on food that is served raw or added to the food after preparation. Water purification methods such as chlorination and filtration are effective in incapacitating most pathogens and toxins. An attack on a water supply would be successful only if it occurred after the water treatment process. The agents could be plant pathogens used to destroy crops. The consequences of such an attack could devastate the food chain and cause famine. The difficulty of using plant pathogens is that plants are grown over an extensive area. It is a difficult task to spread a pathogen over large areas. This makes an attack with a plant pathogen more difficult.

Livestock and other animals, on the other hand, are easier targets because they tend to herd or flock. Our most important sources of meat are beef, pork, and chicken, and an attack on these food sources would have a severe economic consequence. One need only look at the aftermath of the naturally occurring outbreaks of mad cow disease, bovine spongiform encephalopathy (BSE), in the U.K. in 2000[2] or the hoof-and-mouth outbreak in the U.K. in 2001[3] to judge the consequences of a biological attack on livestock.

Aerosolized delivery of BW agents over large geographic areas can produce mass casualties. The epidemic produced by the agent could quickly overwhelm the local health systems. This would, in turn, reduce the ability of emergency response teams and emergency medical providers to respond. Another consequence would be the overloading of limited medical resources such as intensive care units and the quick exhaustion of special medications early on in a biological weapon attack. Even the threat of a biological weapon attack can cause fear and panic, which in itself is a potential strategic goal.

The list of potential biological agents is large; however, the agents of highest risk are shown in Table 4.2.

Biological agents can be (a) bacteria; (b) rickettsiae (a small, nonmobile parasite), chlamydiae, and fungi; (c) biological toxins; and (d) viruses. Each type of organism has unique properties. Infectious organisms such as bacteria, rickettsiae, and viruses have incubation times that last from days to weeks, while toxins can act in a matter of minutes to hours. There is a high degree of variability in the stability of infectious agents, but toxins are stable. Additionally, there is a high degree of variability in the effectiveness of treatments for infectious agents while toxins have no effective treatment. The properties and effects of some biological agents are shown in Table 4.3. Similarly, Table 4.4 shows the properties and effects of some rickettsiae, chlamydiae, and fungi; Table 4.5 focuses on some biological toxins; and Table 4.6 presents information on some viruses.

4.2 PRODUCTION EQUIPMENT AND METHODS

Biological organisms can be grown in several ways. The most widely used method is fermentation. Humankind has used fermentation

Table 4.2 Biological Weapon Agents, Scientific Names or Toxin Source, and Type

Agent	Infectious Agent or Source	Type	CDC Category[a]	Weaponized
Anthrax	*Bacillus anthracis*	Bacteria	A	Yes
Tularemia	*Francisella tularenius*	Bacteria	A	Yes
Plague	*Yersinia pestis*	Bacteria	A	Probable
Argentine hemorrhagic fever (Junin)	*Tacaribe virus complex arenavirus*	Virus	A	Probable
Bolivian hemorrhagic fever (Muchupo)	*Tacaribe virus complex arenavirus*	Virus	A	Probable
Chikungunya hemorrhagic fever	*Alphavirus*	Virus	A	Probable
Crimean-Congo hemorrhagic fever (CCHF)	*Nairovirus*	Virus	A	Probable
Korean hemorrhagic fever (Hantaan)	*Bunyavirus*	Virus	A	Probable
Omsk hemorrhagic fever	*Flavivirus*	Virus	A	Probable
Lassa fever	*Arenavirus*	Virus	A	Probable
Smallpox	*Orthopoxvirus*	Virus	A	Probable
Dengue fever	*Flavivirus*	Virus	A	Unknown
Marburg	Filovirus	Virus	A	—
Ebola	Filovirus	Virus	A	Unknown
Yellow fever	*Flavivirus*	Virus	A	—
Botulinum toxins	*Clostridium botulinum*	Biotoxin	A	Yes
Brucellosis	*Brucella abortus, B. melitensis, B. suis, B. canis*	Bacteria	B	Yes
Glanders	*Burkholderia mallei*	Bacteria	B	Probable
Melioidosis	*Pseudomonas pseudomallei*	Bacteria	B	Possible
Salmonellosis	*Salmonella typhimurium, S. enteritidis*	Bacteria	B	—
Cholera	*Vibrio cholerae*	Bacteria	B	Unknown
Typhoid fever	*Salmonella typhi*	Bacteria	B	Unknown
Q fever	*Coxiella burnetii*	Rickettsia	B	Yes

Table 4.2 (continued) Biological Weapon Agents, Scientific Names or Toxin Source, and Type

Agent	Infectious Agent or Source	Type	CDC Category[6]	Weaponized
Epidemic typhus	*Rickettsia prowazekii*	Rickettsia	B	Probable
Scrub typhus	*Rickettsia tsutsugamushi*	Rickettsia	B	Probable
Psittacosis	*Chlamydia psittaci*	Chlamydia	B	Possible
Influenza	Influenza virus	Virus	B	Probable
Hepatitis A	—	Virus	B	Unknown
Eastern equine encephalitis (EEE)	*Alphavirus*	Virus	B	—
Western equine encephalitis (WEE)	*Alphavirus*	Virus	B	—
Russian spring-summer encephalitis	*Flavivirus*	Virus	B	—
Venezuelan equine encephalitis (VEE)	*Alphavirus*	Virus	B	—
Rift Valley fever	*Phlebovirus*	Virus	B	—
Coccidioidomycosis	*Coccidioides immitis*	Fungal	B	—
Histoplasmosis	*Histoplasma capsulatum*	Fungal	B	—
Cryptosporidiosis	*Cryptosporidium* spp.	Protozoan	B	Unknown
T-2 mycotoxins (yellow rain)	Mycotoxins of the trichothecence group	Biotoxin	B	Probable
Aflatoxin	—	Biotoxin	B	Yes
Ricin	Seed of castor plant	Biotoxin	B	Yes
Staphylococcal enterotoxins (SEB)	Staphylococcus aureus	Biotoxin	B	Probable
Microcystins	Blue-green algae	Biotoxin	B	Possible
Anatoxin A	Blue-green algae	Biotoxin	B	Unknown
Tetrodotoxin	Pufferfish	Biotoxin	B	Possible
Saxitoxin	Marine dinoflagellate	Biotoxin	B	Possible
Clostridium perfringens toxins	*Clostridium perfringens*	Biotoxin	B	Probable

Table 4.2 (continued) Biological Weapon Agents, Scientific Names or Toxin Source, and Type

Agent	Infectious Agent or Source	Type	CDC Category[6]	Weaponized
Palytoxin	Marine soft coral	Biotoxin	B	—
Abrin	Rosary pea	Biotoxin	B	—
Tetanus toxin	*Clostridium tetani*	Biotoxin	B	—
Modeccin	—	Biotoxin	B	—
SARS (severe acute respiratory syndrome)	*Coronavirus*	Virus	C	—
Shigellosis	*Shigella*	Bacteria	C	Unknown
Rocky Mountain spotted fever	*Rickettsia rickettsii*	Rickettsia	C	Unknown
Nipah virus	*Paramyxoviridae*	Virus	C	—
Hantavirus	—	Virus	C	—

[a] Centers for Disease Control, Bioterrorism Agents/Diseases, CDC, Atlanta; http://www.bt.cdc.gov/agent/agentlist-category.asp#; accessed 1/27/04.
Source: U.S. Army, *The Medical NBC (Nuclear, Biological, Chemical) Battlebook: 21st Century Guide to Nuclear, Biological and Chemical Terrorism*, Department of Defense Publications, Washington, D.C., 1991, pp. 4-20–4-21.

over countless centuries for the production of beverages and foods such as beer and wine or cheese and yogurt. The idea of fermentation was to provide a food source, such as sugar, for a medium for bacterial growth. In the cases of foods or medicine, the bacterium that is grown is beneficial. Bacteria that are deadly can also be grown through fermentation for use in bioweapons technology. Viral agents require DNA in order to replicate. Thus, the remaining methods of growth provide live cells. These cells can come from embryos in fertilized chicken eggs, live tissue, or live animals. These processes are the foundation of the biotechnology industry. As such, the knowledge base for food and pharmaceuticals production is well established with dynamic industries and a well-educated work force. Equipment and technical personnel from the biotechnology industry can be adapted to a bioweapons program. The dual-use potential of equipment from the biotechnology industry makes the detection of a bioweapons program difficult.

The pharmaceutical industry has its foundation in the 1930s when the large-scale production of sulfa drugs began. Many of the early pharmaceuticals were produced by direct chemical synthesis. However, pharmaceuticals can also be extracted from their biological origins in animals, plants, and microorganisms.

Table 4.3 Properties and Effects of Bacterial Agents

Disease	Likely Methods of Dissemination	Transmissibility Human to Human	Infectivity	Incubation Time*	Duration of Illness	Lethality	Persistence	Vaccination	Antimicrobial Therapy	Antiserums
(Inhalation) Anthrax	Spores in aerosols	No	Moderate	1–6 days	3–5 days	High	Spores are highly stable	Yes	Effective early; otherwise little effect	Experimental
Brucellosis	1. Aerosol 2. Sabotage (food supply)	Via contact with lesions	High	5–60 days	Weeks to years	Low	Long persistence in wet soil and food	No	Moderately effective	No
Cholera	1. Sabotage (food/water supply) 2. Aerosol	Negligible	Low	1-5 days	1 or more weeks	Moderate to high	Unstable in aerosols & pure water. More persistence in polluted water	Yes	Moderately effective	No
Melioidosis	Aerosol	Negligible	High	Days to year	4–20 days	Variable	Stable	None	Moderately effective	No
(Pneumonic) plague	1. Aerosol 2. Infected vectors	High	High	2–3 days	1–2 days	Very high	Less important because of high transmissibility	Yes	Moderately effective	No
Tularemia	Aerosol	No	High	2–10 days	2 or more weeks	Moderate if untreated	Not very stable	Yes	Effective	No
Typhoid fever	1. Sabotage (food/water supply) 2. Aerosol	Negligible	Moderate	7–21 days	Several weeks	Moderate if untreated	—	Yes	Moderately effective	No

* Incubation applies to infectious diseases. With toxins, its application refers to the period between exposure and appearance of the symptoms and signs of poisoning.

Source: U.S. Army, *The Medical NBC (Nuclear, Biological, Chemical) Battlebook: 21st Century Guide to Nuclear, Biological and Chemical Terrorism*, Department of Defense Publications, Washington, D.C., 1991, p. 4-22.

Table 4.4 Properties and Effects of Rickettsiae, Chlamydiae, and Fungal Agents

Disease	Likely Methods of Dissemination	Transmissibility Human to Human	Infectivity	Incubation Time*	Duration of Illness	Lethality	Persistence	Vaccination	Antimicrobial Therapy	Antiserums
Epidemic typhus	1. Aerosol 2. Infected vectors	No	High	6–16 days	Weeks to months	High	Not very stable	No	Effective	No
Q fever	1. Aerosol 2. Sabotage (food supply)	No	High	10–20 days	2 days to 2 weeks	Very low	Stable	Yes	Effective	No
Rocky Mountain spotted fever	1. Aerosol 2. Infected vectors	No	High	3–10 days	2 weeks to months	High	Not very stable	No	Effective	No
Scrub typhus	1. Aerosol 2. Infected vectors	No	High	4–15 days	Up to 16 days	Low	Not very stable	No	Effective	No
Psittacosis	Aerosol	Negligible	Moderate	4–15 days	Weeks to months	Very low	Stable	No	Effective	No
Coccidioidomycosis	Aerosol	No	High	1–2 weeks	Weeks to months	Low	Stable	No	Not very effective	No
Histoplasmosis	Aerosol	No	High	1–2 weeks	Weeks to months	Low	Long persistence in soil	No	Not very effective	No

* Incubation applies to infectious diseases. With toxins, its application refers to the period between exposure and appearance of the symptoms and signs of poisoning.

Source: U.S. Army, *The Medical NBC (Nuclear, Biological, Chemical) Battlebook: 21st Century Guide to Nuclear, Biological and Chemical Terrorism*, Department of Defense Publications, Washington, D.C., 1991, p. 4-23.

Table 4.5 Properties and Effects of Toxins

Disease	Likely Methods of Dissemination	Transmissibility Human to Human	Infectivity	Incubation Time*	Duration of Illness	Lethality	Persistence	Vaccination	Anti-microbial Therapy	Anti-serums
Botulinum toxin	1. Sabotage (food/water supply) 2. Aerosol	No	—	Variable (hours to days)	24–72 hours; months if lethal	High	Stable	Yes	Not effective	Yes
Clostridium Perfringens toxins	1. Sabotage 2. Aerosol	No	—	8–12 hours	24 hours	Low	Stable	No	Not effective	No
Trichothecene mycotoxins	1. Aerosol 2. Sabotage	No	—	Hours	Hours	High	Stable	No	Not effective	No
Palytoxin	1. Aerosol 2. Sabotage	No	—	Minutes	Minutes	High	Stable	No	Not effective	No
Ricin	Aerosol	No	—	Hours	Days	High	Stable	Under development	Not effective	No
Saxitoxin	1. Sabotage 2. Aerosol	No	—	Minutes to hours	Minutes to days	High	Stable	No	Not effective	No
Staphylococcal enterotoxin B	1. Aerosol 2. Sabotage	No	—	1–6 hours	Days to weeks	Low	Stable	Under development	Not effective	No
Tetrodotoxin	1. Sabotage 2. Aerosol	No	—	Minutes to hours	Minutes to days	High	Stable	No	Not effective	No

* Incubation applies to infectious diseases. With toxins, its application refers to the period between exposure and appearance of the symptoms and signs of poisoning.

Source: U.S. Army, *The Medical NBC (Nuclear, Biological, Chemical) Battlebook: 21st Century Guide to Nuclear, Biological and Chemical Terrorism*, Department of Defense Publications, Washington, D.C., 1991, p. 4-24.

Table 4.6 Properties and Effects of Viral Agents

Disease	Likely Methods of Dissemination	Transmissibility Human to Human	Infectivity	Incubation Time*	Duration of Illness	Lethality	Persistence	Vaccination	Antimicrobial Therapy	Antiserums
Chikungunya fever	Aerosol	None	High	2–6 days	2 weeks	Very low	Relatively stable	Experimental	Not effective	No
Crimean-Congo hemorrhagic fever	Aerosol	Moderate	High	3–12 days	Days to weeks	High	Relatively stable	Experimental (Bulgaria)	Effective	Yes (Bulgaria only)
Dengue fever	Aerosol	None	High	3–6 days	Days to weeks	Low	Relatively unstable	Experimental	Not effective	No
Eastern equine encephalitis	Aerosol	None	High	5–15 days	1–3 weeks	High	Relatively unstable	Yes	Not effective	No
Ebola	Aerosol	Moderate	High	7–9 days	5–16 days	High	Relatively unstable	No	Not effective	No
Korean hemorrhagic fever (Hantaan)	Aerosol	None	High	4–42 days	Days to weeks	Moderate	Relatively stable	Experimental	Effective	No
Lassa fever	Aerosol	Low to moderate	High	10–14 days	1–4 weeks	Unknown	Relatively stable	No	Effective	Experimental
Omsk hemorrhagic fever	1. Aerosol 2. Water	Negligible	High	3–7 days	7–10 days	Low	Relatively unstable	Experimental	Not effective	No

Table 4.6 (continued) Properties and Effects of Viral Agents

Disease	Likely Methods of Dissemination	Transmissibility Human to Human	Infectivity	Incubation Time*	Duration of Illness	Lethality	Persistence	Vaccination	Antimicrobial Therapy	Antiserums
Rift Valley fever	1. Aerosol 2. Infected vectors	Low	High	2–5 days	Days to weeks	Low	Relatively stable	Yes	Not effective	No
Russian spring-summer encephalitis	1. Aerosol 2. Milk	None	High	8–14 days	Days to months	Moderate	Relatively unstable	Yes	Not effective	Yes
Smallpox	Aerosol	High	High	10–17 days	1–2 weeks	High	Stable	Yes	Not effective	Yes
Western equine encephalitis	Aerosol	No	High	1–20 days	1–3 weeks	Low	Relatively unstable	Yes	Not effective	No
Venezuelan equine encephalitis	1. Aerosol 2. Infected vectors	Low	High	1–5 days	Days to weeks	Low	Relatively unstable	Yes	Not effective	No
Yellow fever	Aerosol	None	High	3–6 days	1–2 weeks	High	Relatively unstable	Yes	Not effective	No

* Incubation applies to infectious diseases. With toxins, its application refers to the period between exposure and appearance of the symptoms and signs of poisoning.

Source: U.S. Army, *The Medical NBC (Nuclear, Biological, Chemical) Battlebook: 21st Century Guide to Nuclear, Biological and Chemical Terrorism*, 1991, pp. 4-25–4-26.

Animal-based pharmaceuticals use tissues or live beings for generation. Examples include

- Insulin (used to treat diabetes) produced from porcine/bovine pancreatic tissue
- Human growth hormone (used to treat short stature) produced from human pituitaries
- Blood coagulation factors (used to treat hemophilia) produced from human blood
- Polyclonal antibodies (used for immunization) produced from the serum of immunized animals/humans
- H Bs Ag (vaccination for hepatitis B) produced from the plasma of hepatitis B carriers
- Steroid (sex) hormones (used for various purposes) produced from gonads
- Corticosteroids (anti-inflammatory agent, immunosuppressant) produced from the adrenal cortex
- Adrenaline (used for anaphylaxis) produced from the adrenal gland

About 25% of all prescription drugs sold in North America are made from plants or modified forms of chemicals derived from plants. Plant-derived drugs come from several chemical families:

- Alkaloids: atropine (pupil dilator) made from *Atropa belladonna* (deadly nightshade), codeine made from *Papaver somniferum* (opium poppy), cocaine made from *Erythoxylum coca* (coca leaves)
- Flavonoids: chrysoplenol B (antiviral for rhinovirus) made from vascular plants
- Terpenes and terpenoids: taxol (used for ovarian and breast cancer) made from *Taxus brevifolia* (western yew tree)
- Steroids: digoxin (used to increase heart muscle contraction) made from *Digitalis purpurea*
- Coumarins: dicoumarol (anticoagulant) made from *Melilotus officinalis*
- Salicylates: aspirin produced by *Salix alba* (white willow tree) or *filipendula ulmaria* (meadowsweet)
- Xanthines: theophylline (used as anti-asthmatic or diuretic) made from *Camellia sinensis*

About 3 billion people worldwide use plant-derived medicines as their primary source of healthcare.

Perhaps the most significant body of pharmaceuticals is derived from microorganisms. The wide variety of secondary metabolites from microorganisms has demonstrated antibiotic properties. Antibiotics have had the most significant impact on human health care of any pharmaceutical. About 10,000 antibiotic substances have been isolated and characterized. One of the most prolific microorganisms for antibiotic production is the bacterial order Actinomycertales, producing more than 50% of the known antibiotics. The most famous antibiotic, penicillin, comes from a fungus (*Penicillium notatum*).

During the 1950s, research uncovered a number of naturally produced proteins, such as interferons and interleukins, which have therapeutic value. These proteins impacted the human immune response system with growth factors such as erythropoietin, that stimulates red blood cell production, and neurotrophic factors that regulate the development of neural tissues. These naturally produced proteins were initially made in small quantities because they were extracted from the human body. With the development of recombinant DNA technology and monoclonal antibody technology, the quantity and the technology for mass production of new pharmaceuticals has greatly expanded.

4.2.1 Methods

The pharmaceutical industry uses many methods of production. The commonality of these methods is the need to maintain high standards of quality control and cleanliness. Particularly, there is a need for clean-room technology and ultrapure water.

4.2.2 Characteristics of Equipment

4.2.2.1 Clean Room

The clean room is designed to limit the entry of unwanted materials that could contaminate contained processes. Clean rooms use air-filtration systems that prevent dust and microbes from entering the process space to maintain an aseptic environment. The air entering the room is filtered with a high-efficiency particulate air (HEPA) filter. There are many companies that can build clean rooms, including portable units. In Europe, the capability of a clean room is classified as A, B, C, or D in order of decreasing cleanliness (Table 4.7). In the U.S. clean rooms are classified as class 100 (equivalent to A/B), class 10,000 (grade C), or class 100,000 (grade D).[4]

Table 4.7 European Specifications for Clean-Room Ratings

Grade	Maximum number of particles of 0.5-μm diameter per m³ of clean air	Maximum number of particles of 5-μm diameter per m³ of clean air	Maximum number of microorganisms per m³ of clean air
A	3,500	0	<1 (statistically)
B	3,500	0	5
C	350,000	2,000	100
D	3,500,000	20,000	500

Many organizations still use the U.S. Federal Standard 209, which was replaced in 2001 by the International Organization for Standardization (ISO) 14644-1 standard entitled "Cleanrooms and associated controlled environments." According to Federal Standard 209, a clean room rated as "Class 10,000," will have no more than 10,000 particles larger than 0.5 microns in any given cubic foot of air. A clean room rated as "Class 1000" will have no more than 1000 particles larger than 0.5 microns in any given cubic foot of air. A clean room rated as "Class 100," will have no more than 100 particles larger than 0.5 microns in any given cubic foot of air.[5]

The ISO standards that have been adopted worldwide are related to Federal Standard 209 by the following: ISO Class 3/209 = Class 1; ISO Class 4/209 = Class 10; ISO Class 5/209 = Class 100; ISO Class 6/209 = Class 1,000; ISO Class 7/209 = Class 10,000; and ISO Class 8/209 = Class 100,000. The specifications of the ISO standards can be seen in Table 4.8.

Table 4.8 ISO Standard 14644-1

ISO Class	Maximum Concentration Limits in Air for Various Particle Sizes (particles/m³)					
	≥0.1 μm	≥0.2 m	≥0.3 μm	≥0.5 μm	≥1 μm	≥5.0 μm
1	10	2	—	—	—	—
2	100	24	10	4	—	—
3	1,000	237	102	35	8	—
4	10,000	2,370	1,020	352	83	—
5	100,000	23,700	10,200	3,520	832	29
6	1,000,000	237,000	102,000	35,200	8,320	293
7	—	—	—	352,000	83,200	2,930
8	—	—	—	3,520,000	832,000	29,300
9	—	—	—	35,200,000	8,320,000	293,000

Because of the strict standards for cleanliness, people who work in clean rooms must wear special protective clothing, commonly referred to as "bunny suits." These suits are designed to not give off lint particles and to prevent human skin and hair particles from entering the room's atmosphere. In addition, all of the furnishings in the room need to be made of materials, such as smooth stainless steel, that can be easily kept clean. Materials and personnel enter the clean room through an air lock.

To facilitate production of safe products, the pharmaceutical industry has set procedures for cleaning, decontamination, and sanitation.

4.2.2.2 Water Supply

Water must be highly purified for processes used in the pharmaceutical and biopharmaceutical industries. There are two categories of water: purified water and water for injection (WFI). Purified water and WFI require a multistep purification process. The water is first pumped through a depth filter, an organic trap, and a carbon filter. Second, it goes through deionization (both cation and anion exchangers). At this point, the water is purified. In order to remove microorganisms, the water must go through additional processing. This includes filtration through a 0.45-μm filter followed by exposure to UV light (at 254-nm wavelength). The water then goes through a 0.22-μm filter to remove UV-inactivated microorganisms. The water is then either distilled or passed through a reverse osmosis unit to make it WFI quality.[6] WFI is used in the processing of pharmaceuticals and biopharmaceuticals. Water purification equipment is widely available.

4.2.2.3 Fermentation Systems

4.2.2.3.1 Microbial Cell Culture

Recombinant proteins can be induced in cells in which they normally do not occur. The most common microbe used to produce protein is *Escherichia coli*. As a recombinant production system, the growth of *E. coli* is critical. There are other production systems beside *E. coli*, such as yeasts and fungi.

Microbial cell fermentation has been used for processing nearly half of all biopharmaceuticals that have been approved by the Food and Drug Administration. Industrial-scale fermentation systems for bacteria and yeast have been used for commercial purposes for a very long time. The fermentation system is simple

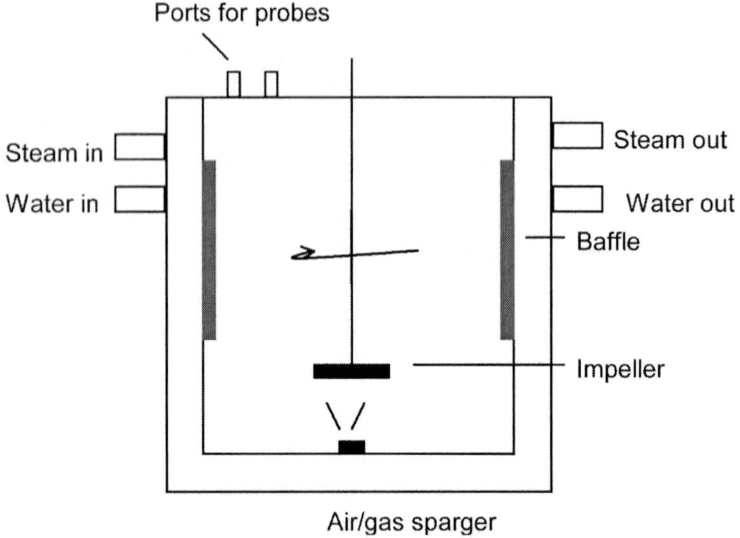

FIGURE 4.2 General jacketed fermentation vessel for microbial cells.

in concept (Figure 4.2). It consists of a jacketed vessel, usually made of stainless steel. There are steam and water inputs and outputs that are used to heat the vessel in order to sterilize it. The vessel typically has ports for probes or the addition of materials (nutrients or acids and bases to control the medium's pH). An impeller that stirs the mixture of nutrients and microorganisms is driven by an external motor. Baffles are placed on the side of the vessel to prevent the formation of a vortex during the stirring process. The goal of fermentation is to provide an environment (temperature, pH, nutrients, and oxygen level) for the optimum growth of the microbe. Some dangerous microbes such as anthrax require an anaerobic (no oxygen) system.

Fermentation systems are widely available in a variety of sizes. As pointed out, the most common uses for such systems are in the production of food or medicine.

Once the cells have grown in the fermentation system, the useful materials have to be extracted and purified (Figure 4.3).

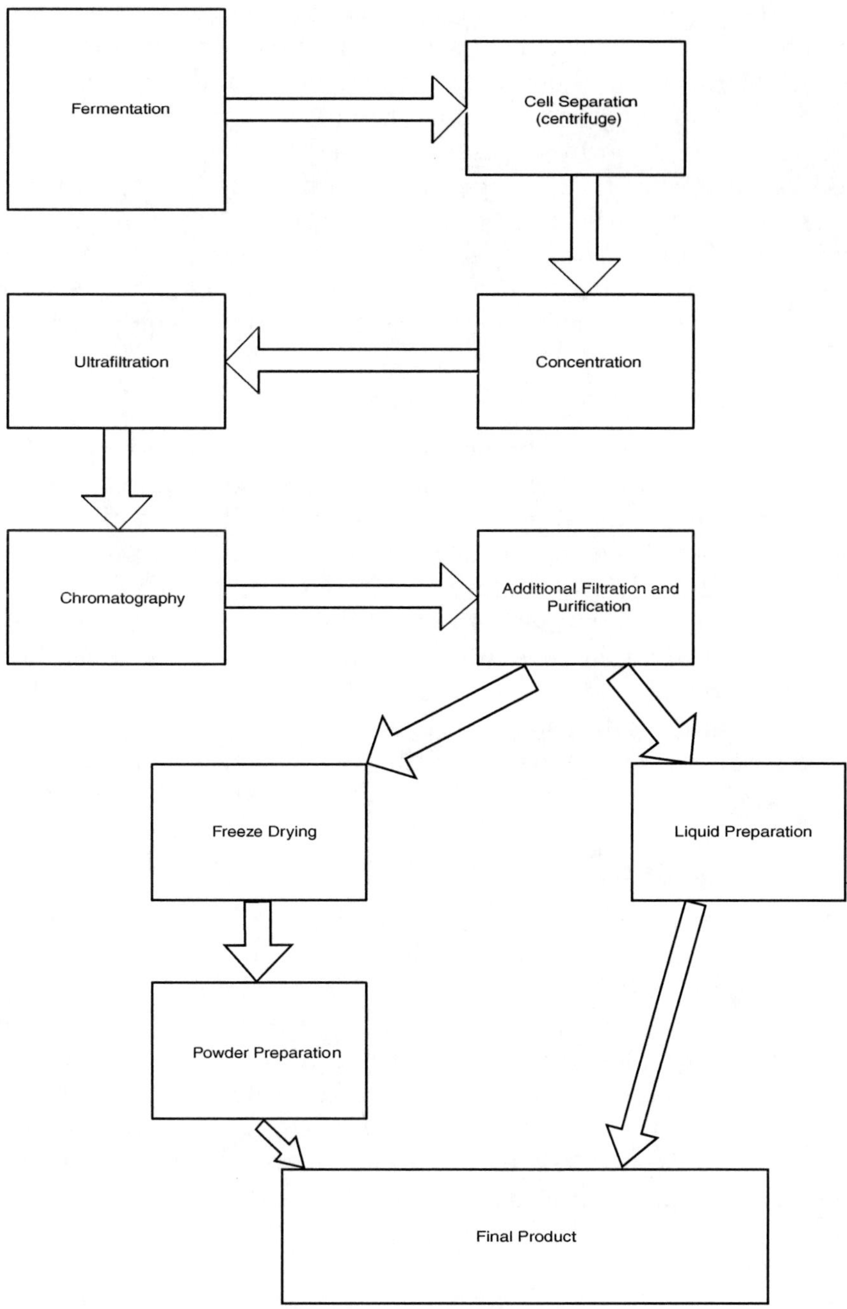

FIGURE 4.3 Diagram of processing procedure employed to produce biopharmaceuticals.

This process requires many steps. The first step is to collect the cellular material. This is done with a centrifuge. The product must be concentrated and then filtered. Filtration is typically done with ultrafiltration membranes and chromatographic purification. Ultrafiltration separates molecules based on their size and shape. Additionally, removal of solvents in the product is accomplished by freeze-drying, where the solvent is removed from a solution while in a frozen state. Ultrafiltration systems, chromatographic purification equipment, and freeze-drying equipment are readily available either as newly manufactured or surplus equipment.

4.2.2.3.2 Mammalian Cell Culture

Mammalian cells (e.g., Chinese hamster ovary and baby hamster kidney) can be used as a medium for growth. Animal cells have been used to produce vaccines and monoclonal antibodies. This method differs from microbial cells because it is a much more complex culture, it is slower due to animal cell growth rates, and the cells are more fragile than microbial cells due to the lack of an outer cell wall. The reactor is much different from the microbial fermentor because of the fragility of the mammalian cells.[7] For example, rather than using an impeller, the mammalian cell reactor is bottle-shaped and is rolled. Rolling is a more gentle form of mixing. It takes thousands of roller bottles for industrial production.

4.2.2.3.3 Yeast and Fungal Cell Culture

Yeast (*Saccharomyces cerevisiae*) has been used in fermentation systems to produce recombinant biopharmaceuticals. Examples of therapeutic recombinant proteins that are manufactured in this way are Novolog (short-acting insulin), Leukine (used in bone marrow transplants), Recombivax (vaccination), Revasc (anticoagulant), Fasturtec (hyperuricemia), and Regranex (diabetic ulcers).

Fungi have also been examined for recombinant protein production. To date, no pharmaceutical based on a fungal production method has been approved by the FDA.

4.2.2.4 Live Tissue

Live tissue or cells can be used for the production of biopharmaceuticals. Transgenic systems will be primarily discussed where the genome is altered by the transfer of a gene to produce a valuble product.

4.2.2.4.1 Transgenic Animals

Transgenic animals are typically grown by injecting the desired DNA into an egg cell. Sometimes the genetic material will be incorporated into the egg cell. The egg is then fertilized and implanted into a surrogate mother. Once the transgenic animal is born, the modified DNA will be passed on to future generations. Transgenic animals have the genes to produce useful proteins that can be harvested for pharmaceutical production. One of the methods of harvesting is to specifically target the mammary glands of an animal so that the desired protein is produced in the milk of that animal. Goats, rabbits, pigs, sheep, and cows have been successfully used as transgenic animals. A wide variety of proteins have been produced by transgenic animals. One of the more widely publicized transgenic animal products is spider silk.[8] A company called Nexia is using goats to produce spider silk proteins in their milk. The proteins from the milk will be assembled into spider silk, which will be marketed as a product called Biosteel.[9] Humankind has been trying to mass-produce spider silk for thousands of years (e.g., silkworms have been used for thousands of years to produce silk). Spider silk is stronger and more flexible than steel, and it offers a lightweight alternative to carbon fiber, which is used in the fabrication of composite materials.

4.2.2.4.2 Transgenic Plants

Transgenic plants have been a subject of research over the past decade or so. Even though no pharmaceuticals using transgenic plants have been approved, there are a number of promising drugs being developed.

4.2.2.4.3 Insect Cells

Insect cells can also be used as a medium for recombinant protein production. Successful production has occurred only on a laboratory scale.

4.2.2.5 Vaccines

Vaccines can be produced for bacteria and for viral agents. When producing a vaccine for a bacterial agent, the bacterial cells are generally grown by a suitable method such as fermentation, and the cells are deactivated (killed) using chemical treatment, heat, or radiation.

Table 4.9 Some Viral Vaccines and Production Methods

Virus	Cell Culture System
Yellow fever	Fertilized chicken eggs
Measles	Chicken embryo cells
Mumps	Chicken embryo cells
Polio	Monkey kidney tissue
Rubella	Duck embryo cells

A virus requires DNA to replicate. Generally a virus is grown in a suitable animal cell culture. One of the most common methods of growth is in fertilized eggs or in cultures of chick embryo tissue. Once the viral material is produced, it is separated by centrifuge, concentrated, filtered, and purified using techniques and equipment previously described.[10] Examples of viral vaccines produced are shown in Table 4.9.

4.3 USES OF BIOLOGICAL AGENTS AS A WEAPON

As with any technology, the benefit for humankind must be balanced with the potential for evil applications. Biotechnology makes possible the enormous benefits of pharmaceuticals and vaccines, but this technology can be used for very harmful purposes. The equipment used in either case is virtually the same. Pharmaceuticals and vaccines or bioweapons can be produced in the same facilities. The dual use of these facilities makes it very difficult to determine the purpose of the facility.

Biotechnology is used by every state in the world for the purpose of creating medicines and vaccines. The equipment that is required to run a pharmaceutical or vaccine facility is widely available to any nation with minimal restrictions agreed upon by the Australia Group (see Chapter 7). Furthermore, an educated workforce is also widely available. Virtually every college or university in the world has some level of biotechnology available in its curriculum. Most secondary schools in the world teach basic skills of biotechnology in the biology curriculum. The technology can be scaled to any size, ranging from small laboratory hand-sized vessels to industrial-scale systems.

Biological weapons are inexpensive to develop. In 1969 the United Nations commissioned a study on the cost of causing 50% casualties over a 1-km^2 area. The results were:

- Conventional weapon ≈\$6000
- Nuclear weapon ≈\$2400
- Chemical weapon (sarin gas) ≈\$1800
- Biological weapon (anthrax) ≈\$3

Biotechnology is available to individuals, groups, industries, and nations. The potential lethality of some of the naturally occurring organisms described in Table 4.2, Table 4.3, Table 4.4, and Table 4.5, indicates a WMD technology that is impossible to control. Furthermore, some of the tools that are being developed in biotechnology will eventually be advanced enough to produce a designer virus.[11] We have seen the beginnings of this capability when Dr. Eckard Wimmer and his team from the University of New York at Stony Brook built the polio virus from scratch using its genome sequence taken off the Internet.[12] The human-made virus was injected into a mouse that later died from the effects of polio, proving that the virus was alive. Polio is a very simple virus and easier to synthesize than smallpox. Nonetheless, it demonstrates that the tools and knowledge of the genome have advanced to the point where life forms can be assembled from strands of DNA that can be ordered from a variety of laboratory supply companies.[13] As technology progresses, the capability to engineer new viral forms will be developed.

4.3.1 Means of Delivery

Making an infectious agent is only one step in the weaponization of biological agents. For optimum dispersal, into the largest human population possible, the agent needs to be breathed by the victims. The average human breathes air at a rate of about 20 l/min. This is the means by which the agent enters the human respiratory system. In order to be trapped in the lungs, the agent must be in the form of an aerosol (e.g., small dustlike particles). The particle sizes that are dangerous to the human respiratory system are on the order of 1 to 5 μm. One micrometer (μm) is 0.00000254 in., and it would require an electron microscope to see a particle that small. If the particles are larger than 5 μm, then the human defense mechanisms will stop them. If the particles are smaller than 1 μm, then they will not be trapped in the lungs and will be expelled with each breath (Figure 4.4).

To make a biological agent into an aerosol of the correct size distribution is a challenge. This would require a milling step at the tail end of the biological agent production process. Another

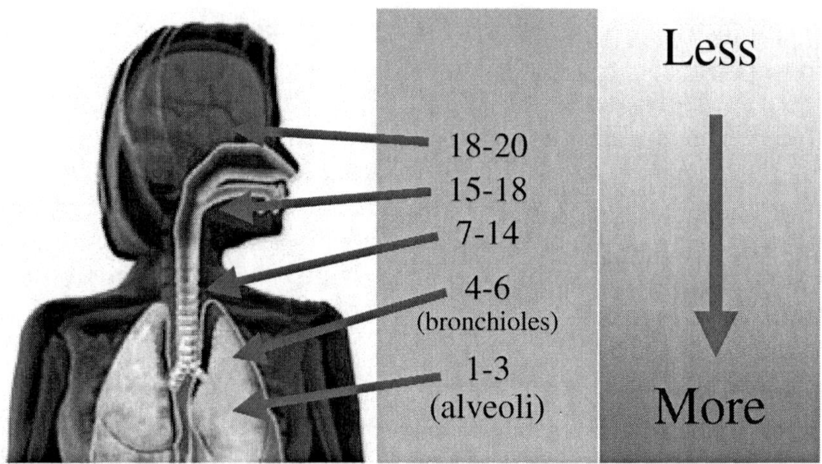

FIGURE 4.4 The size of particles and where they are filtered in the human respiratory system.

problem with small particles is that they tend to attract one another, other particles, or molecules in the atmosphere. The particles will then agglomerate and precipitate out of the air. To prevent this from happening, the particles must be covered with a special (anhydroscopic) coating. This is a challenge and requires some additional expertise, but it is not beyond the capabilities of the higher educational system. For example, the authors' institution is home to the first center dedicated to the study of aerosols, the Particulate Systems Research Center. There are several other centers in this area that have been formed later. Students who study in these centers develop the necessary skill sets to tackle the coating problem.

The product from the production process can be in either a dry powder form or a liquid form. The U.S. and the USSR have developed sophisticated delivery systems to maximize the lethality of either form of bioweapon.[14] Both programs have developed munitions for delivering dry powders and sprayers for delivering either powders or liquids.

Dry powders can be delivered by a variety of methods available to groups or individuals, including off-the-shelf dry-powder garden sprayers (with weapons-grade powders). The key to a successful delivery method is to have some understanding of how air currents will distribute the particles. A weapons-grade powder should float on the air currents.

Liquids require a sprayer such as a modified liquid garden sprayer. The key to this technology is to develop a fine spray with the correct particle-size distribution.

4.3.2 Uses for a State

The U.S. bioweapons program started during World War II and was unilaterally dismantled in 1969. During this period of time, the U.S. was able to parameterize the effects of biological weapons. What is clear from these studies is that biological weapons can be dispersed over large areas (tens of thousands of square miles). The problem with biological agents is that it takes days for the agents to act due to the long incubation times. For a military planner, this time delay limited the value of the weapon militarily.

The USSR viewed biological weapons as an additional weapon in their arsenal for mutually assured destruction.[15] Hence, the USSR put a great deal of effort in developing antibiotic- and vaccine-resistant strains of agents and a very large production capability. The problem with having such a large program is that when the USSR collapsed in 1991, the scientists involved in the program were discarded. Thus, the technology and the expertise in the USSR presented opportunities for unscrupulous states and groups.

In general, a state would use these weapons as deterrents. Two Chinese colonels in 1996, Qiao Liang and Wang Xiangsui, suggested that if China were to go to war with the U.S., it would resort to unrestricted warfare to counter the U.S. military superiority.[16] Unrestricted warfare is not unknown to the world. About 2400 years ago Sun Tzu wrote *The Art of War*,[17] which described how a weak opponent can turn the strengths of its opponent to its favor. What unrestricted warfare entails is up to the imagination, but it is safe to say that all bets are off. For example, states could work with terrorist organizations to deliver weapons of mass destruction on the soil of their mutual opponent. In a world with state-supported or sponsored terrorism, the rules of war have changed.

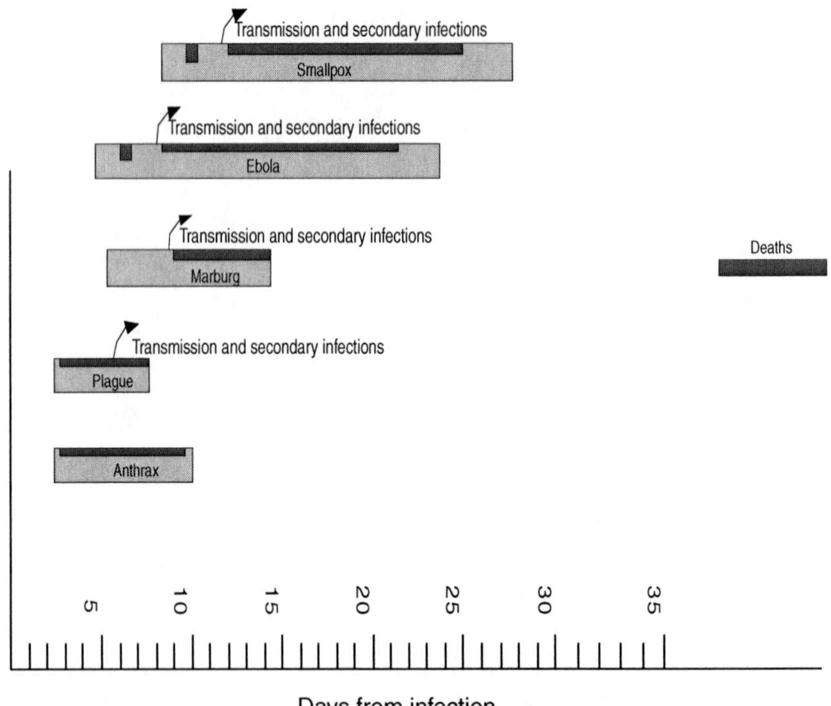

FIGURE 4.5 Incubation period and event timeline for various biological agents.

4.3.3 Uses in Terrorism

Bioweapons are within the capabilities of terrorist groups. The weapons can be simple, such as a suicide terrorist infected with SARS spreading it in the U.S. If the group has access to technologies developed by a supportive state, then more sophisticated attacks are possible. Bioweapons, due to their incubation time, are almost a perfect terrorist weapon. They are small, lethal, and undetectable and give the perpetrator a long time to get away (Figure 4.5).

4.4 CONCLUSION

Biological weapons represent the greatest threat to humankind from any weapons of mass destruction technology. The reasons for this claim are many. First of all most of the agents exist in nature so they are easily obtainable. Second the biotechnology, pharmaceutical and vaccine industries are widely distributed around the world. Thus there is a large inventory of new and low cost used equipment available in the marketplace. Also, there is a knowledgeable and widely distributed workforce that can provide know how. Third, the technology is very difficult to regulate due to its dual uses. Fourth, the implementation of treaties and agreements are virtually impossible to regulate due to a number of factors. Foremost among these is the potential of industrial espionage in the lucrative biotechnology and pharmaceutical industries. Finally, the rapid development of new techniques and methods is making possible the development of ever more sophisticated products. These same tools can also be used to make better biological weapons.

REFERENCES

1. Ghosh, T.K., Prelas, M.A., Viswanath, D., and Loyalka, S., eds., *Science and Technology of Terrorism and Counter Terrorism*, Marcel Dekker, New York, 2002.
2. CNN, Mad Cow Disease, Counting the Cost; http://www.cnn.com/SPECIALS/2000/madcow/; accessed 2/24/04.
3. Oakley, R., Six Months of Foot-and-Mouth Disease in UK, *CNN,* Aug. 20, 2001; http://www.cnn.com/2001/WORLD/europe/08/20/farmer.sixmonths/index.html; accessed 2/24/04.
4. Walsh, G., *Biopharmaceuticals: Biochemistry and Biotechnology*, 2nd ed., Wiley and Sons, New York, 2003.
5. Federal Standard 209E; http://www.aeromechindia.com/faq/federal_standard_209E_class_limits.htm; accessed 3/7/04.
6. Pall Incorporates Revolutionary Technology into Water Treatment Systems. *Waternunc.com*, Jan. 01, 2001; http://www.waternunc.com/gb/pall01.htm; accessed 3/7/04; Boswell, C., *Chemical Reporter*, Aug. 12, 2002; http://www.findarticles.com/cf_dls/m0FVP/5_262/90623766/print.jhtml.
7. Fritchman, K., BD Cell™ MAb Medium: Grow Your Cells for Up To 21 Days Without Medium Changes, *The Cell Line*, 11(1), 1–3, 2001; http://www.bdbiosciences.com/discovery_labware/technical_resources/cellline/issues/cellline_v11_n1.pdf; accessed 3/8/04.
8. Lazaris, A., Arcidiacono, S., Huang, Y., Zhou, J.-F., Duguay, F., Chretien, N., Welsh, E.A., Soares, J.W., and Karatzas, C.N., Spider Silk Fibers Spun from Soluble Recombinant Silk Produced in Mammalian Cells, *Science*, 295 (5554), 472–476, 2002.

9. Nexia Biotechnologies Inc., Vaudreuil-Dorion, QC, Canada; http://www.nexiabiotech.com/en/00_home/index.php; accessed 3/8/04.

10. Prelas, M., The Classification and Manufacture of Biological Agents, in *The Science and Technology of Terrorism and Counterterrorism*, Ghosh, T.K., Prelas, M.A., Viswanath, D., and Loyalka, S.K., eds., Marcel Dekker, New York, 2002.

11. See note 10 above.

12. BBC, First Synthetic Virus Created, *BBC News,* July 11, 2002; http://news.bbc.co.uk/2/hi/science/nature/2122619.stm; accessed 03/09/04.

13. Cello, J., Paul, A.U. and Winman, E., Dangerous Virus Made from Mail-Order Kits: Should This Have Been Done? *Cell News*, July 11, 2002; http://www.geocities.com/giantfideli/cellnews_dangerous_virus_made_from_mail-order_kits.html; accessed 3/9/04.

14. Prelas, M., Weaponization and Delivery Systems, in *The Science and Technology of Terrorism and Counterterrorism*, Ghosh, T.K., Prelas, M.A., Viswanath, D., and Loyalka, S.K., eds., Marcel Dekker, New York, 2002.

15. Alibek, K.W. and Handelman, S., *Biohazard: The Chilling True Story of the Largest Covert Biological Weapons Program in the World Told*, Dell, 2000.

16. Pomfret, J., China Ponders New Rules of "Unrestricted War," *Washington Post*, Aug. 8, 1999.

17. Giles, Lionel, trans., *Sun Tzu on the Art of War*; http://www.kimsoft.com/polwar.htm; accessed 3/9/04.

5

Characteristics of Chemical Weapons

Chemical weapons (CWs) deliver quantities of toxic substances to cause morbidity or mortality over large populations. CWs were widely deployed during the First World War. The most infamous incident occurred when the German army released chlorine gas at Ypres, Belgium, on April 23, 1915.[1] This surprise attack was so successful that it caused a break in the French line, but the Germans failed to take full advantage because they did not anticipate the magnitude of the disorientation. The panic disabled even well-disciplined soldiers, leading about 5000 troops to perish in the attack. The technology, know-how, and equipment to produce CWs are widely available today.

Chemical weapons technology used in the First World War predominantly consisted of standard explosive munitions with a toxic payload. These munitions typically used payloads with industrial chemicals or variants. One of the first CW uses simply involved release of industrial containers of chlorine gas by the Germans. The French followed by adapting artillery munitions with phosgene. The war drove CW technological improvements, leading to the deployment of mustard gas. Mustard had the ability to challenge protective measures in place at the time. By the war's end, about 113,000 tons of CWs had been used, resulting in the deaths of about 92,000 people and 1.3 million injuries. Following the war, the Geneva Protocol attempted to ban the future use of poison gas and bacteriological weapons on the battlefield.[2]

The Geneva Protocol was initially ratified by the League of Nations in 1925. Under the protocol, most nations agreed to prohibited CW use in warfare. Several signatories, including the U.S., reserved the right of retaliation if CWs were first used against them. Even though the protocol was developed in 1925, the U.S. did not ratify the treaty until 1975. Interestingly, CWs were later deployed by signatory nations, including the Italians in Ethiopia and the Japanese in Manchuria and China. Despite the existence of considerable CW stockpiles, CWs were not deployed during World War II.

During World War II, the Germans developed a new class of CWs, the nerve agents. By the end of the war, the Germans had stockpiled up to 30,000 tons of the nerve agent tabun. The allies discovered several chemical production plants after invading Germany. The British built on the German technology and developed additional nerve agents from the processes used for industrial insecticides. The British research led to the devolvement of the nerve agent VX during the 1950s. VX had greater lethal properties than any other known agent at the time. The U.S. also built on this technology and began large-scale VX manufacturing during the 1960s. The U.S. developed and deployed defoliating agents such as Agent Orange, Agent Purple, Agent Blue, and Agent White during the Vietnam conflict.

5.1 CHEMICAL AGENTS

Chemical weapons contain substances intended to incapacitate the targeted individuals by causing morbidity or mortality. Those who deploy CWs also exploit the indirect physiological effects of panic and disorientation that accompanies CW use. Certain classes of CWs are designed to dispatch large numbers of people. Such weapons classes fall into the category of weapons of mass destruction (WMDs).

CW effectiveness is dependent on the physical properties, biological effects, method of release, and the meteorological conditions at the time. Agents vary in persistence. Some materials disperse rapidly after release and present an immediate, short-duration hazard. These agents are usually released as airborne particles, liquids, and gases, and incapacitation usually results from inhalation. Other materials continue to present a hazard for a considerable time after delivery and remain a contact hazard or produce an inhalation hazard by vaporizing over a period of time. CW effectiveness is measured by the capability to maximize the number of casualties with the least amount of agent. In addition to biological responses, meteorological factors present at the time of dispersal will influence the effectiveness of the weapon. For example, the amount of wind and ground topography will affect dispersal. High temperatures may decrease the persistence of agents and result in greater vaporization. Low temperatures may increase agent persistence. Some agents may be susceptible to freezing, thus reducing contact effectiveness. Rain may dilute and promote hydrolysis of certain agents.

CW agents may enter the body by several routes. Gases, vapors, and aerosols may enter the body by inhalation and be absorbed by the mucosa of the nose, eyes, or lungs. Aerosols larger than 5 μm tend to be retained in the upper respiratory tract, while those with droplets smaller than 1 μm tend not to be retained by the body. Liquids may be absorbed directly through the skin and mucous membranes. Toxic compounds can produce their effects when deposited on the skin as solid or liquid particles. Agents that penetrate the skin may form temporary reservoirs, thus delaying the onset of symptoms. CW agents may also contaminate food and water and be absorbed inadvertently in the gastrointestinal tract.

Four classes of chemical agents have been weaponized, and their deployment has the potential of causing widespread morbidity and mortality:

1. Pulmonary agents
2. Vesicants or blister agents
3. Cyanide or blood agents
4. Nerve agents

5.1.1 Pulmonary Agents

Pulmonary agents directly attack lung tissue and result in respiratory distress, including pulmonary edema. This class includes phosgene, diphosgene, chlorine, and chloropicrin. Of this class, phosgene is the most dangerous and the most likely to be used in the future. Phosgene was used for the first time in 1917, and it was responsible for a majority of CW-related fatalities during World War I.[3]

Inhalation of pulmonary agents results in an acute chemically induced lung injury and varying degrees of pulmonary edema. The onset of symptoms is usually delayed by a varying duration as a function of the amount of agent exposure. This chemical agent affects the alveolar-capillary membrane, the blood-air barrier in the lungs. While the U.S. no longer maintains military phosgene stockpiles, about 3 million tons of phosgene are produced worldwide each year for industrial uses.[4] Phosgene or perfluoroisobutylene (PFIB) is a toxic pyrolysis product of tetrafluoroethylene polymers used in Teflon®.

Phosgene, first synthesized in 1812, is used in the plastics and pesticides[5] industries. Phosgene can be formed when certain compounds, such as some types of plastics, are exposed to heat. At room temperature, phosgene is a poisonous gas. Phosgene gas can be liquefied for shipping and storage. A colorless gas with a low boiling point of 8.2°C, phosgene is an extremely volatile and nonpersistent agent. Because phosgene has a vapor density about 3.4 times greater than air, it can collect in low-lying areas. Phosgene is readily soluble in organic solvents and fatty oils and undergoes rapid hydrolysis in water to form hydrochloric acid and carbon dioxide. Liquid phosgene quickly vaporizes when exposed to the atmosphere. The plume is heavier than air and stays close to the ground.

Phosgene was developed as a CW agent during the early 20th century. Germany first deployed phosgene on the battlefield during World War I at Verdun in 1917. Later, both sides in the conflict used phosgene either alone or mixed with chlorine in artillery munitions. Both sides subsequently deployed phosgene during the war. Phosgene is transported as a liquid, and military dispersion during the war usually began with the explosion of liquid-filled shells. The gas subsequently vaporized and formed a white cloud due to its slight solubility in an aqueous environment. Phosgene has a characteristic odor of sweet, newly-mown hay.

Phosgene exposure risk is highly dependent on proximity to the release. The gas can be absorbed through skin, eyes, or lungs. Exposure is also possible by contact with phosgene-contaminated water or food. Phosgene irritates the skin, eyes, nose, throat, and lungs immediately following exposure. Subsequent symptoms include coughing, a burning sensation in the throat, blurred vision, difficulty breathing or shortness of breath, nausea, and vomiting. Skin contact results in frostbitelike lesions. Mortality primarily occurs from pulmonary edema within about two to six hours of exposure. However, onset of symptoms may be delayed up to 48 hours following exposure. Secondary exposures can occur from contaminated clothing.[5]

Phosgene produces pulmonary edema following a latent period that is a function of the intensity of exposure and the physical activity of the exposed individual. The victim experiences worsening respiratory distress following the latent period. Pulmonary edema and death may follow. During the time preceding the appearance of shortness of breath, individuals exposed to particularly high concentrations of organohalides may report symptoms associated with mucous membrane irritation. Exposure to large quantities of phosgene may irritate moist mucous membranes due to the generation of hydrochloric acid from the hydrolysis of phosgene. Irritation of the larynx by very large concentrations of the agent may lead to sudden choking and death.

In industrial settings, chemical toxicity is defined in terms of the quantity that is immediately dangerous to life and health (IDLH). For chemical vapors or gases, the concentration that is expected to result in the death of 50% of those exposed is defined as the LC_{50}, and the amount of liquid exposure expected to result in the death of 50% of those exposed is referred to as LD_{50}.[6] The IDLH concentration of phosgene is 2.0 parts per million (ppm).[7] Phosgene's odor of newly mown hay, has an odor threshold that is below dangerous concentrations. The odor threshold for phosgene is about 1.5 mg/m^3, and phosgene irritates mucous membranes at 4 mg/m^3. The LC_{50} of phosgene is approximately 3200 mg·min/m^3, which is about half the LC_{50} (6000 mg·min/m^3) of chlorine, the first gas used on a large scale in World War I.

Phosgene is commonly manufactured within the chemical industry as an intermediate chlorinating agent. A number of production processes have been documented in the chemical processing literature. Chlorination is one of the most common reactions in the chemical process industry. A suitable phosgene facility could be purchased with an investment of $10 million to $14 million.[8] An existing chemical production facility could easily be refitted to produce phosgene munitions.

Phosgene is also a chemical precursor used in the production of other CWs.[9] Phosgene can be combined with thionyl chloride dimethylmethylphosphonate to produce DC (methylphosphonyl dichloride). DC is one of the fundamental building blocks for the syntheses of some G and V nerve agents. Because of its common use in the chemical industry, the equipment for the production of phosgene is widely available. Additionally, there is a large pool of people skilled in the assembly and operation of this type of equipment.

5.1.2 Vesicants or Blister Agents

Vesicant CWs were developed not only to produce battlefield casualties, but also to harass opposing forces by requiring the opponent to wear full protective equipment. Vesicant agents are chemicals that can cause blistering of the skin and extreme irritation of the lungs and eyes, leading to blindness. These agents were designed to incapacitate, but vesicants in large doses can also kill. Vesicant agents can be thickened to create a persistent contaminate that can be applied to terrain, ships, aircraft, vehicles, or other equipment. Vesicants will burn and blister the skin or any other part of the body they contact. They will also permeate through most clothing and attack mucous membranes, lungs, skin, and blood-forming organs. Vesicants are biologically activated by moisture created by perspiration. They also damage the respiratory tract when inhaled and cause vomiting and diarrhea if ingested.

The basic vesicant agent is mustard gas, which was used extensively during World War I. Mustard gas, or diphosgene, causes shortness of breath (lung irritant), nausea, and blindness. Later during the war, a number of modifications were made to mustard gas to make it more toxic and lethal. These modifications were called nitrogen mustard and lewisite.

Militarized vesicant CWs can be deployed as vapor, aerosol, or liquid. Vesicants attack exposed skin, airways, and mucous membranes. First synthesized in the early 1800s, vesicants were first deployed by the Germans during World War I. Vesicants were also used by the Italians in the 1930s against Abyssinia, by the Egyptians in the 1960s against Yemen, and by the Iraqis in the 1980s against Iran and the Kurds.

There are three major families of blister agents (vesicants): sulfur mustard (HD) and nitrogen mustard (HN); the arsenical vesicants such as lewisite (L) (sometimes mixed with HD); and the halogenated oximes (CX). Most of the vesicants (except CX) are relatively persistent.

The vesicant class of CWs includes

1. Mustard (sulfur mustard, H, HD)
2. Lewisite (L)
3. Phosgene oxime (CX)

The biological effects of vesicant agents are listed in Table 5.1

5.1.2.1 Mustard (2,2′-dichloroethyl sulfide)

Mustard was extensively deployed during the First World War. Nonpermeable clothing in addition to respiratory protection was

Table 5.1 Biological Effects of Vesicant Agents

Chemical agent	IDLH (mg/m^3)	LC_{50} vapor (mg·min/m^3)	LD_{50} liquid (mg/kg)
H: sulfur mustard	0.003	1500	100
L: lewisite	0.003	1500	30
CX: phosgene oxime	Undefined	1500–2000	25

Source: U.S. Army Medical Research Institute of Chemical Defense, *Medical Management of Chemical Casualties Handbook*, 3rd ed., MCMR-UV-ZM, USAMRICD, Chemical Casualty Care Division, Aberdeen Proving Ground, MD, 2000; http://ccc.apgea.army.mil/reference_materials/handbooks/Red-Handbook/001TitlePage.htm; accessed 4/6/02.

required to protect troops against exposure. The agent caused extensive, slow-healing skin lesions. Mustard was first synthesized in 1822, and its vesicant properties were discovered in the middle of the 19th century. Mustard was first used as a CW in 1917 near Ypres, Belgium, which accounts for its French name (yperite). Mustard was also known by the name "lost" in German.

Sulfur mustard (H), the main blistering agent used in warfare, is an oily liquid at room temperature with a garlic odor and ranges in color from clear to dark brown, depending on purity.[10] Sulfur mustard can be readily absorbed by the skin and most clothing and is fairly persistent in the environment, presenting a hazard for days or even weeks, depending on the weather. Compared with the more toxic nerve agents, sulfur mustard is relatively easy to produce and to load into munitions. Sulfur mustard can be stockpiled for decades — especially when distilled — either as bulk agent or in weaponized form. The primary drawbacks of sulfur mustard as a CW agent are that it

- Must be used in relatively high concentrations to produce significant casualties
- Freezes at a relatively high temperature, about 14°C (57°F) for distilled mustard
- Tends to polymerize when stored for long periods (unless distilled to high purity), forming solids that precipitate out of solution, thus reducing the efficiency of dissemination

Sulfur mustard has diffused toxic effects on the body, taking up to 3 hours for symptoms to manifest. The primary biological effect of sulfur mustard is painful skin blistering and eye and lung irritation. The indirect effect is the large number of casualties, who place an enormous burden on medical services. Heavy exposure to an aerosol of mustard or mustard vapor causes the lungs to fill with fluid, "drowning" the victim from within.[11] Nevertheless, only 2 to 3% of hospitalized American and British mustard casualties in World War I died. A similarly low death rate was reported for Iranian mustard casualties during the Iran-Iraq War.[12] Seven to ten days after exposure, sulfur mustard can also cause a delayed impairment of the immune function that increases vulnerability to bacterial infection, which may lead to other serious medical complications.

5.1.2.1.1 Biological Effects of Mustard

Sulfur mustard is a powerful irritant and blistering agent that damages the skin, eyes, and respiratory (breathing) tract. It also damages DNA, a vital component of cells in the body.

Mustard rapidly forms cyclic ethylene sulfonium ions after contact with moisture on the body. Mustard binds irreversibly to tissue within several minutes after contact. Cyclic ethylene sulfonium is very reactive and readily binds to intracellular and extracellular enzymes, proteins, and other cellular components. This leads to cellular death and inflammation. Penetration through clothing is enhanced by body heat and sweat.

Mustard exposure initially results in irritation of the eyes, nose, sinuses, and pharynx. Moist, exposed skin is the most susceptible to mustard exposure. Symptoms vary from mild burning to serious inflammation and usually occur between 2 to 48 hours after exposure. The eyes are particularly sensitive to mustard. Swelling and loosening of corneal epithelial cells lead to corneal edema and clouding with white blood cells. Blindness may result from inflammation of the inner eye. The gastrointestinal tract is also very susceptible to mustard damage, resulting in nausea, with or without vomiting. The blister fluid is clear, at first thin and straw-colored, but later yellowish and tending to coagulate. Mustard produces airway lesions. Damage to the trachea and upper bronchi cause a sputum-producing cough. The damage propagates from the upper airways to the lower pulmonary region and may damage the alveoli in the lungs. Mortality occurs from respiratory failure within 24 hours following exposure. Additional mortalities occur from secondary bacterial infections.

5.1.2.1.2 Production of Mustard

Thousands of tons of mustard agent were produced from alcohol, bleaching powder, and sodium sulfite during World War I. Following the war, two common industrial methods were developed using sulfur monochloride and ethylene as base materials. A mustard agent plant using this technology could use the existing process equipment at an oil refinery. Modern mustard production uses thiodiglycol, a sulfur-based industrial organic solvent.[13] Thiodiglycol is also used in the manufacture of ink, lubricant additives, and plastics as well as in the photographic developing industry. Mustard can also be produced directly from the chlorination of thiodiglycol by addition of hydrochloric acid, another readily available industrial chemical. This process, the Victor Meyer-Clarke process, does not require sophisticated equipment. The process lends itself to the use of less corrosive chlorination agents than hydrochloric acid, sacrificing efficiency for avoidance of corrosion-resistant reactors and pipes. The end product is purified by either distillation or solvent extraction. The process requires adequate ventilation for worker protection.

Thiodiglycol is produced by five U.S. and eight foreign chemical suppliers. The Chemical Weapons Convention (CWC) places controls on the export of thiodiglycol. However, thiodiglycol can be produced by reacting ethylene oxide with hydrogen sulfide; both of these ingredients are widely available. Hydrogen sulfide can be extracted from natural gas or crude oil, where it is often present as an impurity, or derived from elemental sulfur. Ethylene oxide is readily produced from ethylene, a major product of petroleum refining.

5.1.2.2 Lewisite (2-chlorovinyldichloroarsine)

Lewisite (L) is a vesicant that also damages the eyes, skin, and airways by direct contact in a similar manner to mustard. After absorption, it causes an increase in capillary permeability to produce a loss of blood volume, shock, and organ damage. Exposure to lewisite causes immediate pain or irritation, although lesions require hours to become full-blown. Dr. Wilford Lee Lewis first synthesized lewisite in 1918, too late for deployment during World War I. There have been allegations that it was used by Japan against Chinese forces in the late 1930s[14]; however, there are no confirmed reports that it has been used in warfare, although it may be stockpiled by some countries. Destruction of U.S. stockpiles of chemical agents, including lewisite, was mandated by the CWC to take place before April 2007.

Lewisite has been used to increase the effectiveness of mustard agent dispersion. Like mustard, lewisite can penetrate ordinary clothing and even rubber. Absorption through the skin can be fatal.

In its pure form, lewisite is an oily, colorless liquid, although it can appear amber to black in its impure form. Lewisite has an odor like geraniums and contains arsenic, a poisonous element. Mustard-lewisite mixtures have been used for ground dispersal and aerial spraying. The mixture was developed to lower the mustard freezing point.

5.1.2.3 Phosgene Oxime (dichloroform oxime)

Phosgene oxime (CX) is considered an irritant agent because skin contact produces intense itching and a rash similar to hives. First produced in 1929, phosgene oxime has never been used on the battlefield. Specific information on this chemical is limited.

Colorless in its solid form and yellowish-brown when it is a liquid, phosgene oxime has a disagreeable, irritating odor. Phosgene oxime causes pain on contact with the skin followed by formation of a ring after 30 sec and by a wheal in about 30 min. The extreme pain can persist for days. The agent can also cause extreme eye pain. The damage is similar to that caused by lewisite. Phosgene oxime is also very irritating to the upper airways. This agent causes pulmonary edema if inhaled.

In warfare, CX would likely be deployed as a thermal fog. However, phosgene oxime has been combined with other chemicals, including mustard and VX, to increased permeability of these agents.

A chemical researcher wrote in 1934 that there are few substances in organic chemistry that exert such a violent effect on the human organism as this phosgene oxime.[15] In addition to having very rapid action, phosgene oxime is known to have superior ability to penetrate rubber-based protective garments. While not a true blister agent (in the sense that its effects on the skin are different from mustard or lewisite), phosgene oxime produces almost immediate and extremely painful irritation to skin, eyes, and respiratory system. A full body rash can result from even limited contact with phosgene oxime.[16] Symptoms may linger for as long as a year. Sores and lesions on the skin require an extensive healing period, and like wounds from other blister agents, these can serve as focal points for secondary infections.

5.1.3 Blood Agents (Cyanogen Agents, AC, CK)

Cyanide is a rapidly acting lethal agent, with fatality occurring within 6 to 8 min following inhalation. Inhalation of cyanide-containing gases presents the greatest risk to individuals. However, cyanide ingestion is also toxic. In either case, cyanide binds to the hemoglobin, preventing oxygenation of the blood.

Cyanide can be a colorless gas such as hydrogen cyanide (HCN) and cyanogen chloride (CNCl), or it can be in a crystal form such as sodium cyanide (NaCN) and potassium cyanide (KCN). Cyanide has been described as having a "bitter almond" smell, but it does not always give off an odor, and not everyone can detect this odor. Materials of interest as chemical agents are hydrogen cyanide (hydrocyanic acid, AC) and the simple cyanogen, cyanogen chloride (CK).

Cyanide has a high affinity for the ferric iron in methemoglobin (a form of hemoglobin that occurs when hemoglobin is oxidized during decomposition). Inhalation, ingestion, or skin absorption of cyanide results in rapid respiration, restlessness, dizziness, weakness, headache, nausea, and vomiting. Higher exposure levels lead to convulsions and a drop in blood pressure followed by loss of consciousness and death.[17]

Cyanide and its compounds historically have had limited use in weaponized forms. Cyanide gas evaporates and disperses quickly in open spaces, making it less harmful outdoors. Released cyanide gas will rise because it is less dense than air. The French deployed about 4000 tons of cyanide during the First World War. The effectiveness was limited by the small munitions size and the high volatility of cyanide. The U.S. maintained a small number of cyanide munitions during World War II. Zyklon B, hydrogen cyanide, was used as a genocidal agent by the Germans in their concentration camps during World War II. Japan allegedly used cyanide against China before and during World War II, and Iraq may have used cyanide against the Kurds in the Kurdish city of Halabja in northern Iraq in the 1980s.[18]

The cyanides exist as liquids in munitions but rapidly vaporize upon detonation. The major human threat is from the vapor. The toxicity of the liquid is similar to that of mustard. Large munitions (bombs, large shells) are required for cyanide to be effective on the battlefield. Smaller weapons will not provide the higher concentrations needed for biological effects.

The U.S. manufactures about 300,000 tons of hydrogen cyanide each year for industrial purposes.[19] Cyanides are used by industry for various chemical syntheses, including electroplating, mineral extraction, dyeing, printing, photography, and agriculture as well as in the manufacture of paper, textiles, and plastics. Cyanide gas is used to exterminate pests and vermin in ships and buildings.

Cyanide is the least toxic of the "lethal" chemical agents. The LC_{50} for AC and CK by inhalation has been estimated to be 2500 to 5000 mg·min/m^3 for AC and about 11,000 mg·min/m^3 for CK. The LD_{50} for hydrogen cyanide has been estimated to be 1.1 mg/kg for intravenous administration and 100 mg/kg after skin exposure. The oral LD_{50} for sodium and potassium cyanide is about 100 and 200 mg/kg, respectively. The IDLH concentration of hydrogen cyanide (AC) is 50.0 parts per million (ppm); for cyanogen chloride (CK), the IDLH concentration is 0.6 mg/m^3. Cyanide salts, in solid form or in solution, are readily absorbed from the gastrointestinal tract after ingestion. Hydrogen cyanide is released as a gas, and the most important route of entry in a battlefield or terrorist scenario would likely be by inhalation.

The central nervous system (CNS) and the heart are susceptible to cyanide.[20] Most clinical effects are of CNS origin and are nonspecific. Inhalation of a high concentration of cyanide will cause abnormally deep or rapid breathing within about 15 sec, followed by the onset of convulsions about 1 min after exposure. Respiratory activity stops 2 to 3 min later, followed by cardiac arrest, leaving the victim dead after 6 to 8 min.

The onset and progression of signs and symptoms after ingestion of cyanide or after inhalation of a lower concentration of vapor are slower. The first effects may not occur until several minutes after exposure, and the time course of these effects depends on the amount absorbed and the rate of absorption. The initial transient breathing problems may be followed by feelings of anxiety or apprehension, agitation, vertigo, a feeling of weakness, nausea with or without vomiting, and muscular trembling. Later, consciousness is lost; respiration decreases in rate and depth; and convulsions, apnea, abnormal heartbeat, and death follow. Because this cascade of events is prolonged, successful treatment is possible. The effects of cyanogen chloride include those described for hydrogen cyanide. Cyanogen chloride is also similar to the riot-control agents (tear gas) in that it causes irritation to the eyes, nose, and airways, marked by the secretion of tears, runny nose, and coughing.

Hydrogen cyanide is a common chemical used in industry. For example, it is used by U.S. producers American Cyanamid Co., Avondale, LA; BP America, Inc., Green Lake, TX; Ciba-Geigy Corp., St. Gabriel, LA; DeGussa Corp., Theodore, AL; Dow Chemical, Freeport, TX; E.I. DuPont de Nemours, Beaumont, TX, Orange, TX, and Victoria, TX; Monsanto Co., Chocolate Bayou, TX; Rohm and Haas Co., Deer Park, TX; and Sterling Chemicals, Inc., Texas City, TX. Hydrogen cyanide is also manufactured worldwide as a chemical intermediate used in the manufacture of acrylic polymers. Cyanide could be diverted for other uses or separately manufactured with minimal investment.

The manufacture of hydrogen cyanide (HCN) has become an important raw material in many chemical processes. Some of the main uses include the manufacture of adiponitrile, acrylonitrile, and sodium cyanide. Adiponitrile is used in the production of nylon; acrylonitrile is used for textile fibers and synthetic rubbers; and sodium cyanide is used to extract gold from ore.

The technologies used to produce cyanides are simple, well known, and require no specialized equipment. The industrial applications of this agent are recognized by the CWC, and they are included on a schedule wherein few restrictions apply.

Four commercial processes are used for the synthesis of hydrogen cyanide. An older synthesis process — the Andrussow process — is commonly used outside of the U.S. The Andrussow process reacts air, ammonia, and natural gas in the presence of a platinum or platinum rhodium catalyst. High temperatures (1100°C) are required to form the hydrogen cyanide. The product gas mixture also contains carbon dioxide, hydrogen, and unreacted ammonium. The products are separated by cooling and cold-water absorption, then the hydrogen cyanide is stripped from the absorber and concentrated. The Andrussow process yields about 75% hydrogen cyanide.

5.1.4 Nerve Agents

Nerve agents are among the most toxic of known chemicals. Weaponized nerve agents can be absorbed into the body by either inhalation or skin contact. Nerve agents inactivate the body's acetylcholinesterase enzyme, resulting in interruption of normal nerve transmission impulses.[21] In either the liquid or vapor state, nerve agents can cause death within minutes after exposure.

Nerve agents fall into two classes — G and V — and can be clustered into three groups:

1. GA: tabun
2. GB/GD: sarin/soman
3. VX

Nerve agents are primarily organophosphorus esters, chemically similar to insecticides. Nerve agents are produced and stored in the liquid phase, with volatility varying between that of gasoline and heavy lubricating oil. The G agents tend to be nonpersistent, whereas the V agents are persistent. Some G agents can be thickened with various substances to increase their persistence.

At room temperature, GB is a comparatively volatile liquid. GA and GD are also significantly volatile and are less persistent. VX is a relatively nonvolatile liquid and exhibits greater persistence. Nerve agents are moderately soluble in water (slow hydrolysis), are highly soluble in lipids, and are rapidly inactivated by strong alkalis and chlorinating compounds. When nerve agents are dispersed as a spray or an aerosol, droplets can be absorbed through the skin, eyes, and respiratory tract. When dispersed as a vapor, the nerve agent is absorbed primarily through the respiratory tract. If enough agent is absorbed, local effects are followed by generalized systemic effects. The rapidity with which effects occur is directly related to the amount of agent absorbed in a given period of time and temperature. Nerve agents can be deployed from conventional weapons such as missiles, bombs, and artillery, or they can be released by spray tanks.

The G-class nerve agents were first developed by the German firm IG during pesticide research in 1936.[22] The Germans produced and weaponized GA (tabun) during World War II. Two years later Germany developed the more toxic GB (sarin). Because this class of compounds was much more toxic than previously developed CWs, the Germans had planned to deploy the nerve agents against the English using the V-1 rocket. However, due to the limited payload of the V-1, the Germans determined that conventional explosives would result in a greater number of casualties. As a result, CWs were not used by Germany during the war. After the war, several industrial nations produced and stocked various nerve agents. The U.S. and the former Soviet Union produced large quantities of both nerve agent classes during the 1950s and 1960s. The Iraq-Iran conflict remains the only known battlefield deployment of nerve agents.

5.1.4.1 Biological Effects of Nerve Agents

Biological effects from nerve agent exposure begin within seconds to several minutes after exposure. Loss of consciousness and onset of seizure activity have occurred within 1 min of exposure to a high concentration. Low-concentration exposures result in constriction of the pupil of the eye and other effects after 15 to 30 min. Unlike other CWs, nerve agents do not have a latent period following exposure. However, people may become indirectly exposed from contact with contaminated clothing. While effects may continue to progress for a period of time, usually the most profound affects are seen within minutes following exposure (Table 5.2).

Nerve agents act as organophosphorus cholinesterase inhibitors. They attack red cells. The acute reaction rate is a function of received dose and absorption route, inhalation or skin. The IDLH and LD_{50} thresholds are shown in Table 5.3. Exposure to lethal quantities results in rapid loss of consciousness, convulsive activity, apnea, and muscular flaccidity. Even small exposures of nerve agent aerosol or vapor will affect the eyes, nose, and airway.

Twitching of the skeletal muscles is the first outward indication of nerve agent exposure. Large acute exposures produce

Table 5.2 Summary of Nerve Agents and Their Routes of Absorption and Effects

Nerve Agent	Types of Effects	Routes of Absorption	Description of Effects
Vapor	Local	Lungs	Rhinorrheal nasal hyperemia, tightness in chest, wheezing
Vapor	Local	Eyes	Miosis, conjunctival hyperemia eye pain, frontal headache
Vapor	Systemic	Lungs or eyes	Muscarinic nicotinic and central nervous system effects
Liquid	Local	Eyes	Same as vapor effects
Liquid	Local	Ingestion	Gastrointestinal
Liquid	Local	Skin	Local sweating and muscular twitching
Liquid	Systemic	Lungs	Tightness in the chest, occasional wheezing; cough dyspnea substernal tightness
Liquid	Systemic	Eyes	Same as for vapor effects
Liquid	Systemic	Skin	Generalized sweating
Liquid	Systemic	Ingestion	Gastrointestinal

Source: Office of the Surgeon General, *The Medical NBC Battlebook*, Tech Guide 242, U.S. Army, Washington, D.C., May 2000.

Table 5.3 Toxicity of Nerve Agents — LD_{50}[24]

Nerve Agent	Vapor Toxicity (mg/m^3)	Liquid Toxicity (mg)
GA (tabun)	0.0001	1000
GB (sarin)	0.0001	1700
GD (soman)	0.0003	50
GF	0.0001	30
VX	0.0001	10

Source: U.S. Army Medical Research Institute of Chemical Defense, *Medical Management of Chemical Casualties Handbook*, 3rd ed., MCMR-UV-ZM, USAMRICD, Chemical Casualty Care Division, Aberdeen Proving Ground, MD, 2000; http://ccc.apgea.army.mil/reference_materials/handbooks/Red-Handbook/001TitlePage.htm; accessed 4/6/02.

fatigue and muscle weakness followed by loss of muscle tone. This effect can be seen near the site of skin droplet contamination, and generalized twitching is common after a large exposure. The central nervous system quickly responds by seizure, apnea, and loss of consciousness. Small exposures are indicated by forgetfulness, an inability to concentrate fully, insomnia, irritability, impaired judgment, and depression.

Eye contact results in rapid tearing within seconds of an acute exposure. The tearing is often accompanied by pain, blurred vision, nausea, and occasionally, vomiting. The exposed individual may have eyeball or headache pain. This is followed by pupil constriction and corresponding poor vision. A runny nose and coughing may also occur, depending on the exposure dose. Longer-term effects include glandular secretions in the gastrointestinal tract, resulting in nausea, vomiting, and diarrhea.

5.1.4.2 Production of Nerve Agents

The technologies required for the production of nerve agents have been known for more than 40 years and are within the capabilities of any moderately advanced chemical or pharmaceutical industry. The technology for nerve agent production is very similar to that associated with commercial products such as organophosphorus pesticides.

Nerve agent production requires greater industrial sophistication than the techniques used to produce pulmonary, vesicant, or blood agents. Specialized corrosion-resistant process equipment is needed for the highly corrosive chlorination and fluorination production steps. Also, the product is very hazardous by nature, requiring special handling to keep the workforce safe.

5.1.4.2.1 GA (Tabun)

GA was the first militarized nerve agent. The first production facilities were built by the Germans during the 1930s.[25] The Germans produced up to 3000 tons of GA a month during the war. GA synthesis has an advantage over other nerve agents in that it does not require corrosive materials or produce highly reactive intermediates. GA production is a two-step process involving blending precursors and a basic carrier solvent. The exothermic reaction requires cooling of the reaction vessel and air filtration systems to protect workers from gaseous hydrochloric acid generated as a by-product. Critical material used in GA production is phosphorus oxychloride or phosphorus trichloride, sodium cyanide, dimethylamine, and ethyl alcohol. The production facilities must consider the cyanation reaction in which a cyanide group is added to the central phosphorus. This step uses the highly toxic hydrogen cyanide (HCN) gas as the reagent.

Most of the ingredients for GA are widely available. Ethanol and sodium cyanide are commodity chemicals that are manufactured and sold in vast quantities; dimethylamine and phosphorus oxychloride are produced by companies in several countries for commercial applications in the production of pharmaceuticals, pesticides, missile fuels, and gasoline additives.

5.1.4.2.2 GB (Sarin) and GD (Soman)

Sarin (GB) and soman (GD) production are similar. Both use a semibatch process with the same basic reaction steps. GB uses phosphorus trichloride, methylphosphonyldifluoride DF, DC, hydrogen fluoride, and isopropanol. GD uses also uses phosphorus trichloride, DC, and hydrogen fluoride, but a different alcohol (pinacolyl alcohol). Production of GB/GD involves the use of highly corrosive hot hydrochloric acid and hydrogen fluoride. Both processes require expensive corrosion-resistant equipment made of Hastelloy or silver. The synthesis uses the alkylation reaction to form a phosphorus-carbon bond from a methyl group or an ethyl group added the central phosphorus. Oxidation, fluorination, and esterification reactions are also used in the synthesis of these nerve agents. A large amount of power also needs to be available. If the agent is to be stored, then the final product must be concentrated by distillation (removal of hydrogen fluoride) and stabilized.

5.1.4.2.3 VX (Aminoethyl Alkyl Phosphonothiolates and Corresponding Alkylated or Protonated Salts)

The V class of nerve agents was originally discovered in 1948 by British scientists engaged in pesticide research.[23] The U.S. and the USSR followed up with military development and production of VX in the 1960s. VX is an oily liquid that has greater persistence than the G-class agents and can last for weeks or longer in the environment. VX is primarily absorbed through the skin.

VX has a persistent phosphorusmethyl (P-CH3) bond and a phosphorus-sulfur bond, but no fluorine. There are at least three industrial processes to synthesize V agents that are readily available to proliferating nations. As with G agents, production of VX involves a difficult alkylation. However, the VX process avoids the use of the corrosive HF gas. After the alkylation steps, the remaining synthesis is uncomplicated. VX uses an Amiton process conducted in solution requiring an inert atmosphere and high-temperature methylation equipment.

5.1.4.2.4 DC (Methylphosphonyl Dichloride)

Methylphosphonyl dichloride (DC), a precursor used in the synthesis of GB and GD,[27] is the fundamental building block of significant portions of G and V agents. The process requires thionyl chloride or phosgene or phosphorus pentachloride. The production of G agents involves the use of partially fluorinated DC. This mixture is reacted with alcohol and degassed. The product is further distilled if it is to be stored instead of being deployed right away. The processes are common in the chemical industry, and both sovereign states and subnational states are capable of producing the materials.

Once distilled, DC is stable with a long shelf life and can be produced in militarily significant quantities in small facilities. A DC ancillary support facility would cost approximately $25 million without expectation that U.S. environmental laws would be met.[28] DC synthesis requires corrosion-resistant equipment, glass-lined reactor vessels, and storage tanks. This specialized equipment is similar to that used in the pesticide or fertilizer industry.

5.1.4.2.5 DMMP (Dimethylmethylphosphonate)

There are many available production processes for DMMP. These processes require glass-lined vessels and glass-lined distillation columns. For example, DMMP may be synthesized by the chlorination of sodium fluoride with phosphorus pentachloride and methylphosphonyl dichloride. The resulting methylphosphonyl difluoride and methylphosphonyl dichloride may be reacted with isopropyl alcohol to produce Sarin.

5.2 CW MUNITIONS

The effectiveness of a CW is limited by the ability to disseminate the toxic materials to the target. Toxic agents have been effectively weaponized by placement in bombs, sub-munitions, projectiles, warheads, and spray tanks. Explosive agents have been the principal dispersion method used. However, care must be taken to maximize the aerosol produced by the explosion and to concentrate the dispersion on the target. Other physical parameters such as vapor pressure, particle size, and viscosity of the agent must be considered. In the case of flammable aerosols, the dispersion cloud can sometimes become ignited (flashing) in the process. Most modern chemical agents are not very volatile. The most volatile of the G agents is GB (sarin), which has a volatility resembling that of water.

Delivery systems can be designed to perform the final mixing of CW precursors immediately prior to or during use. Binary agents are those consisting of two relatively nontoxic chemical components that react to form a lethal agent when mixed together. A binary agent is a more attractive design because it is inherently safer to handle and produce. The use of a binary design reduces the consequences of a toxic spill or premature detonation. The U.S. included three different binary munitions within its CW arsenal. These binary weapons included a GB projectile (a 155-mm artillery shell), an aerial bomb producing VX, and a medium-range missile warhead (for the multiple launch rocket system [MLRS]) containing an agent of intermediate volatility.

Iraq attempted a binary design during the Gulf War. They kept one part of the binary material in the munitions. The other part of the binary was kept in jerry cans. When the munitions were used, a suited technician would take the plug off the munitions and add the chemicals from the jerry can just prior to release of the weapon.

CW capabilities can vary greatly in sophistication. A crude CW arsenal might contain only one or two agents combined with an agricultural sprayer. The Iran-Iraq War of the 1980s saw the first protracted use of chemical weapons since World War I and the first use of nerve agents. CWs may have contributed to 50,000 Iranian casualties, including about 5,000 deaths. The growing availability of CW technology and production equipment, with the globalization of chemical trade, has given more than 100 countries the capability — if not necessarily the intent — to produce simple chemical weapons such as phosgene, hydrogen cyanide, and sulfur mustard. A smaller number have the capability to produce nerve agents such as GA (tabun), GB (sarin), GD (soman), and VX because while mustard-gas production is very simple (particularly if thiodiglycol is available as a starting material), making nerve agents involves more complex and difficult reaction steps.

Technologies and processes used to produce CW are difficult to distinguish from those used to manufacture commercial chemical compounds. Many of the technologies that enable CW production are dual use and widely available. Legitimate commercial chemical facilities can produce CW agents. Technical hurdles associated with the production process include the cyanation reaction for tabun and the alkylation reaction for the other nerve agents. Alkylation requires high temperatures or highly corrosive reagents. Chemical plants capable of manufacturing organic phosphorus pesticides or flame retardants could be converted over a period of weeks to the production of CW agents, although this would not be a simple process. Conversion of multipurpose plants would be easier to convert than single-purpose plants. The hurdles to acquiring a CW production capability are lower if a proliferating country seeks to produce only low-quality agents for immediate use and is willing to cut corners on agent shelf life, safety, and environmental protection. Additional production of CW agents still requires several steps for an operational CW capability. The weapon program also requires the design of effective munitions, the filling of such munitions, and a delivery system.

Although hundreds of thousands of toxic chemicals have been examined over the years for their military potential, only about 60 have been weaponized. Unlike nuclear weapons, which require a large, specialized, and costly scientific industrial base, CW agents can be made with commercial equipment generally available to any industrialized country. The current synthesis processes for mustard and nerve agents were developed between the two World Wars. The vast majority of the U.S. stockpile (in terms of tonnage) was produced during the 1950s and 1960s. The routes of production are generally known, and they can be pursued by relatively primitive proliferating countries who seek to acquire a fully integrated CW capability. Such nations would pursue the following strategy:

- Based on end use, choose a CW agent and a process.
- Acquire process equipment.
- Acquire precursors and stock materials.
- Procure relevant expertise.
- Build a pilot facility to work out technical details of the synthetic process.
- Scale up to a production plant.
- Procure suitable munitions and delivery systems.
- Build a dual-use or dedicated clandestine facility.

The globalized economy has resulted in international distribution of dual-use chemicals (Table 5.4). Many of the basic feedstock chemicals — ammonia, ethanol, isopropanol, sodium cyanide, yellow phosphorus, sulfur monochloride, hydrogen fluoride, and

TABLE 5.4 Dual-Use Chemicals

Dual-Use Chemical	CW Agent	Commercial Product
Thiodiglycol	Sulfur mustard	Plastics, dyes, inks
Thionyl chloride	Sulfur mustard	Pesticides
Sodium sulfide	Sulfur mustard	Paper
Phosphorus oxychloride	Tabun	Insecticides
Dimethylamine	Tabun	Detergents
Sodium cyanide	Tabun	Dyes, pigments, gold recovery
Dimethyl methylphosphonate	G agents	Fire retardants
Dimethyl hydrochloride	G agents	Pharmaceuticals
Potassium bifluoride	G agents	Ceramics
Diethyl phosphite	G agents	Paint solvent

Source: Snidle, G.A., United States Effort in Curbing Chemical Weapons Proliferation, Expenditures and Arms Transfers 7939, U.S. Arms Control and Disarmament Agency, U.S. Government Printing Office, Washington, DC, 1990, p. 23.

sulfur — have legitimate commercial use and can be used in the production of nerve agents. Monitoring commerce under the CWC provides little intelligence value because the imprecision of international trade data would make it impractical to detect the diversion of militarily significant quantities. Hydrogen fluoride, for example, is used at many oil refineries and can be purchased commercially in large quantities; it is also easily derived from phosphate deposits, which usually contain fluorides.

5.3 CW USE BY STATES

5.3.1 Iraq

The Iraqi chemical industry rebuilt some of its chemical production infrastructure for commercial use following the Gulf War. U.S. intelligence has suspected that some of the infrastructure has CW dual-use capability. Indeed, the United Nations Special Commission (UNSCOM) discovered evidence of persistent nerve agents (VX) in missile warheads in 1998. At that time, however, the Iraqi government denied that they had weaponized VX.[29] Iraq had not ratified the CWC.

Some of Iraq's dual-use facilities have the potential to be converted to CW production. Prior to the war, Iraq was suspected of producing and stockpiling mustard, tabun, sarin, and VX. In 1998, UNSCOM reported to the UN Security Council that Iraq continued to withhold information related to its chemical program.[30] UNSCOM cited an example where Baghdad seized a document discovered by UNSCOM inspectors, which indicated that Iraq had not consumed as many chemical munitions during the Iran-Iraq War as had been declared previously by Baghdad. This document suggests that Iraq may have an additional 6000 chemical munitions hidden. Similarly, UNSCOM discovery in 1998 of evidence of VX in Iraqi missile warheads showed that Iraq had lied to the international community for seven years when it repeatedly said that it had never weaponized VX.[31] However, these stockpiles were not located by U.S. forces after the invasion of Iraq in 2003.

5.3.2 Iran

Iran started developing CWs during the Iran-Iraq War and was suspected to have directed limited deployments against Iraqi troops. Iran has maintained CW stockpiles and delivery systems and has continued its development of precursor production and CW capability. Iran has ratified the CWC, and in May 1998 it acknowledged the existence of past CW programs, including deployment during the Iran-Iraq War. Tehran has manufactured and stockpiled blister, blood, and choking chemical agents and has weaponized some of these agents. Iran is also believed to continue clandestine development of nerve agents. Tehran asserted that Iran's CW programs were "terminated" following the conclusion of the war. However, Iran has continued to seek CW technology and precursor chemicals from Russia and China.

5.3.3 Syria

Syria has not signed the CWC; it has produced and stockpiled nerve agents and is continuing to improve its chemical infrastructure. Damascus already has a stockpile of sarin and has developed the capability to deploy the CW by either aircraft or ballistic missile. Syria also has continued with a CW development program with the goal of expanding this capability. Damascus remains dependent on foreign sources for CW precursor materials and chemicals as well as sophisticated processing equipment. Syria has a combined total of several hundred SCUD B, SCUD C, and SS-21 SRBMs. Syria is believed to have chemical warheads available for a portion of its SCUD missile force. Damascus continues to acquire SCUD-related equipment and materials from Iran and North Korea, including considerable North Korean help producing SCUD Cs.

5.3.4 Libya

Libya has not signed the CWC. During the 1980s, Libya produced blister and nerve CWs at Rabta and deployed chemical agents against Chadian troops in 1987.[32] Libya is dependent on foreign suppliers for precursor chemicals, process equipment, and technical expertise for their CW programs. The UN imposed sanctions against Libya in the 1990s to limit foreign support. Following the suspension of UN sanctions in April 1999, Libya reestablished contacts with foreign sources of expertise and precursor chemicals for their CW programs. Prior to the UN embargo, Libya produced about 100 t of CW, including mustard and some nerve agents, at a chemical facility near Rabta. Libya suspended production there in 1990 due to intense international media attention and the threat of military intervention.

5.3.5 India

India was an original signatory to the CWC. In 1997, India acknowledged that it had a dedicated CW program. India stated that all CW facilities would be open for inspection and later hosted all required CWC inspections. India committed to destroy all their CW stockpiles. However, India's extensive chemical industry would enable production of a wide variety of CW precursors with only moderate facility modifications. India's sizable chemical industry could also be a source of dual-use chemicals for proliferators. India's dual-use facilities continue to be a CW proliferation concern.[33]

5.3.6 Pakistan

Pakistan has ratified the CWC but has not declared any CW production facilities. Pakistan has continued commercial chemical industry improvements that could support dual-use facilities and the production of CW precursors. Pakistan has opened its facilities for inspection while continuing to seek foreign equipment and technology to expand its biotechnical infrastructure. Pakistan has also developed various CW delivery methods.

5.3.7 China

While China has ratified the CWC, intelligence suggests that Beijing has not revealed the full extent of its CW program. China has demonstrated the ability to adapt its chemical industry to produce a wide variety of CWs but probably has not produced any. However, the Chinese chemical industry has the capability to produce many of the CW precursors sought by rogue states, and Beijing has viewed foreign sales as a source of much needed trade. While the Chinese government has imposed and enforced some restrictions on sales of precursors, these efforts have yielded mixed results. China declared under the CWC that the nation no longer maintains a CW inventory. However, many nations believe that the Chinese possess a moderate CW stockpile.

5.4 CW USE IN TERRORISM

On March 20, 1995, a terrorist group released the nerve agent sarin (GB) in a Tokyo subway tunnel. The attack injured over 5500 people. The terrorist group Aum Shinrikyo cult was accused of this attack. The group had a large membership and financial assets of over $1 billion to build and operate a large facility for the manufacture of CW and biological agents. The synthesis technology for CWs is generally available, and CW agents can readily be synthesized by a skilled chemist. Some agents require specialized industrial equipment, such as a corrosion-resistant reaction vessel.

5.5 CW USE BY INDIVIDUALS

No cases of chemical WMD deployment by individuals have occurred. However, some crimes, such as the 1982 Chicago Tylenol product-tampering case, have involved the use of chemical agents. The Tylenol case left seven people dead. Each tainted capsule contained about 65 mg of potassium cyanide, many times the lethal dose. Another example was the 1986 case of Stella Nickell, who killed her husband with cyanide-laced Excedrin in order to collect his life insurance. In an attempt to disguise her crime, she also killed a complete stranger by placing three packages of tampered Excedrin and Anacin capsules on the shelves of local stores. While heinous, these crimes are outside the scope of WMDs.

5.6 CONCLUSIONS

The technology, equipment, and skilled personnel for the production of chemical weapons are readily available. The main barrier to the deployment of chemical weapons is the volume of material that is necessary to mount an attack, even over a few city blocks (about 1 metric ton).[34]

REFERENCES

1. Cirincione, J., Wolfsthal, J.B., and Rajkimos, M., *Deadly Arsenals*, Carnegie Endowment for International Peace, Washington, DC, 2002, p. 51.
2. Cirincione, J., *Deadly Arsenals*, Carnegie Endowment for International Peace, Washington, DC, 2002, p. 52.
3. U.S. Department of Health and Human Services, Facts about Phosgene, Fact Sheet, Centers for Disease Control and Prevention, Atlanta, Mar. 17, 2003.

4. IPCS International Programme on Chemical Safety, Phosgene Health and Safety Guide, IPCS Health and Safety Guide, No. 106, World Health Organization, Geneva 1998; http://www.inchem.org/documents/hsg/hsg/hsg106.htm.

5. U.S. Army Medical Research Institute of Chemical Defense, *Medical Management of Chemical Casualties Handbook*, 3rd ed., MCMR-UV-ZM, USAMRICD, Chemical Casualty Care Division, Aberdeen Proving Ground, MD, 2000; http://ccc.apgea.army.mil/reference_materials/handbooks/Red-Handbook/001TitlePage.htm; accessed 4/6/02.

6. See note 5 above.

7. National Institute for Occupational Safety and Health, NIOSH *Pocket Guide to Chemical Hazards*; http://www.cdc.gov/niosh/.

8. Federation of American Scientists, Technical Aspects of Chemical Weapon Proliferation 2, Washington, DC; http://fas.org/spp/starwars/ota/934404.pdf.

9. Organization for the Prohibition of Chemical Weapons (OPCW), Organisation for the Prohibition of Chemical Weapons, texts of the Chemical Weapons Convention; http://www.opcw.org/cwcdoc.htm.

10. Department of the Army, Department of the Air Force, U.S. Marine Corps, FM 3-6/FMFM 7-11-H/AFM 105-7, Washington, DC, Nov. 3, 1986.

11. See note 5 above.

12. See note 1 above.

13. See note 8 above.

14. Croddy, E., China's Role in the Chemical and Biological Disarmament Regimes; http://cns.miis.edu/pubs/npr/vol09/91/91crod.pdf.

15. See note 14 above.

16. NATO, Handbook on the Medical Aspects of NBC Defensive Operations, AMEDP-6(B) Part III — Chemical; http://www.Globalsecurity.Org/Wmd/Library/Policy/Army/Fm/8-9/3toc.htm.

17. See note 16 above.

18. See note 1 above.

19. The Innovation Group, Custom Chemical Profiles: Hydrogen Cyanide; http://www.the-innovation-group.com/Chem-Profiles/Hydrogen%20Cyanide.htm.

20. See note 16 above.

21. Office of the Secretary of Defense, Chemical and Biological Defense Primer, prepared by the deputy assistant to the secretary of defense for chemical and biological defense, Washington, DC, Oct. 2001.

22. Anon., Biological and Chemical Weapons, Agents, and Proliferation, in Deadly Arsenals, Carnegie Endowment for International Peace, Washington, DC, 2002; www.ceip.org.

23. Cirincione, J., Wolfsthak, J.B., and Rajkomas, M., *Deadly Arsenals: Tacking Weapons of Mass Desruction,* CE for IPN, Washington, D.C., 2002.

24. Office of the Surgeon General, *The Medical NBC Battlebook, Tech Guide 242,* U.S. Army Center for Health Promotion and Preventative Medicine, Washington, D.C., May 2000.

25. See note 8 above.

26. See note 1 above.

27. HCTL, Weapons of Mass Destruction Technologies, part 2 of *Militarily Critical Technologies List (MCTL)*, Mar. 1999.

28. Office of the Secretary of Defense, Proliferation: Threat and Response, OSD, Washington, DC, Jan. 2001; http://www.defenselink.mil.

29. See note 28 above.

30. See note 28 above.

31. See note 28 above.

32. See note 28 above.

33. See note 28 above.

34. Prelas, M., Weaponization and Delivery Systems, in *The Science and Technology of Terrorism and Counterterrorism*, Ghosh, T., Prelas, M., Viswanath, D., and Loyalka, S., eds., Marcel Dekker, New York, 2002, pp. 95–108.

6

Effectiveness of Arms Control

Two rival superpowers — the U.S. and the USSR — engaged in a dangerous nuclear arms race until the fall of the USSR. Bilateral and multilateral treaties kept the two superpowers from engaging in an unwinnable war. After the fall of the USSR, the role of treaties diminished. As discussed in Chapter 2, the rivalry between the USSR and the U.S. escalated the development of WMD technology, which proved to be expensive for both parties. In many cases, it was easier and less expensive for other states to play the superpowers against each other in order to get what they wanted, rather than investing directly in WMD technology. Today the political landscape has changed, and the forces that favor the proliferation of WMDs have gained strength.

6.1 NONPROLIFERATION PROBLEMS IN THE PRESENT

Looking at the issues that dominate the world today, the nuclear programs in North Korea,[1] Iran,[2] and Libya[3] have generated the most interest. Both North Korea and Iran have appeared to have accelerated their nuclear weapons programs. Libya, on the other hand, has agreed to cooperate with the West in dismantling its WMD program. The motivations for the development of a weapons program are complex, but a consistent component is for deterrence. During the Cold War, if one superpower became aggressive with a country, appeals for help would be made to the other superpower. This served as an effective deterrent and restored balance. Today, the lack of a rival to balance the U.S. precipitates the need for

WMDs by other states. Without a counterbalance, President Bush's "axis of evil" speech,[4] which specifically identified Iraq, Iran, and North Korea, may have had an effect opposite of what was intended. Being identified as a potential target of the U.S. may have provided additional motivation for WMD proliferation in these countries.

Another factor accelerating the Iranian and North Korean nuclear weapons programs was the lack of an effective counterbalance to U.S. world influence. The Iranian and North Korean governments saw the U.S. lead in the Kosovo (1999) and Iraq (2003) police actions, without UN backing. Prior to the U.S. actions in Kosovo and Iraq, UN resolutions had been passed: Resolution No. 1199 for Kosovo passed on Sep. 23, 1998, and Resolution No. 1441 for Iraq passed on Nov. 8, 2002. In both cases, the UN did not sanction military action. In the case of Kosovo, the U.S. persuaded the NATO allies to take military action because of Serbian noncompliance with Resolution 1199. With Iraq, the U.S. persuaded key allies to join it in a military action because of Iraqi noncompliance with Resolution 1441. Some believe that the U.S. actions were inconsistent with Article 53 of the UN Charter. Article 53 forbids member states from initiating military action to enforce UN Resolutions without the approval of the UN Security Council.

Historically, political or military action provokes a reaction. For example, U.S. development of nuclear technology during the Cold War provoked a reaction by its main rival, the Soviet Union. The USSR accelerated its nuclear weapons program after the U.S. demonstrated its nuclear weapons at the end of World War II. The Soviet Union responded by testing its own nuclear weapons, which brought China into the arena. China — motivated to action by its long history of border conflicts with Russia — countered the Soviet threat by developing its own nuclear weapons. This domino effect continued with India, which also had numerous border conflicts with China. India began a program to develop nuclear weapons in the 1950s and detonated its first nuclear weapon in 1974. Intense international pressure caused India's program to go outwardly dormant until 1998, when India reinitiated nuclear testing. Pakistan, which had a long history of border conflicts and had fought several wars with India over the Kashmir territory, began its nuclear program after India's 1974 nuclear test. When India reinitiated nuclear testing in 1998, Pakistan quickly countered this move with nuclear development.

The stakes are very high if North Korea becomes a nuclear state. Stability in East Asia is one of the main objectives of U.S. foreign policy. North Korea could initiate a new domino effect in East Asia. One concern is how the Japanese will react. Japan is an industrial powerhouse with a well-developed nuclear technology. The Japanese have built several nuclear power reactors, and they reprocess the spent reactor fuel, which is a major step in producing weapons-grade plutonium. The Japanese also have isotope-separation capability and an enormous industrial complex. The Japanese have not developed nuclear weapons because it is inconsistent with their constitution. Instead, Japan has relied on the 1960 U.S.-Japan Security Treaty as the foundation of its foreign policy and for strategic defense. However, the Japanese have been under increasing pressure to reinterpret Article 9 of their constitution to allow greater latitude in providing for their own security. If North Korea declares itself a nuclear state, this will catalyze a change in Article 9. The reason behind this potential change in Article 9 stems from a historical animosity between Korea and Japan.[5] Many believe that the people of Japan originally migrated from Korea (a belief not shared by the Japanese). The Japanese and Koreans both believe that they were the conquerors of the other around 300 to 700 A.D., when archeological evidence has indicated that people and material objects moved between Japan and Korea. What is known is that Japan mounted a particularly brutal invasion of Korea during the 16th century. When Japan annexed Korea in 1910 and remained until the end of World War II, the Japanese tried to eradicate the Korean culture and to replace the Korean language with Japanese in schools. The contempt and bitterness between these two countries still remains in the subconscious of its peoples. It is difficult for most Americans to understand historical consciousness, but it does play an important role in world politics.

Treaties thus far have limited the number of nuclear states by reducing the motivation for states to develop nuclear weapons. Alliances and treaties have been stabilizing based on the U.S. guarantees for the security of countries in East Asia. In addition to the 1960 U.S.-Japan Security Treaty, the U.S. and South Korea are allied by the 1954 Mutual Defense Treaty and the 1954 Southeast Asia Collective Defense Treaty, which allies Australia, France, Great Britain, New Zealand, Pakistan, the Philippines, Thailand, and the U.S. In order for this treaty structure to work effectively, the allies must continue to have confidence that the U.S. can guarantee their security. North Korea's nuclear weapons program has shaken that confidence.

North Korea became a signatory of the Non-Proliferation Treaty (NPT)[6] as a nonnuclear weapons state in 1985. In 1992, North and South Korea issued a joint denuclearization statement. Problems in coming to an agreement with the International Atomic Energy Agency (IAEA) for developing an inspection agreement led to North Korea's withdrawal from the NPT in March 1993. The UN Security Council issued a resolution in May 1993 urging North Korea to cooperate with the IAEA and continue implementation of the North-South Denuclearization Statement. As part of the diplomatic process, the U.S. engaged North Korea in talks between October 1993 and October 1994. These talks resulted in an agreement at the 1994 Geneva Agreed Framework. As part of this agreement, North Korea would freeze its nuclear program and allow IAEA inspections. In return, the U.S. agreed to cooperate in replacing North Korea's electric power reactors. Additionally, the U.S. agreed to work with North Korea to store and eventually dispose of the plutonium-laden spent fuel from North Korea's graphite-moderated reactors. All sides agreed to normalize political and economic relations, to bring peace and security to the Korean Peninsula, and to strengthen the international nuclear nonproliferation regime. The U.S. followed by easing economic sanctions in 1995. The U.S. and North Korea began canning the spent fuel in 1995, and the canning was declared complete in April 2000.

However, many experts believed that this agreement was reached hastily and that there were holes that could be exploited. Problems began in 1998, when the U.S. identified an underground site in Kumchangni that was suspected of being a nuclear site. After several rounds of negotiation, the U.S. was allowed to send in a team to verify the contents of the site. By October 2000, the issue had been resolved.

When the Bush administration formulated foreign policy, following the 2001 inauguration, they made the decision to engage North Korea on a number of issues. These issues included reducing North Korea's conventional military force, restricting missile development, limiting the export of missile technology, and human rights improvement and humanitarian issues. The Bush administration also became aware that North Korea had begun uranium enrichment for the purpose of developing nuclear weapons. When the secretary of state for East Asian and Pacific affairs, James A. Kelly, led a delegation in October 2002, North Korea acknowledged the uranium-separation effort. This was in direct conflict with the NPT obligation and the North-South Denuclearization Declaration. The U.S. demanded that the program be eliminated and suspended much of the 1994 framework until North Korea complied with its demands. North Korea reacted by expelling the IAEA inspectors, withdrawing from the NPT, and resuming reprocessing of spent nuclear fuel.

The U.S. has advocated talks with North Korea involving North Korea's neighbors. These talks have been referred to as the six-party talks (North Korea, U.S., China, South Korea, Japan, and Russia). The initial meeting between North Korea, China, and the U.S., held in April 2003, began a series of talks that is still progressing at the time of this writing. In August 2003, the six-party talks yielded some progress. North Korea agreed to the eventual elimination of its nuclear program if the U.S. would sign a bilateral nonaggression treaty, provide aid, and normalize relations. The U.S. stance was that the resolution should be multilateral.

North Korea as a declared nuclear state sets a dangerous precedent because, as discussed earlier in this chapter, Japan has the capability to build nuclear weapons. This, coupled with rhetoric described in Chapter 2 by Japanese officials (Defense Agency Director General Shigeru Ishiba and Deputy Chief Cabinet Secretary Shinzo Abe), is cause for concern.

South Korea also has an advanced nuclear capability that it might exploit. Additionally, Taiwan potentially could develop nuclear weapons. Treaties have provided a belief that all nations can be secure without the need for nuclear weapons. This complex set of alliances, understandings, and agreements has developed a crack in its foundation due to the North Korean position. If regional destabilizing forces continue eroding confidence, then the potential exists for Japan, South Korea, and Taiwan to withdraw with the justification that the North Korean threat is too great to trust their security to others.

Coupling all of these concerns together, this is a dangerous situation. North Korea has been likened to a starving wolf with a 1-million-man army and nuclear capability. It is a country with insufficient resources to support its population. In the past, North Korea has sought and gained concessions by accelerating development of its nuclear program, a form of nuclear blackmail. Due to the disproportionate amount of resources used to support military objectives, very little has been invested in the people themselves. This puts North Korea under tremendous political stress. This was also a contributing factor to the breakup of the USSR in 1991. The Soviet government invested in a military buildup at the expense of investments for the basic needs of its people, a choice that ultimately destabilized the government. As the morale and confidence of the Soviet people dropped, so did their productivity and creativity. The USSR was no longer able to support itself. The bottom line is that the USSR failed to recognize that people are the most important resource that any nation has. North Korea is following the same path. The government has chosen to put its resources into unproductive military expenditures. It continually chooses to engage in nuclear blackmail to solve problems rather than addressing the structural flaws that created the problems.

U.S. policy has focused on Afghanistan and Iraq from 2001 to 2003, and during that time North Korea has been placed on the back burner. Once the Iraq War was declared concluded by the Bush Administration, the focus of the administration shifted to the North Korean and Iranian nuclear programs. Both the North Korean and Iranian programs received a substantial amount of technical assistance from Pakistan.[7] It is known that Pakistan sold an atomic bomb–making kit to Libya that contained all of the elements needed to make a highly enriched uranium nuclear bomb. This included UF_6, advanced centrifuges, and detailed operational instructions and plans for bomb assembly. It is believed that similar kits were sold to North Korea and Iran. The full extent of Pakistan's technology transfer is still being sorted out.

6.2 NONPROLIFERATION PRIOR TO THE FALL OF THE USSR

Since the fall of the Soviet Union, international negotiations and treaties have changed. When the Soviet Union and the U.S. were pitted against one another, other countries felt more secure and were less willing to invest in expensive WMD technology. In that world, a series of bilateral and multilateral treaties was sufficient to control the spread of WMDs.

The arms races of the 1940s, 1950s, and 1960s resulted in a tremendous buildup of weapons-grade nuclear materials (see Table 6.1). There are hundreds of tons of plutonium and highly enriched uranium stockpiled around the world. As discussed in Chapter 3, it takes about 10 kg of plutonium and about 50 kg of

Table 6.1 Estimated Weapons-Grade Plutonium and Uranium Inventory for Various Countries

Country	Estimated Plutonium Inventory (metric tons)[8]	Estimated Highly Enriched Uranium Inventory (metric tons)[9]
U.S.	97	500–600
Russia	125–160	520–920
U.K.	2.8	5–15
France	6.0	10–20
China	1.5–3	10–20
India[10]	0.3	Unknown
Pakistan[10]	Unknown	0.42–0.68
Israel[11]	0.24–0.41	Unknown
North Korea[12]	0.006–0.028	Unknown
Iran[13]	Unknown	Unknown

highly enriched uranium to make a nuclear explosive. Tracking 10- to 50-kg quantities of materials from this large inventory of weapons-grade material has been challenging. It is absolutely critical that mechanisms to reliably secure this material be continually improved. All nations with nuclear weapons need to have similar levels of safeguards in order to protect the interests of everyone, which is not the case today.

U.S. sources have estimated that the USSR has produced over 600 metric tons of fissile material[14] since the 1940s. The security of nuclear materials in the states from the former Soviet Union continues to be of great concern. One proliferation path is to use the technical expertise and materials from a country like Russia. The investment to make an atomic weapon has been estimated to be between $1 billion and $20 billion. In addition, the investments for nuclear weapon delivery systems such as missiles, bombers, and submarines are even greater. Rather than having to make these huge investments, these materials could be purchased at reduced cost. We have heard reports of briefcase bombs developed by the USSR being sold on the black market.[15] Recently, Pakistani journalist Hamid Mir had a televised interview with Ayman al-Zawahri that was broadcast by the Australian Broadcasting Corp. In this interview al-Zawahri claimed that al Qaeda had purchased "smart briefcase bombs" that were available on the black market.[16]

The USSR also had substantial programs in chemical and biological weapons development.[17] The Russian chemical weapon stockpile is about 40,000 t. The stockpile has 32,300 t of sarin, soman, and other nerve gases; 7,700 t of lewisite and mustard gas;

and 5 t of mustard gas. The biological weapons program had over 60,000 people involved, with hundreds of tons of anthrax and dozens of tons of smallpox and plague stockpiled.[18]

The Russian transfer of technology and expertise in nuclear, chemical, and biological technology is of concern. There have been dual-use projects that can contribute to biological, chemical, and nuclear weapons. Iran continues to pursue a nuclear fuel cycle for a civilian and military program while it continues to move toward self-sufficiency in its biological and chemical weapons programs. For example, Iran continues to seek foreign assistance in building chemical production plants for commercial chemicals that have dual-use capabilities and could be used for production of nerve agents. Finally, Iran has tried to sell some of its artillery rockets, ballistic missiles, and related technologies on the open market. Beyond country-country interactions, Russian WMD materials and technology also are vulnerable to theft or diversion.

6.3 TREATIES AND THEIR HISTORICAL IMPACT

6.3.1 Toxic Materials

The use of toxic materials in warfare, as discussed in Chapters 4 and 5, dates back to at least 600 B.C. Poisoning of water supplies was used as a military tactic in the American Civil War, and as a consequence, the U.S. War Department issued General Order 100 on April 24, 1863, forbidding the use of poisons of any type. The problem was tackled on a global level when, on July 29, 1899, the Hague Convention II declared that "it is especially prohibited … to employ poison or poisoned arms."[19]

Unfortunately, the Hague Convention did not prevent the use of chemical weapons in World War I. After World War I, the 1925 Geneva Protocol treaty prohibited "the use in war of asphyxiating, poisonous, or other gases and of all analogous liquids, materials or devices." Additionally, it banned "bacteriological methods of warfare." The Geneva Protocol was the first important multilateral agreement regarding chemical and biological weapons. It is considered a part of customary international law that binds even states that are not parties to it. However, this did not prevent the use of chemical weapons by Italy against Libya (late 1920s), Italy against Ethiopia (1935–1936), Egypt against Yemen (1963–1967), Iraq against Iran (1983–1988),[20] Libya against Chad (1987), Iraq against Iraqi Kurds (1988), and Sudan against Sudanese rebels

(1989).[21] Nor did it deter the possible use of USSR-supplied trichothecene mycotoxins by Vietnam against Laos in 1975.[22]

In 1954, West Germany renounced the manufacture of nuclear, chemical, or biological weapons in the Revised Brussels Treaty.[23] By 1972, the Biological Weapons Convention had been developed as a declaration by a large number of states renouncing the use of germ weapons against humans, animals, and plants.[24] However, the 1972 convention did not provide mechanisms for enforcement of the treaty. The treaty did provide for review conferences, which have been ongoing. In 1995, negotiations were initiated for an agreement among states for a legally binding instrument to strengthen verification and other compliance-supporting measures. The fifth review conference opened on November 19, 2000, but was adjourned due to a lack of progress on the issues.[25] Primary among the concerns was how to protect the biotech industries of participating states from industrial espionage in a compliance regime. Industrial espionage cost the U.S. between $100 billion to $250 billion in 2000.[26] A main target for industrial espionage is the biotechnology industries. In 2003, a new process began in order to address the compliance issues.[27] The secretary general of the United Nations has some degree of empowerment to investigate the use of chemical and biological weapons as a means of strengthening the 1925 Geneva Protocol, but to date this has not been an effective deterrent.

In 1988, the U.S. and the Soviet Union signed the Wyoming Memorandum of Understanding, which initiated talks on bilateral verification and a data exchange on their respective chemical programs. The 1993 Chemical Weapons Convention Treaty prohibits the use of toxic chemicals on humans or animals.[28] The treaty prohibits development, production, and stockpiling of chemical weapons or assistance in acquiring them. Each member must have in place compliance measures that include penalties. Additionally, each state participates in a verification regime operated by an international agency called the Organization for the Prohibition of Chemical Weapons (OPCW).[29] Many view the compliance regime of the Chemical Weapons Convention (CWC) as a test bed for how compliance issues can be addressed for the Biological Weapons Convention (BWC). Even though industrial espionage is a concern for the chemical industry, the economic consequences of intellectual property theft is not as significant for the chemical industry as it is for the biotechnology industry.[30] Biotechnology is one of the driving forces behind the U.S. economy, and verification will not be an easy issue to accommodate within the BWC.

Nuclear treaty regimes have been relatively successful, due in part to the high cost and complexity of nuclear technology. Development of nuclear technology requires a significant financial commitment, an educated workforce, and a strong industrial infrastructure. Treaty development also addressed nuclear weapons delivery systems. These strategic delivery systems include ballistic missiles, bombers, submarines, and cruise missiles. The same critical factors — financing, know-how, and infrastructure or access to critical components supplied by third parties — are necessary to develop efficient delivery systems. North Korea has been willing to export missile technology. However, conventional delivery systems are best used for deterrence rather than an offensive threat. For example, no nation could survive a direct confrontation with the U.S. because its strategic capabilities are so overwhelming. North Korea and Iran are accelerating their nuclear capabilities, due in part to the fear that the U.S. might attempt regime changes in their countries, similar to what happened in Iraq. The U.S. role in the second Gulf War has created anxiety among several nations. For example, China has expressed an ongoing concern about the Taiwanese Democratic Progressive Party, which supports Taiwan statehood. During the 2000 election won by Chen Shui-bian, of the opposition Democratic Progressive Party, China placed 2.5 million military personnel on alert. China warned Taiwan that it would not tolerate a declaration of independence and that it would invade should such a declaration be made.[31] Had President Chen declared Taiwan independent, it would have triggered an invasion, and the U.S. would have had to make an uncomfortable decision whether to continue to support an Asian democracy and historical friend. The same ordeal reoccurred in the 2004 elections.[32]

Given the U.S. actions in Kosovo and Iraq, China would have to view the U.S. as a superpower with a history of invading countries experiencing internal strife and without international support. China views its relations with Taiwan as an internal matter. In order to prepare for this potential threat, China eventually will have to deploy more nuclear weapons as a countermeasure. China may also adopt a policy of unrestricted warfare if forced to go to war with the U.S.[33] Such a policy could put any imaginable scenario into play, ranging from commandos delivering weapons of mass destruction to strategic targets on U.S. soil to direct support of anti-U.S. terrorist groups. In other words, the unthinkable becomes possible.

6.3.2 Nuclear Weapons

The arms race almost went out of control when the U.S. and the USSR had a showdown over Soviet nuclear missiles being placed in Cuba in 1962.[34] The Cuban Missile Crisis nearly led to a nuclear exchange. Following the crisis, both governments realized that unchecked growth of the arms race could be disastrous. In 1964 a small but significant breakthrough occurred at the Geneva-based 18-nation disarmament committee talks. The U.S. proposed that the number of strategic delivery systems be decoupled from the number of warheads. Prior to this, the issues surrounding the limitation of both delivery systems and warheads had been highly contentious. By focusing on a single issue, breakthroughs were made. Strategic delivery systems were based on ballistic missiles, nuclear submarines with missile platforms, and long-range bombers. Each delivery system was capable of carrying nuclear weapons and delivering the weapons to a long-range target. Perhaps the catalyst for the first substantial treaty breakthrough was the nuclear weapon test conducted by China. The unpredictability of a nuclear China was a potential destabilizing force.

The technical issues involved in the development of a strategic nuclear force are complex. An arms race perpetuates as both sides try to gain advantage over the other by developing offensive and defensive technologies. With nuclear weapons, the first step was taken by the U.S., which developed the first nuclear weapon and a means of delivery. Initially, the weapons were very large and required a large long-range bomber to deliver them to the targets (e.g., Hiroshima and Nagasaki). After the U.S. demonstrated the use of nuclear weapons in war, the USSR was forced to counter by developing its own nuclear weapons program.

After World War II, both the U.S. and the USSR began working on the more powerful thermonuclear weapons and the more sophisticated delivery, detection, and defensive systems. It is no surprise that after the war, the USSR, England, and the U.S. took apart the German advanced rocket and jet airplane programs and carted off the equipment and personnel for the purpose of developing more-advanced delivery systems. There are several types of delivery systems: strategic (long range), intermediate range missiles, and tactical (short range).[35]

Strategic systems form a triad that includes long-range bombers, intercontinental ballistic missiles, and submarine-launched ballistic missiles.[36] The missiles depend upon different types of launch systems. Intercontinental ballistic missiles (ICBMs) can be land based and can use silos, rail-mobile launch systems, or road-mobile launch systems. Submarine-launched ballistic missiles (SLBMs) use submarines as the launch platform. Intermediate-range systems have ranges between 300 to 3400 miles, such as ground-launched ballistic missiles and cruise missiles.[37]

As thermonuclear weapons technology progressed, the development focus was to reduce the size of the weapon. Size became the critical parameter when combined with the new long-range delivery systems that were being developed. The first missiles were incapable of carrying large payloads. However, unlike in cases involving slower-moving aircraft, countermeasures to stop a missile reentering the atmosphere were next to impossible. The development of jet aircraft added speed to the long-range bomber, which shortened the detection and reaction time that a countermeasure would need to stop it.

As delivery systems improved, countermeasures focused on hardening targets and exploiting delivery-system inaccuracies. For example, the U.S. Air Force was able to superharden silo launching systems by burying them deep underground. These hardened silos were capable of withstanding 25 to 100 lb/in.^{2} overpressures. Data from aboveground nuclear tests also provided information about the distance a nuclear blast must be from the silo to take it out. This research revealed that a silo would require a virtually direct hit by a nuclear weapon to neutralize it.[38] At that time, the guidance systems used by the USSR were not accurate enough to detonate a nuclear weapon close enough to the silo to destroy it. The U.S. guidance systems, on the other hand, were very accurate and could take out Soviet silos. This forced the USSR to counter with road- and rail-mobile missile launchers. Eventually, Soviet guidance systems improved, and that led the U.S. to develop the MX missile that could be launched from a silo or a rail-mobile launching system. (As part of the START I treaty, the U.S. no longer deploys rail-mobile launch capability.)

SLBMs, on the other hand, were difficult to defend against. These missiles were deployed on large submarines that were very difficult to detect. A submarine with a ballistic missile could park off a coast and launch missiles at targets inland. The only effective

Table 6.2 Classification of Ballistic Missiles

U.S. Classification System			USSR Classification System	
Classification	Designation	Range (km)	Classification	Range (km)
Intercontinental ballistic missile	ICBM	Over 5500	Strategic	Over 1000
Intermediate-range ballistic missile	IRBM	3000–5500	Operational strategic	500–1000
Medium-range ballistic missile	MRBM	1000–3000	Operational	300–500
Short-range ballistic missile	SRBM	Up to 1000	Operational tactical	50–300
			Tactical	Up to 50

Source: Federation of American Scientists, Ballistic Missile Basics; http://www.fas.org/nuke/intro/missile/basics.htm; accessed 4/18/04.

countermeasure was another submarine designed to find and attack the ballistic missile submarines.

Antiballistic missile (ABM) systems have also been developed since the 1950s as a countermeasure to the ballistic missile. The initial intent of the ABM was to reduce the probability that a ballistic missile system would hit its designated target. Early ABM systems used missiles to target incoming warheads. The early missile systems were not very accurate, and one strategy was to place a nuclear warhead on the tip of the missile.[39] Ballistic missiles are categorized based on the distance they can travel from the point of launch to the target (Table 6.2).

The speed and accuracy of the missile-detection ability depends on the missile classification. For example, ICBMs have three stages of flight: boost, ballistic, and reentry. During the boost phase, the missile is accelerated by rocket engines. This is the most vulnerable phase of the flight. During the ballistic phase, the vehicle coasts. During the reentry phase, the vehicle reenters the Earth's atmosphere. The speed of the reentry vehicle (RV) reaches about 20,000 miles per hour during the reentry phase.[40] Countermeasures for each flight phase have been developed.[41] The easiest countermeasure system is the boost-phase interceptor.[42] A high-speed interceptor, such as an airborne laser[43] or a high-speed missile,[44] can catch the ballistic missile and target its high-temperature exhaust. The problem in implementing a boost-phase interceptor is that it must be located within a few hundred miles of the launch site (under the line of the missile trajectory). The vehicle is difficult to track and hit after reaching high speeds. During the ballistic phase, the rockets no longer provide a heat source for sensors to track. A high-speed interceptor such as a laser beam from a space-based laser would have the capabilities of hitting a high-speed target.[45] The technical issues involved in developing a space-based laser are difficult and will take many years of research and a lot of money to solve.

Current national missile defense strategy has three main components.[46] The first is early-warning satellites with infrared (IR) sensors. These sensors identify the hot exhaust from the ballistic missile rockets. About 3 min following liftoff, the rocket motors shut down and warheads and decoys are released. These components are above the atmosphere and are tracked with ground-based radar. At this stage, the RV and the decoys travel at the same speed, making it difficult to distinguish between them. About 10 min after the launch of the ballistic missiles, high-speed interceptor missiles can be launched. These missiles carry above the atmosphere, an exoatmospheric kill vehicle designed to neutralize the RV about 18 min following launch. The kill vehicle uses an onboard infrared telescope to track the RV and decoys. About 600 km from the target, the kill vehicle has less than 1 min to distinguish the RV from the decoys. It then maneuvers itself using a rocket engine to destroy the RV by ramming it. There have been many questions raised about the viability of this plan, and these have been vigorously debated for years.[47] In the authors' opinion, the arguments against the missile interceptor as a viable national missile defense system outweigh the arguments in favor. Breakthroughs in tracking technology could potentially change the equation. But for every breakthrough in interceptor-system technology, there are also breakthroughs in countermeasures.

The simplest antiballistic missile countermeasure is to overwhelm the system's capacity by launching more missiles than it can handle. This adds a destabilizing influence to arms control because it encourages the proliferation of warheads. Furthermore, nuclear weapons can be delivered by a means that renders an ABM defense system ineffective. For example, unless the U.S. suspected that an attack was about to occur, cargo ships could carry nuclear-tipped cruise missiles into U.S. waters relatively easily. Before the U.S. could respond, many of these cruise missiles could be launched against coastal targets. Another method might include the smuggling of small warheads into the U.S. As a free society, the U.S. border control policies allow relatively easy access into the country. A nuclear weapon could be smuggled into the U.S. through holes in the nuclear sensors net. These sensors monitor the radiation signatures from HEU and plutonium. However, the sensor net cannot cover the entire U.S. border.

ABM systems were designed for the Cold War, where the threat and defensive goals were much different. Primarily, an ABM system was meant to increase the uncertainty of a missile's hitting a given target. The decreased probability of hitting a target added deterrence. However, in the present circumstance, an ABM system is envisioned to counter a limited number of ballistic missiles. The current threat is from countries such as North Korea and Iran, and the goal of such a system would be to counter a limited ballistic missile capability launched from China (about 20 to 30 missiles). Having an ABM system would allow the U.S. to take a more rigid stance in its policies toward these countries. However, as described above, a determined adversary could overcome an ABM system.

Despite the problems, treaties were effective in controlling proliferation during the Cold War (Table 6.3). After the Geneva-based Eighteen-Nation Disarmament Committee met in January 1964, the U.S. proposed that the number and characteristics of the strategic nuclear offensive and defensive delivery systems be decoupled from the comprehensive disarmament proposals. By 1966, China had developed nuclear weapons, and both the USSR and the U.S. were engaged in the development of antiballistic missile systems. In 1967, it became clear that the nuclear arms race was unmanageable, and President Johnson and Premier Kosygin indicated a willingness to reengage in arms control discussions. By July 1, 1968, the Non-Proliferation Treaty was signed, and the U.S. and USSR agreed to initiate discussions on the limitation and reduction of both strategic nuclear weapons delivery systems and defense against ballistic missiles.

The Strategic Arms Limitation Talks (SALT I) occurred from November 1969 to May 1972. SALT I ended when both the U.S. and the USSR signed the Anti-Ballistic Missile Treaty on May 26, 1972, and developed the Interim Agreement on Strategic and Offensive Arms (agreed to begin talks for a more comprehensive nuclear arms treaty), which led to the SALT II talks and the signing of the SALT II treaty on June 18, 1979. The SALT II treaty would have limited nuclear delivery vehicles (missiles, bombers, and air-to-surface antiballistic missiles) to 2400 units. Although the treaty was not brought to the U.S. Senate for ratification, both

TABLE 6.3 Summary of Treaties and Agreements

Treaty	Date Signed	Date Ratified	Purpose
Accidents Measures Agreement[48]	Sep. 30, 1971	Sep. 30, 1971	Reduce the risk of outbreak of nuclear war
African Nuclear-Weapon-Free Zone Treaty (The Treaty of Pelindaba)[49]	July 21, 1964	Apr. 11, 1996	Protect African states against possible nuclear attacks on their territories
Antarctic Treaty[50]	Dec. 1, 1959	June 23, 1961	Ban nuclear weapons in the Antarctic
Anti-Ballistic Missile (ABM) Treaty[51]	May 26, 1972	Oct. 3, 1972	Limit antiballistic missile systems
Ballistic Missile Launch Notification[52]	May 31, 1988	May 31, 1988	Notify 24 h in advance of test launches of missiles
Biological Weapons Convention[53]	Apr. 10, 1972	Mar. 26, 1975	Control biological weapons
Comprehensive Test Ban Treaty[54]	Sep. 30, 1996	—	Ban nuclear testing
Confidence- and Security-Building Measures[55]	Sep. 19, 1986	—	Increase openness and predictability about military activities in Europe
Convention on the Physical Protection of Nuclear Material[56]	Mar. 3, 1980	Feb. 8, 1987	Provide physical protection during international transport of nuclear material
Geneva Protocol[57]	June 17, 1925	Feb. 8, 1928	Prohibit the use of asphyxiating, poisonous, or other gases and of bacteriological methods of warfare
Hot-Line Agreement[58]	June 20, 1963	June 20, 1963	Establish lines of communication
Hot-Line Expansion Agreement[59]	July 17, 1984	July 17, 1984	Expand the 1963 agreement
Hot-Line Modernization Agreement[60]	Sep. 30, 1971	Sep. 30, 1971	Supplement the 1963 agreement

TABLE 6.3 (continued) Summary of Treaties and Agreements

Treaty	Date Signed	Date Ratified	Purpose
Incidents at Sea Agreement[61]	May 25, 1972	May 25, 1972	Prevent incidents on and over the high seas
Intermediate-Range and Short-Range Nuclear Forces (INF) Treaty[62]	Dec. 8, 1987	June 1, 1988	Eliminate intermediate-range missiles
Latin American Nuclear-Free Zone Treaty[63]	Feb. 14, 1967	Apr. 22, 1968	Obligate Latin American parties to abjure nuclear weapons
Limited Test Ban Treaty[64]	Aug. 5, 1963	Oct. 10, 1963	Ban nuclear weapon tests in the atmosphere, in outer space, and underwater
Memorandum of Agreement on the Establishment of a Joint Center for the Exchange of Data[65]	June 4, 2000	—	Exchange of data from early-warning systems and notifications of missile launches
Memorandum of Understanding on Notifications of Missile Launches (PLNS MOU)[66]	Dec. 16, 2000	—	Establish a pre- and post-launch notification system
Missile Technology Control Regime[67]	Jan. 7, 1993	—	Limit the risks of proliferation of weapons of mass destruction (i.e., nuclear, chemical, and biological weapons) by controlling transfers that could contribute to delivery systems
Moscow Treaty[68]	May 24, 2002	—	Establish strategic offensive reductions
Nuclear Non-Proliferation Treaty[69]	July 1, 1968	Mar. 5, 1970	Prevent the spread of nuclear weapons

Table 6.3 (continued) Summary of Treaties and Agreements

Treaty	Date Signed	Date Ratified	Purpose
Nuclear Risk Reduction Centers[70]	Sep. 15, 1987	Sep. 15, 1987	Establish nuclear-risk-reduction centers
Outer Space Treaty[71]	Jan. 27, 1967	Oct. 10, 1967	Restrict outer space to peaceful uses
PNE Treaty[72]	May 28, 1976	Dec. 11, 1990	Govern underground nuclear explosions for peaceful purposes
Prevention of Nuclear War Agreement[73]	June 22, 1973	June 22, 1973	Reshape U.S.-USSR relations on the basis of peaceful cooperation
Seabed Arms Control Treaty[74]	Feb. 11, 1971	May 18, 1972	Prohibit the emplacement of nuclear weapons and other WMDs on the seabed and the ocean floor
South Pacific Nuclear Free Zone Treaty[75]	Aug. 6, 1985	—	Prohibit the manufacture, acquisition, possession, or control of any nuclear explosive device by any means anywhere inside or outside the South Pacific Nuclear-Free Zone
Strategic Arms Limitation Talks (SALT I) (narrative)[76]	Nov. 1969 to May 1972	—	Establish an interim agreement on certain measures with respect to the limitation of strategic offensive arms
Strategic Arms Limitation Talks (SALT II)[77]	June 18, 1979	—	Limit strategic nuclear delivery vehicles
Strategic Arms Reduction Treaty (START)[78]	July 31, 1991	—	Limit warheads to 6000

TABLE 6.3 (continued) Summary of Treaties and Agreements

Treaty	Date Signed	Date Ratified	Purpose
Strategic Arms Reduction Treaty (START II)[79]	Sep. 26, 1997	—	Limit warheads to between 3800 and 4250
Threshold Test Ban Treaty[80]	July 3, 1974	Dec. 11, 1990	Establish a treaty to limit underground nuclear weapons tests
U.S.-IAEA Safeguards Agreement[81]	Nov. 18, 1977	Dec. 9, 1980	Establish an agreement between the U.S. and the International Atomic Energy Agency (IAEA) for the application of safeguards in the U.S.
U.S.-Russia Strategic Offensive Reductions Treaty (see the Moscow Treaty)[82]	May 24, 2002	—	Implement substantial reductions in strategic offensive weapons

countries agreed to abide by the provisions. President Reagan stated that the USSR was not in compliance with SALT II in 1986 and asked to USSR to join with the U.S. in mutual restraint. One of the major issues with SALT II was verification, a theme that persists to this day.

Arms control made progress in the 1980s through the Intermediate-Range Nuclear Forces (INF) Treaty that was signed on December 8, 1987. The Strategic Arms Reduction Treaty (START I) was undertaken with regard to strategic offensive arms in Article VI of the Treaty on the Non-Proliferation of Nuclear Weapons of July 1, 1968; Article XI of the Treaty on the Limitation of Anti-Ballistic Missile Systems of May 26, 1972; and the Washington Summit Joint Statement of June 1, 1990. The START I treaty was signed in Moscow on July 31, 1991. With START I, the U.S. and Russia agreed to reduce strategic nuclear warheads to 6000. In December 1991, the USSR disbanded and became the Commonwealth of Independent States (CIS). On May 7, 1992, each of the commonwealth states that housed nuclear weapons agreed, along with the U.S., to abide by START I in the Lisbon Protocol. START II was designed to reduce the level of strategic nuclear warheads to 3500 and was signed on January 3, 1993. However, START II has not yet been ratified by the U.S., although it has been ratified by Russia. The Comprehensive Nuclear Test-Ban Treaty (CTBT), which halts nuclear testing, was signed on September 24, 1996, but it was rejected by the U.S. Senate in 1999.

When the USSR dissolved and the CIS arose, the future of the treaties that served as the foundation of arms control came into question. The first issue was how to deal with START I, since some of the states other than Russia in the CIS housed nuclear weapons. The Lisbon Protocol was initiated to validate that these states still agreed to the conditions in the START I treaty. Additionally, these states agreed to transfer control of the nuclear weapons on their territory to Russia. The next issue dealt with the security of nuclear materials and with the large number of scientists engaged in the nuclear weapons enterprise for the former Soviet Union (FSU). One of the first steps was the creation of the International Science and Technology Center (ISTC) by President Bush in 1992. The goal of the ISTC was to support FSU scientists engaged in the production of nuclear, chemical, and biological weapons in projects for peaceful uses and economic development. The U.S., Japan, and the European Community (EC) committed $75 million to initiate the program. In addition, the Soros Foundation provided a large amount of money to support FSU scientists. Soros eventually started the International Science Foundation to support FSU scientists, and this project eventually evolved into the Civilian Research Development Fund. To safeguard FSU nuclear stockpiles, the Nunn-Lugar bill (S. 2026), authorized funds for proliferation threat reduction projects. It supported efforts to foster Russian warhead dismantlement, to work on disposition options for surplus fissile material, to establish lab-to-lab cooperative nonweapons projects with Russian nuclear scientists, and to support the Russian highly enriched–uranium purchase agreement. In addition, the U.S. provided funding to the Mayak Production Association for the construction of a plutonium storage facility. The goal of these and other efforts was to help Russia secure its nuclear materials stockpile. To date, the program has been successful in a number of areas. It has provided support to critical FSU scientists in order to secure their scientific know-how for the production of nuclear weapons, and it has helped Russia with funding to develop better methods of nuclear stockpile stewardship.

While the two superpowers were reducing their stockpiles, other nations were building theirs up, although not to the same levels. These large numbers lead to the possibility that not all weapons have been fully accounted for, and that there may be unrecognized theft from storage or during weapon transfers. The best strategy here is to reduce nuclear stockpiles, account for all weapons, and share and adopt good security practices.

6.4 NUCLEAR, CHEMICAL, AND BIOLOGICAL WEAPONS SAFEGUARDS

Controlling the proliferation of WMDs is in the interest of all civilized countries. A critical aspect in achieving this goal is to develop agreements and safeguards. As described in this and previous chapters, the technologies for each weapon system are vastly different, as are the issues associated with the weapon system. Countermeasures against the nuclear threats must be both general and very specific. Both short- and long-term steps are needed, and these must be vigorously implemented. The greatest concern is to limit the acquisition of weapons-grade nuclear materials and the spread of technologies that make it possible to produce these materials from the abundant resources of natural uranium. There are also concerns regarding the spread of expertise of weapon making, but given the large number of trained scientific and technical personnel and scientific/industrial facilities and laboratories these days, there is only so much that can be done in this area. In the short run, the countermeasures must protect nuclear weapons. All nuclear nations safeguard their nuclear weapons, but the unevenness of these efforts must be addressed.

In order to safeguard nuclear weapons, a number of additional agreements have to be developed in the area of transparency. The importance of transparency has been well illustrated with the recent developments in the North Korean and Iranian nuclear programs. Both countries have signed the NPT while effectively hiding parts of their nuclear programs. For nations that have the capability of developing nuclear weapons, those that have signed the Non-Proliferation Treaty must be held accountable. For nations that have not signed the NPT, appropriate incentives must be developed.

6.4.1 Biological Weapons

The large-scale production of biological weapons is very difficult to detect, because they are produced using the same methods that are employed by the legitimate vaccine and pharmaceutical industries. This has made it difficult to implement the Biological Weapons Convention. Detailed inspections of vaccine or pharmaceutical production facilities are required to detect the production of biological weapons. Because the biotechnology and the pharmaceutical industries use proprietary technology, the open inspection of these industries could have important strategic and economic consequences. For example, economic espionage, including the theft of trade secrets, costs the U.S. about $250 billion per year. The FBI has recently identified 23 countries involved in this practice, targeting U.S. industries including pharmaceutical companies. Much of the intellectual property of a U.S. pharmaceutical company is in trade secrets. The strict inspection regime of the BWC would expose these trade secrets to espionage. Hence, it is unlikely that the U.S. pharmaceutical industry would favor the BWC inspections.

The only means currently available to address the proliferation of biological weapons is through the Australia Group, an informal community of nations focused on minimizing proliferation of materials and technology that could be used for development or production of chemical and biological weapons. The Group includes 38 member nations and the European Commission. The Group annually makes recommendations to the international community for export controls. Many goverments have voluntarily incorporated the Group's recommendations into export licensing requirements.

In the view of the authors, biotechnology will present a more dangerous and complex nonproliferation problem than any other technology for the production of WMDs.

6.4.2 Chemical Weapons

The proliferation of chemical weapons is very difficult to control. The main problem is that facilities producing pesticides and fertilizers could also be used to produce chemical weapons. The dual use of these common chemical technologies makes the Chemical Weapons Convention difficult to implement. The single most important element of the CWC is transparency, a significant component of which is a comprehensive inspection regime.

There are technical issues with chemical weapons that make them unattractive to potential proliferators. For example, the quantity of material needed to attack even a modest area is large. In modern warfare, it is important that weapons be small and stealthy. More importantly, the best safeguard is to deal with the motivations for developing WMDs, as discussed in Chapters 7 and 8.

6.5 CONCLUSIONS

Arms control was very effective in controlling the proliferation of nuclear weapons prior to the fall of the USSR. The cost of the technology played an important role, and countries were able to play the U.S. and the USSR against one another to gain favorable situations. There was little motivation to invest in nuclear weapons. The landscape has changed since the fall of the USSR. The policies of the U.S., which has sought regime change in other countries without support from the United Nations, have introduced uncertainties in the global balance of power. These uncertainties appear to be a factor in the acceleration of the North Korean and Iranian nuclear weapons programs.

In a time of uncertainty, it is important to build a consensus among nations on policies to curb the proliferation of weapons of mass destruction. Countries pursue WMDs when they perceive a threat to their security. The forces that present these threats need to be addressed and moderated by a coalition of like-minded nations. Admittedly, there will always be rogue nations who do not respond to standard motivations to curb proliferation. But even in these cases, pressure by a majority of the world's nations can be an effective tool. Arms-control measures must evolve to deal with the multidimensional world that currently exists.

REFERENCES

1. CNN, North Korea Nuclear Talks Make Scant Progress, Feb. 28, 2004; http://www.cnn.com/2004/WORLD/asiapcf/02/28/nkorea.talks/index.html; accessed 3/11/04; CNN, Timeline: North Korea's Nuclear Weapons Development, July 17, 2003; http://www.cnn.com/2003/WORLD/asiapcf/east/02/07/nkorea.timeline.nuclear/index.html; accessed 3/11/04.
2. Otterman, S., Iran Nuclear Weapons, *Council on Foreign Relations,* Nov. 25, 2003; http://www.cfr.org/background/iran_nuclear.php; accessed 3/11/04; CNN, Iran Warns That It May Renege on Nukes, Mar. 10, 2004; accessed 3/11/04; Smith, C.S., Alarm Raised over Quality of Uranium Found in Iran, *New York Times*, Mar. 11, 2004; http://www.nytimes.com/2004/03/11/international/middleeast/11NUKC.html; accessed 3/11/04.

3. CNN, Libya Signs Snap Checks Agreement, Mar. 10, 2004; http://www.cnn.com/2004/WORLD/europe/03/10/iaea.meeting /index.html; accessed 3/11/04; BBC, Libya Ships out Last WMD Parts, BBC News, Mar. 7, 2004; http://news.bbc. co.uk/2/hi/africa/ 3539799.stm; accessed 3/11/04.
4. President Delivers State of the Union Address, Jan. 29, 2002; http://www.whitehouse.gov/news/releases/2002/01/20020129-11. html; accessed 3/11/04.
5. Diamond, J., Japanese Roots, *Discover Magazine,* http://www2.gol. com/users/hsmr/Content/East%20Asia/Japan/History/roots.html; accessed 3/14/04.
6. U.S. Department of State, Treaty on the Non-Proliferation of Nuclear Weapons, July 1, 1968; http://www.state.gov/t/np/trty/16281.htm; accessed 3/15/04.
7. Sanger, D.E., U.S. Sees More Arms Ties between Pakistan and Korea, *New York Times*, Mar. 14, 2004; http://www.nytimes. com/ 2004/03/14/international/asia/14KORE.html; accessed 3/18/04; Sanger, D.E. and Broad, W.J., Pakistani's Nuclear Earnings: $100 Million, *New York Times,* Mar. 16, 2004; http://www.nytimes.com/ 2004/03/16/international/asia/16NUKE.html; accessed 3/18/04.
8. Albright, D., Berkhout, F., and Walker, W., *World Inventory of Plutonium and Highly Enriched Uranium*, Oxford University Press, Oxford, 1993, pp. 25–38.
9. Albright, D., Berkhout, F., and Walker, W., *World Inventory of Plutonium and Highly Enriched Uranium*, Oxford University Press, Oxford, 1993, pp. 47–60.
10. Albright, D., India and Pakistan's Fissile Material and Nuclear Weapons Inventory, End of 1998, Institute for Science and International Security, Oct. 27, 1999; http://www.isis-online.org/publications/ southasia/stocks1099.html; accessed 3/22/04.
11. Albright, D., A Proliferation Primer, *Bull. Atomic Scientists,* June 1993; http://www.thebulletin.org/issues/1993/j93/j93Al-bright.html; accessed 3/22/04.
12. Norris, R.S., North Korea's nuclear program, 2003, *Bull. Atomic Scientists*, 59 (2), 74–77, 2005; http://www.bullatomsci.org/issues/ nukenotes/ma03nukenote.html; accessed 3/22/04.
13. International Atomic Energy Agency, Implementation of the NPT Safeguards Agreement in the Islamic Republic of Iran, report, Feb. 2004; http://www.fas.org/nuke/guide/iran/nuke/; accessed 3/22/04.

14. Spector, L.S., Missing the Forest for the Trees: U.S. Non-Proliferation Programs in Russia, Arms Control Association, June 2001; http://www.armscontrol.org/act/2001_06/specjun01.asp; accessed 3/22/04.

15. Staff, New York Nuclear Bomb Scare Kept Secret for Months, *Space Daily,* Mar. 3, 2002; http://www.spacedaily.com/news/nuclear-black-market-02c.html; accessed 3/22/04.

16. Associated Press, Al-Qaeda Leader Says They Have Briefcase Nukes, AP-NY, Mar. 22, 2004; http://aolsvc.news.aol.com/news/article.adp?id=20040321100309990001; accessed 3/22/04.

17. Alibek, K. and Handelman, S., *Biohazard: The Chilling True Story of the Largest Covert Biological Weapons Program in the World — Told from Inside by the Man Who Ran It*, Random House, New York, 1999; Vogel, K., Viewpoint: Ensuring the Security of Russia's Chemical Weapons: A Lab-to-Lab Partnering Program, *Nonproliferation Rev.*, Winter 1999; http://cns.miis.edu/pubs/npr/vol06/62/vogel62.pdf; accessed 3/24/04.

18. U.S. Congress, Terrorist and Intelligence Operations: Potential Impact on the U.S. Economy, statement by Dr. Kenneth Alibek (program manager of Battelle Memorial Institute) before the Joint Economic Committee United States Congress, May 20, 1998; http://www.house.gov/jec/hearings/intell/alibek.htm; accessed 3/22/04.

19. Harvard Sussex Program, Declaration on the Use of Projectiles the Object of Which Is the Diffusion of Asphyxiating or Deleterious Gases, July 29, 1899; http://www.sussex.ac.uk/spru/hsp/Hague1899.html; accessed 4/1/04; Harvard Sussex Program, Laws and Customs of War on Land (Hague IV), Oct. 18, 1907; http://www.sussex. ac.uk/spru/hsp/Hague1907.html; accessed 4/1/04.

20. Stockholm International Peace Research Institute, Chemical Warfare in the Iraq-Iran War, May 1984; http://projects. sipri.se/cbw/research/factsheet-1984.html; accessed 4/13/04.

21. Monterey Institute of International Studies, Reported Use of Chemical Weapons, Ballistic Missiles, and Cruise Missiles in the Middle East; http://cns.miis.edu/research/wmdme/timeline.htm; accessed 4/14/04.

22. Tucker, J.B., Conflicting Evidence Revives "Yellow Rain" Controversy, Monterey Institute of International Studies; http://cns.miis.edu/pubs/week/020805.htm; accessed 4/13/04.

23. European Defense, Revised Brussels Treaty — 23 October 1954; http://www.european-defence.co.uk/directory-t.html; accessed 4/13/04.

24. Harvard Sussex Program, The 1972 Biological and Toxin Weapons Convention (BWC); http://www.sussex.ac.uk/spru/hsp/BWCpreamble.html; accessed 4/13/04.

25. Pearson, G.S., Strengthening the Biological Weapons Convention, Review Conference Paper No. 6 in *Return to Geneva: The United Kingdom Green Paper*, Pearson, G.S. and Dando, M.R., eds., Department of Peace Studies, University of Bradford, Bradford, U.K., June 2002.

26. Office of the National Counterintelligence Executive, Annual Report to Congress on Foreign Economic Collection and Industrial Espionage, 2001; http://www.nacic.gov/pubs/reports/fy01.htm#a; accessed 4/13/04.

27. U.S. Department of State, Decision of the Fifth Review Conference of the States Parties to the Convention on the Prohibition of the Development, Production, and Stockpiling of Bacteriological (Biological) Weapons and on Their Destruction, Dec. 12, 2002; http://www.state.gov/t/ac/rls/or/2002/15725.htm; accessed 4/13/04.

28. Harvard Sussex Program, 1993 Chemical Weapons Convention (CWC); http://www.sussex.ac.uk/spru/hsp/CWCpreamble.html; accessed 3/23/04.

29. Organization for the Prevention of Chemical Weapons; http://www.opcw.org/; accessed 4/13/04.

30. Harvard Sussex Program, Overview of the CBW regime; http://www.sussex.ac.uk/spru/hsp/regime-overview.html; accessed 3/23/04.

31. CNN, Taiwan Voters Elect New President; Chinese Troops on Alert, Mar. 18, 2000; http://www.cnn.com/2000/ASIANOW/east/03/18/taiwan.elex.01/index.html; accessed 4/13/04.

32. Chinoy, M., Thousands Gather for Taiwan Rally, CNN, Mar. 27, 2004; http://www.cnn.com/2004/WORLD/asiapcf/03/26/taiwan.election/index.html; accessed 4/13/04.

33. Pomfret, J., China Ponders New Rules of "Unrestricted War," *Washington Post*, Aug. 8, 1999.

34. George Washington University, The Cuban Missile Crisis, 1962: The 40th Anniversary, National Security Archives, GWU; http://www.gwu.edu/~nsarchiv/nsa/cuba_mis_cri/; accessed 4/13/04.

35. Federation of American Scientists, Nuclear Weapons in Russia: Safety Security and Control Issues; http://www.fas.org/spp/starwars/crs/IB98038.pdf; accessed 4/14/04.

36. Federation of American Scientists, Strategic Nuclear Forces; http://www.fas.org/nuke/guide/usa/doctrine/dod/95_nuc.htm; accessed 4/14/04.

37. Federation of American Scientists, Intermediate-Range Nuclear Forces; http://www.fas.org/nuke/control/inf/; accessed 4/14/04.

38. Strategic-Air-Command.com, Minuteman Missile History; http://www.strategic-air-command.com/missiles/Minuteman/Minuteman_Missile_History.htm; accessed 4/14/04.

39. Baal, B. and Trendafilovski, V., Russian Anti-Ballistic Guided Missile Systems, Radar and Missile Analysis Group (R&MAG); http://www.wonderland.org.nz/rusabgm.htm; accessed 4/18/04.

40. Federation of American Scientists, Intercontinental Ballistic Missiles; http://www.fas.org/nuke/intro/missile/icbm.htm; accessed 4/19/04.

41. PBS, The Technology: Can It Work?, *Frontline*; http://www.pbs.org/wgbh/pages/frontline/shows/missile/technology/; last accessed 4/19/04.

42. Federation of American Scientists, Boost-Phase Intercept; http://www.fas.org/spp/starwars/program/bpi.htm; accessed 4/19/04.

43. Federation of American Scientists, Airborne Laser; http://www.fas.org/spp/starwars/program/abl.htm; accessed 4/19/04.

44. Federation of American Scientists, Kinetic Energy Boost Phase Intercept; http://www.fas.org/spp/military/docops/defense/actd_mp/BPI.htm; accessed 4/19/04.

45. Federation of American Scientists, Space Based Laser (SBL); http://www.fas.org/spp/starwars/program/sbl.htm; accessed 4/19/04.

46. Postol, T., Why Missile Defense Won't Work, *Frontline*, PBS, April 2002; available on-line at http://www.pbs.org/wgbh/pages/frontline/shows/missile/etc/ postol.html; accessed 4/26/04.

47. PBS, Missile Wars: The Technology, Can It Work? *Frontline*; http://www.pbs.org/wgbh/pages/frontline/shows/missile/technology/; accessed 4/19/04.

48. U.S. Department of State, Agreement on Measures to Reduce the Risk of Outbreak of Nuclear War between the United States of America and the Union of Soviet Socialist Republics; http://www.state.gov/t/ac/trt/4692.htm; accessed 4/26/04.

49. U.S. Department of State, African Nuclear-Weapon-Free Zone Treaty (the Treaty of Pelindaba); http://www.state.gov/ac/trt/4699.htm; accessed 4/26/04.

50. U.S. Department of State, Antarctic Treaty; http://www.state.gov/t/ac/trt/4700.htm; accessed 4/26/04.

51. U.S. Department of State, Treaty between the United States of America and the Union of Soviet Socialist Republics on the Limitation of Anti-Ballistic Missile Systems; http://www.state. gov/t/np/trty/16332.htm; accessed 4/26/04.

52. U.S. Department of State, Agreement between the United States of America and the Union of Soviet Socialist Republics on Notifications of Launches of Intercontinental Ballistic Missiles and Submarine-Launched Ballistic Missiles; http://www.state. gov/t/ac/trt/4714.htm; accessed 4/26/04.

53. U.S. Department of State, Convention on the Prohibition of the Development, Production and Stockpiling of Bacteriological (Biological) and Toxin Weapons and on Their Destruction; http://www.state.gov/t/ac/trt/4718.htm; accessed 4/26/04.

54. U.S. Department of State, Comprehensive Test Ban Treaty; http://fpc.state.gov/documents/organization/9071.pdf; accessed 4/26/04.

55. U.S. Department of State, Document of the Stockholm Conference on Confidence- and Security-Building Measures and Disarmament in Europe Convened in Accordance with the Relevant Provisions of the Concluding Document of the Madrid Meeting of the Conference on Security and Cooperation in Europe; http://www.state.gov/t/ac/trt/4725.htm; accessed 4/26/04.

56. U.S. Department of State, Convention on the Physical Protection of Nuclear Material, Document of the Stockholm Conference on Confidence- and Security-Building Measures and Disarmament in Europe Convened in Accordance with the Relevant Provisions of the Concluding Document of the Madrid Meeting of the Conference on Security and Cooperation in Europe; http://www.state. gov/t/ac/trt/5079.htm; accessed 4/26/04.

57. U.S. Department of State, Protocol for the Prohibition of the Use in War of Asphyxiating, Poisonous or Other Gases, and of Bacteriological Methods of Warfare; http://www.state.gov/t/ac/trt/4784.htm; accessed 4/26/04.

58. U.S. Department of State, Memorandum of Understanding between the United States of America and the Union of Soviet Socialist Republics Regarding the Establishment of a Direct Communications Link; http://www.state.gov/t/ac/trt/4785.htm; accessed 4/26/04.

59. U.S. Department of State, Agreement between the United States of America and the Union of Soviet Socialist Republics to Expand the U.S.-USSR Direct Communications Link; http://www.state.gov/t/ac/trt/4786.htm; accessed 4/26/04.

60. U.S. Department of State, Agreement between the United States of America and the Union of Soviet Socialist Republics on Measures to Improve the U.S.A.-USSR Direct Communications Link (with Annex, Supplementing and Modifying the Memorandum of Understanding with Annex, of June 20, 1963); http://www.state.gov/t/ac/trt/4786.htm; accessed 4/26/04.

61. U.S. Department of State, Agreement between the Government of the United States of America and the Government of the Union of Soviet Socialist Republics on the Prevention of Incidents on and over the High Seas; http://www.state.gov/t/ac/trt/4791.htm; accessed 4/26/04.

62. U.S. Department of State, Treaty between the United States of America and the Union of Soviet Socialist Republics on the Elimination of Their Intermediate-Range and Shorter-Range Missiles; http://www.state.gov/t/np/trty/18432.htm; accessed 4/26/04.

63. U.S. Department of State, Treaty for the Prohibition of Nuclear Weapons in Latin America and the Caribbean (Treaty of Tlatelolco); http://www.state.gov/t/ac/trt/4796.htm; accessed 4/26/04.

64. U.S. Department of State, Treaty Banning Nuclear Weapon Tests in the Atmosphere, in Outer Space and Under Water; http://www.state.gov/t/ac/trt/4797.htm; accessed 4/26/04.

65. U.S. Department of State, Memorandum of Agreement between the United States of America and the Russian Federation on the Establishment of a Joint Center for the Exchange of Data from Early Warning Systems and Notifications of Missile Launches (JDEC MOA); http://www.state.gov/t/ac/trt/4799.htm; accessed 4/26/04.

66. U.S. Department of State, Memorandum of Understanding on Notifications of Missile Launches (PLNS MOU); http://www.state.gov/t/ac/trt/4954.htm; accessed 4/26/04.

67. U.S. Department of State, Missile Technology Control Regime; http://www.state.gov/t/ac/trt/5073.htm; accessed 4/26/04.

68. U.S. Department of State, Treaty between the United States of America and the Russian Federation on Strategic Offensive Reductions; http://www.state.gov/t/ac/trt/18016.htm; accessed 4/26/04.

69. U.S. Department of State, Treaty on the Non-Proliferation of Nuclear Weapons; http://www.state.gov/t/np/trty/16281.htm; accessed 4/26/04.

70. U.S. Department of State, Agreement between the United States of America and the Union of Soviet Socialist Republics on the Establishment of Nuclear Risk Reduction Centers (and Protocols Thereto); http://www.state.gov/t/ac/trt/5179.htm; accessed 4/26/04.

71. U.S. Department of State, Treaty on Principles Governing the Activities of States in the Exploration and Use of Outer Space, Including the Moon and Other Celestial Bodies; http://www.state.gov/t/ac/trt/5181.htm; accessed 4/26/04.

72. U.S. Department of State, Treaty between the United States of America and the Union of Soviet Socialist Republics on Underground Nuclear Explosions for Peaceful Purposes (and Protocol Thereto); http://www.state.gov/t/ac/trt/5182.htm; accessed 4/26/04.

73. U.S. Department of State, Agreement between the United States of America and the Union of Soviet Socialist Republics on the Prevention of Nuclear War; http://www.state.gov/t/ac/trt/5186.htm; accessed 4/26/04.

74. U.S. Department of State, Treaty on the Prohibition of the Emplacement of Nuclear Weapons and Other Weapons of Mass Destruction on the Seabed and the Ocean Floor and in the Subsoil Thereof; http://www.state.gov/t/ac/trt/5187.htm; accessed 4/26/04.

75. U.S. Department of State, South Pacific Nuclear Free Zone Treaty; http://www.state.gov/t/ac/trt/5189.htm; accessed 4/26/04.

76. U.S. Department of State, Treaty between the United States of America and the Union of Soviet Socialist Republics on the Limitation of Strategic Offensive Arms (SALT I); http://www.state.gov/t/ac/trt/5191.htm; accessed 4/26/04.

77. U.S. Department of State, Treaty between the United States of America and the Union of Soviet Socialist Republics on the Limitation of Strategic Offensive Arms (SALT II); http://www.state.gov/t/ac/trt/5195.htm; accessed 4/26/04.

78. U.S. Department of State, Strategic Arms Reduction Treaty (START); http://www.state.gov/t/ac/trt/18535.htm; accessed 4/26/04.

79. U.S. Department of State, Strategic Arms Reduction Treaty (START II); http://www.state.gov/t/ac/trt/10425.htm; accessed 4/26/04.

80. U.S. Department of State, Treaty between the United States of America and the Union of Soviet Socialist Republics on the Limitation of Underground Nuclear Weapon Tests (and Protocol Thereto); http://www.state.gov/t/ac/trt/5204.htm; accessed 4/26/04.

81. U.S. Department of State, Agreement between the United States of America and the International Atomic Energy Agency for the Application of Safeguards in the United States (and Protocol Thereto); http://www.state.gov/t/ac/trt/5209.htm; accessed 4/26/04.

82. U.S. Department of State, Treaty between the United States of America and the Russian Federation on Strategic Offensive Reductions; http://www.state.gov/t/ac/trt/10527.htm; accessed 4/26/04.

7

The Future of Weapons of Mass Destruction

One of the historical facts about the evolution of advanced weapons is that the weapon timeline begins as an advantage to the possessor (e.g., the state). This advantage remains as long as the weapon technology remains a state secret. Eventually, other states develop similar or superior weapons to compete or gain advantage, and the weapon technology ultimately becomes available to individuals. Despite the best efforts of a state to slow down this natural evolution, the technology eventually disseminates into the public domain. As discussed in prior chapters, the speed of knowledge flow has been accelerated by the Internet's compression of the dissemination process,[1] thus hastening the evolution of this era's advanced weapons, the weapons of mass destruction (WMDs).

Technology can also be used to protect state secrets, which lengthens the time it takes a state secret to migrate to the public domain. We have no way of knowing how long it will take for the current WMD technology to fully disseminate. What we do know is that in some cases, the process is well along, since state-to-state transfer of WMD technology is occurring (e.g., transfer of nuclear technology from Pakistan to Iran, Libya, and North Korea).

There are economic barriers that play a role in determining how weapons technology migrates. In 1969 the United Nations did a study on the cost of causing 50% casualties over a 1-km^2 area using various weapon systems.[2] Biological weapons were by far the least expensive weapon.

The U.S. nuclear weapons program has been very costly.[3] The U.S. has invested \$5.5 trillion since 1940 and continues to spend about $30 billion each year to maintain its present stockpiles. The costs of even modest nuclear programs are significant. For example, Pakistan sold uranium-enrichment technology — including gas centrifuges, uranium hexafluoride, instructions, and plans for a gun-type nuclear weapon — for about $100 million.[4] The cost of implementing a program once the Pakistan-supplied nuclear kit was in hand was considerably larger, and only a few countries made the purchase (Iran, Libya, and North Korea). In comparison, the Japanese Aum Shinrikyo cult assembled the resources to develop both chemical and biological weapons and perpetrated a chemical weapons attack on a judges' compound in Matsumoto and on the Tokyo subway.[5]

Nations develop WMDs for a variety of reasons. Deterrence is a common motivation to prevent another country from attacking. Aggression is also a motivating factor, where a country might want to initiate an attack for the acquisition of resources. Another factor might be to use WMDs as a tool of persuasion, where disarmament could be a factor in negotiating favorable deals with other nations (such as trade agreements) or in gaining a more prestigious position in world affairs, such as membership in the EU (European Union) or the G8.

G8 is an informal group of eight countries: Canada, France, Germany, Italy, Japan, Russia, the United Kingdom, and the United States of America. The European Union also participates as a permanent non-hosting member. The G8 members hold an annual meeting to discuss macroeconomic and other broad-based agenda items that addresses a wide range of international economic, political and social issues.

In this chapter, nuclear, biological, and chemical weapons will be examined in detail to assess future proliferation threats. The motivations for a nation to develop WMDs will also be discussed. The root motivation for WMDs stems from a growing global population putting an increasing demand on a dwindling resource that is critical to civilization and the global economy — oil.

7.1 NUCLEAR WEAPONS

As discussed in Chapters 2 and 3, the development of nuclear weapons requires a considerable investment in science and technology. A nuclear weapons program also requires a well-educated workforce, an advanced infrastructure, and a considerable economic base. Very few countries possess all of these capabilities.

However, states can cooperate with one another to gain strength in areas where they are weak.

7.1.1 Use by States

Countries are grouped into four categories based on nuclear capabilities. Group A includes countries that have nuclear weapons. As discussed in Chapter 2, the A group includes

U.S.	France
Russia	India
China	Pakistan
England	Israel

The B group comprises countries that can develop nuclear weapons independently but have not yet done so or have not yet declared nuclear capability. The B group countries include

Canada	South Korea
Germany	Sweden
Japan	Taiwan
North Korea	Ukraine

The C group comprises countries that have most of the ingredients for developing nuclear weapons, but would require either assistance and additional time and investment to do so. The C group countries include

Algeria	Brazil
Argentina	Kazakhstan
Australia	Netherlands
Belarus	Switzerland

Group D states have sought or are actively seeking technology and assistance in developing nuclear weapons. The D group countries include

Libya[6]
Iran[7]
Syria[8]

The cost of developing and maintaining a nuclear arsenal is very high. Unless there is a perceived threat that justifies the cost, the development of a nuclear arsenal is a burden that most countries would not wish to bear. In the cases of the North Korean and Iranian nuclear programs, the perceived threat of the U.S. war on terrorism — and their identification as part of the "axis of evil" by the Bush administration — has been at least partially responsible for the acceleration of investments in their programs. Iran also has the additional concern of the Israeli nuclear arsenal.

Most of the First World countries in groups A and B have the resources to develop nuclear weapons. North Korea (in Group B) is a special case, because the country's dictator can squeeze the nation's meager resources to the detriment of its people in order to develop nuclear weapons and advanced missile technology. Given the high cost of developing a nuclear weapons program (see Chapter 2), most countries would prefer investing in their economies and promoting the welfare of their people rather than allocating scarce resources to unproductive ventures such as WMDs. A nuclear weapons program is attractive only if there is a threat or a perception of threat that justifies the diversion of resources.

Countries in groups C and D would have a steeper climb to achieve a viable nuclear weapons program. The required resources are significant and would be hard if not impossible to justify in a democratic or parliamentarian system. However, a dictatorship with access to a resource base such as oil would pose a significant threat.

7.1.2 Delivery Systems

Mid-range missile technology, such as the SCUD, is widely available due to technology transfer from China and North Korea. Additionally, cash-strapped North Korea has shown a willingness to sell its technologies and its long-range missile, the Taepo Dung, which would be an attraction to a group D country contemplating a WMD program.

Cruise missiles and unmanned air vehicles (UAVs) pose a threat for delivery of WMDs. If cruise missiles or UAVs are combined with the ballistic missiles, they could penetrate even the most expensive missile defense systems.[9] UAVs could be relatively inexpensive. Conversion of small airplanes or UAVs into WMD delivery systems would also be inexpensive.

The weapon can also be delivered by other means, for example, a cruise missile launched from a commercial ship navigating within the normal shipping lanes. Weapons could also be smuggled across the U.S. border and delivered to targets by enemy agents.

Nuclear weapons are more effectively used as a deterrent or as a means of influencing foreign policy. Actual deployment of a nuclear weapon would enrage the entire world, regardless of justification of use. No state would risk the backlash of such a move.

7.1.3 Use by Terrorist Groups

Terrorist groups do not have the resources of even a small poor country. The barriers for terrorist groups to develop nuclear weapons are too great to overcome. Nevertheless, there are potential scenarios that have raised concern. One such scenario is a terrorist group buying a nuclear weapon from a rogue nation or from the black market of the former Soviet Union.[10] Of the many possible events reported, none have credibility. The bulk of such sales, if they did occur at all, are confidence games played by unscrupulous gangsters on the buyer. Oftentimes an ignorant buyer will judge the merchandise based on its looks and markings. Additionally, nuclear weapons do have a shelf life (a few years for USSR designs) and most likely would require complete rebuilding in order to make the weapon operational (a difficult task without the resources of a country).

A second concern is state-sponsored terrorism, which involves a nation enlisting the actions of a terrorist group. If a nuclear weapon were delivered by a state-sponsored terrorist group, the technology exists to trace a deployed nuclear weapon back to its origin. It is unlikely that most countries would risk the international backlash of providing a nuclear device to a terrorist group, the exception being that of unrestricted warfare as described in Chapter 6.

Even the most well-financed terrorist group, al Qaeda, has not demonstrated the necessary resources to develop a nuclear weapon. The only source of a nuclear weapon for a group such as al Qaeda is either from a black-market sale or from a rogue nation. As described previously, there are problems and risks that make this scenario unlikely. Even the most organized of terrorist groups has a very limited infrastructure.

Terrorist groups have sent agents into countries to engage in a variety of espionage and reconnaissance activities. Thus, smuggling of a weapon across borders and taking it to a specific target would be the delivery method most likely used.

The most significant effect of a nuclear weapon attack by terrorists would be the aftermath of fear and panic that it would generate. Markets and institutions would suffer unspeakable consequences. We are not making light of the consequences of a nuclear attack. On a local scale, it would be devastating. However, we are more concerned about the instinctual reaction of people around the world and how this would amplify the effects of the nuclear attack, which is just the opposite of what should be done.

Logically, the deployment of a nuclear weapon by a terrorist group, if it occurs at all, would be an isolated event for several reasons: the cost of the weapon, the low probability of a successful detonation, and the lack of resources. However, it will not be logic that governs our response; it will be emotion. Unfortunately, our emotions will be based upon a fear that comes from our media-shaped perceptions of nuclear weapons and radiation. We can examine the effects of irrational fears by looking at the example of dihydrogen monoxide (DHMO). What you will find in reading about DHMO is that it is a formidable material.[11] What is interesting is that when university students are asked to evaluate the risks of DHMO, they are fearful of it for a number of reasons.

- DHMO has killed far more people than any WMD.
- DHMO has killed more people than explosives.
- DHMO is widely available.

They are all surprised to learn that DHMO is water.

We need to step beyond our initial reactions and examine the potential agenda of groups using unfamiliar technology for the purpose of inciting fear or action. This tactic is used all too often. For example, President Dwight D. Eisenhower warned us about the evils of the military-industrial complex before leaving office in 1960. As it turned out, he was right. During the Cold War, a common tactic used for funding military programs was to exaggerate the comparable capability of the Soviets. In truth, the USSR's military used the same exact method. Examples of this behavior can be seen every day. People commonly exaggerate to sell news, to win arguments, and to persuade others into accepting their proposition.

As engineers, the authors have observed this behavior when critics attack the nuclear industry. We have seen facts often replaced by myth in the media and political arenas. These myths promote irrational fears and often have resulted in poor decisions. The purpose of these tactics is to stop the peaceful use of nuclear energy production. However, as stated in Chapter 3, by far the most important contribution of nuclear science is in the medical area, where it has saved countless lives. The unintended consequence of the myths is to create fear in victims who need nuclear-based lifesaving procedures. One example discussed in Chapter 3 is nuclear magnetic resonance (NMR) imaging, which uses the interaction of the hydrogen nucleus with radio-frequency waves to image the human body. The term *nuclear* used in NMR so agitated people that it was dropped from the name, and now the technology is called magnetic resonance imaging (MRI).

Intentional exploitation of irrational fear has also proved to be a problem when dealing with terrorism. The September 11, 2001, terrorist attack was a terrible event. But as a nation, we allowed the fear to go beyond the initial impact and permitted it to invade our national psyche. Our economy was impaired, and many industries were devastated following the 9/11 attack. The real cost of 9/11 can be counted in trillions of dollars. The media and politicians fanned the flames of fear for their own agendas. The terrorists were beneficiaries because the real damage went far beyond the initial attack.

The DHMO example demonstrates how a technical description can be manipulated to invoke fear of a substance as harmless as water. As citizens participating in a democratic process, it is critical that we question information and objectively form our own educated opinions. Otherwise, we leave ourselves open to the manipulation by others, including terrorists.

While the possibility exists, the use of nuclear weapons by a terrorist group is unlikely. The limited availability of such weapons, combined with the effects of the vast damage resulting from a detonation to infrastructure, markets, and institutions, would turn public opinion against the cause of the terrorist.

7.1.4 Use by Individuals

An individual has virtually no access to a nuclear weapon. An individual would encounter the same obstacles as a small country and would have limited resources to call upon. While individuals may have significant wealth, equivalent to a small country, individuals with this kind of wealth are more interested in preserving it. An individual would have virtually no infrastructure to call upon and would have to deploy a nuclear weapon in much the same way that a terrorist group would.

Unlike the terrorist who seeks to redress some perceived injustice, an individual might actually be motivated by the disruption or destruction of world order and institutions.

7.2 DIRTY BOMBS

The threat of radiological dispersion devices (RDDs), or dirty bombs, has been highly overrated in the media. Radiation is most lethal when concentrated. An RDD uses conventional explosives to distribute the radioactive material over a large area. Most of the casualties would be generated from the explosion itself. The cleanup and decontamination following deployment of an RDD would be substantial, but the task is manageable due to available technologies such as nuclear sensors and experience.

The real issue associated with an RDD detonation is the fear and panic it would generate in the general public (see the discussion on use of a nuclear weapon by terrorists). Interestingly, the radioactive source used in an RDD does not have to be particularly dangerous to incite panic. This concept was illustrated when the Green Party attacked British Nuclear Fuels in the media for release of a krypton isotope (Kr-85) while reprocessing spent nuclear fuel. Kr-85 is a noble gas that disperses readily if released and has almost no interaction with human tissue if breathed into the lungs. Kr-85 has virtually no biological effect on the human body. Nuclear power plants routinely release small amounts Kr-85 because it poses no health threat. Nonetheless, the criticisms of the Greens caused great public concern about Kr-85. In contrast, the public overreactions to radiation of any type makes the consequences of an RDD attack that much worse.

7.2.1 Use by States

Most states have the capability of developing RDDs using radioactive isotopes from industry. However, a dirty bomb has virtually no military value, other than inciting panic among the target population.

A dirty bomb would have to be fairly large because of the shielding required to protect people before deployment. The size of the delivery vehicle would limit options to large planes or trucks.

7.2.2 Use by Terrorist Groups

The dirty bomb is a psychological tool rather than an effective weapon. Terrorist groups could use an RDD to exploit public fears of radiation by using radioisotopes that are more commonly available. First of all, obtaining a harmful radioisotope is fraught with problems, but finding harmless radioisotopes would be much easier. For example, one possible radioisotope that might be used in an RDD is depleted uranium. Depleted uranium is available in large quantities, emits very little radiation, is easily handled, requires no shielding, and is feared by the public.

A dirty bomb is within the economic capability of a terrorist group. The infrastructure required to handle radioisotopes would be considerable for a group. A hazardous radioisotope would require some resources, including a shielded area, someone with health physics training, and a remote location. The dirty bomb would require a fairly large delivery vehicle, depending upon shielding needs.

7.2.3 Use by Individuals

A dirty bomb is something within the reach of an individual. The most significant aspect of a dirty bomb is the reaction that it would generate. An individual who is interested in disruption of society on a large scale might take advantage of the public's irrational fears.

7.3 BIOLOGICAL WEAPONS

In many ways, biological weapons are more understandable than other types of WMDs. We have shared human experiences in dealing with colds, flus, and infection. The basics of hygiene are universally taught to children to help them avoid catching disease. Life experience and familiarity tends to mitigate our fear of disease because we have to live with it. In contrast to nuclear threats, the problem is that we become complacent and do not have a healthy fear of biological agents. It is very common for us to go to work or school with a cold or the flu, fully recognizing that we will not take precautions in the workplace or the classroom to protect others or ourselves. A cough or sneeze deposits a biological aerosol on surfaces that others touch, such as desktops and doorknobs. People inevitably transmit biological material and spread the disease to others who touch the desktops or doorknobs and then touch their mouths or eyes. Habits are hard to break, but in order to minimize infection routes, frequent washing of hands and learning not to touch the mouth and eyes are critical. Flus and colds spread through communities and homes rapidly. But the risk of dying from a cold or the flu is small, so we do not think twice about the disease.

What would our reaction be if the infection were SARS (severe acute respiratory syndrome)? SARS, with a 30% mortality rate, is one of several infectious diseases that have the potential to spread rapidly. The World Health Organization keeps a close watch on natural SARS outbreaks and works quickly to intervene when discovered. What would happen if SARS were being spread on purpose by a determined group? If multiple people were purposely infected with SARS and were sent to public places to spread the disease, what could be done to limit its spread? Our complacency to biological agents would work against us.

Biological weapons do not have to be sophisticated to be effective. The numbers are staggering. For example, a highly infectious agent with a 2.5% mortality rate could, if optimally spread around the world, infect a significant portion of the world's population and kill over 100 million people: The 1918 influenza pandemic, for example, killed 20 to 40 million people when the world's population was much smaller.[12] However, as described in Chapter 4, biological weapons can be even more sophisticated and more lethal. As biotechnology flourishes, the means to make agents more sophisticated and lethal will also flourish. Biotechnology has developed a host of tools that many would have thought impossible 50 years ago, such as recombinant genetic engineering. A first-generation genetically modified virus or bacteria might be an enhanced natural agent that has been modified for antibiotic resistance, enhanced invasiveness, toxin production, or an enhanced ability to evade host immune defenses.

Biotechnology is making unheard of leaps and will continue to do so. We can expect many wonderful things. As the human genome is being deciphered, the ability to understand what specific genes do and how to manipulate them will eventually be achieved. Even the basic understanding of chemistry at the molecular level will be developed. Within 30 years or so, sophisticated computer models might be available that can predict the operations of specific gene sequences or drugs and their impact. These achievements will lead to cures for many human maladies. However, in developing this depth of knowledge, we must realize that it can also be used for evil. The risk of a genetically engineered disease spelling the end of mankind is many orders of magnitude greater than the same risk for nuclear or chemical weapons.

7.3.1 Use by States

Every country has some degree of a pharmaceutical, vaccine, and fermentation (wine, beer, and cheese) industry. Thus, the knowledge base and infrastructure for the potential production of bioweapons exists. Basically, as described in Chapter 4, the educated work force, the equipment, and the agents are available to even very poor countries. What is not readily available is the capability of weaponizing the agent (producing an aerosol of weapon quality, as described in Chapter 4).

Biological weapons can be delivered in a variety of ways: sprayers on aircraft, or cruise missiles, munitions, and ballistic missile warheads. Iraq purchased munitions from Spain (R-400) and modified them for delivery of chemical and biological weapons. Biological weapons can also be deployed with limited technology, such as with a garden sprayer or a crop duster, or even dumped from a container into a light wind.

Biological weapons have limited effectiveness as a military tool. Deployment can be dependent on the wind used for dispersing the material, the unpredictability of the weather, and the latent period before infection occurs.

7.3.2 Use by Terrorist Groups

Aum Shinrikyo, a terrorist group that released the nerve agent sarin (GB) in a Tokyo subway tunnel, demonstrated that terrorist groups had the resources to engage in biological weapons development. A large-scale production facility is not necessary for production of biological weapons. When Colin Powell appeared before the UN to present evidence of the Iraqi weapons of mass destruction program on February 5, 2003, he accused Iraq of building mobile bioweapons laboratories.[13] Even though we now know that this was not true,[14] it does show that U.S. experts believed that a bioweapons laboratory could be placed on the back of a truck. As discussed in Chapter 4, production facilities for biological agents can come in any size. Terrorists do not need large-scale facilities.

The cost of developing biological weapons is well within the means of even a moderately funded group. The required equipment is easily obtained, as described in Chapter 4; the knowledge base is widely available, as are the specialized skills.

Delivery systems need not be complex. They can range from jars that are opened and dumped in strategic places, to aerosol spray cans (e.g., hairspray), to garden sprayers, to crop dusters, to infected humans (akin to suicide bombers).

Biological weapons are well suited to terrorist activities because the incubation time for the disease to manifest itself is on the order of days (see Chapter 4). This would give terrorists the opportunity to initiate the attack and to escape before being discovered. A successful biological attack would have an impact far greater than the event itself, as discussed above.

7.3.3 Use by Individuals

The question of whether an individual is capable of developing and using a biological weapon was addressed by the FBI's lead theory about the October 2001 anthrax-mailing case.[15] The FBI has theorized that an individual with germ warfare experience was behind the attack.[16] Whether this theory is true, experts in the U.S. government believe that it is possible.

The cost of developing biological weapons is well within the means of an individual. Because biotechnology equipment is readily available and production can be done on a small scale, the important component is knowledge. This knowledge base is widely available due to the size of the world's pharmaceutical, vaccine, and fermentation industries.

An individual would use delivery systems similar to those of a terrorist group. Unlike terrorists, who want to protect their families and their people, an antisocial individual might have the goal of destroying mankind. An antisocial individual might be willing to unleash dangerous and highly infectious organisms. Terrorists, on the other hand, are unlikely to unleash something that could impact their families or their people.

7.4 CHEMICAL WEAPONS

7.4.1 Use by States

As discussed in Chapter 5, the chemical industry is widely spread among nations of the world. Countries with an agricultural base will also have facilities to produce insecticides and fertilizers. These same facilities can be used for the production of chemical weapons (CWs). Thus, it is no surprise when a country such as Libya, which recently came forward to disband its chemical and nuclear arsenals, discloses that it had stockpiled 44,000 pounds of mustard gas.[17]

The cost of producing CWs is well within the capabilities of most states. The required infrastructure, equipment, knowledge and skill base are widely available from the chemical industry.

Chemical agents can be delivered as vapors, liquids, or aerosols using sprayers from aircraft or cruise missiles, by ballistic missiles, and by other munitions. Many of the smaller-scale delivery systems (such as those described for biological agent delivery) are suitable for chemical agents as well. As with biological weapons, deployment would be impacted by the wind and weather. Most agents are fast acting, resulting in a higher military value than that of biological agents.

7.4.2 Use by Terrorist Groups

Terrorist groups have developed and used chemical weapons. For example, the Aum Shinrikyo group developed a chemical weapon program and attacked the Tokyo subway system.[18] There is no reason to believe that terrorist groups will not continue to pursue chemical weapons. The example of Aum Shinrikyo should serve as a warning. We also know, from documents and videotapes found in Afghanistan, that al Qaeda has sought to expand its capabilities by research into chemical, biological, and nuclear weapons. Terrorist groups certainly have the financial means to pursue chemical weapons, as evidenced by Aum Shinrikyo's success. Infrastructure should not be a significant problem.

Chemical weapons delivery systems can be either simple or complex, offering a range of options for terrorist groups. However, a very large amount of chemical agent is needed to attack a large area effectively (hundreds of kilograms of agent per square kilometer).[19] Given the large amount of material required, chemical weapon attacks will likely be of limited scope, with the hope that the aftermath will damage world markets and institutions.

7.4.3 Use by Individuals

Individuals could gather the resources required to make chemical weapons. However, given the relative amounts of materials required for an effective attack, chemical weapons would not be an attractive strategy.

7.5 OIL AS A DOMINANT FORCE IN PROLIFERATION

The authors believe that oil is one of the strongest forces driving the proliferation of WMDs. Oil is a portable, liquid, high energy–content fuel that has revolutionized the structure of the world. Oil is the world's single most important traded commodity, providing fuel for 95% of all transportation needs and 40% of all commercial energy needs. Oil is also a major feedstock for thousands of manufactured products, serves as the most important feedstock in the chemical industry, and is critical for food production. Looking at its impact from about 1930 onward, oil has become indispensable to our civilization. A particularly intriguing definition of modern agriculture, the use of land to convert petroleum into food, is brought to light by Professor Albert Bartlett of the University of Colorado in his popular lecture "Arithmetic, Population and Energy."[20] He makes the point that it takes about 80 gallons of gasoline or equivalent to produce one acre of corn, in addition to 9 hours of human labor per crop acre. Petroleum also plays a role in the production of the pesticides and fertilizers that are critical for the high yield per acre of modern agriculture.

It is anticipated that the world's population will double in about 36 years, which means that food production must keep pace. In addition to population growth, there are economic pressures on oil. The global economy is based on moderate growth, which is fueled by improvements in the standard of living. As discussed in Chapter 1, economic growth is closely tied to growth in energy consumption. The growth in energy consumption doubles about every decade. The use of energy in food production grows faster than in any other sector of the economy. Countries such as China and India, with populations greater than 1 billion, aspire to improve the standard of living for their people. These burgeoning economic powers, especially China, are driving an unprecedented growth in oil consumption.[21]

Due to its exorbitant energy consumption, the U.S. has held a special distinction which amounts to about 25% of the world's energy usage for about 5% of the world's population. The rest of the world is striving to obtain a similar standard of living. When the people of China reach the same standard of living as Mexico's (measured by per capita energy use), the world's oil consumption will double. In terms of the consumption of the remaining oil, the most credible estimate is that 2000 billion barrels of oil have been formed in the crust of the Earth.[22] We have discovered or used about 1775 billion barrels of oil, and an estimated 150 billion barrels remain to be discovered.[23] The world's oil consumption is about 27.8 billion barrels of oil per year (in 2001) and is growing rapidly.[24] This serves as a backdrop to the understanding of why oil is one of the strongest forces in proliferation of weapons of mass destruction.

The longer it takes for the world to find an acceptable alternative to oil, the closer it teeters toward the Olduvai Gorge theory (a theory of industrial civilization).[25] The Olduvai Gorge theory was developed by Dr. Richard Duncan to describe the rise and fall of civilization. Assuming that no alternative to oil can be developed, look at the total energy used by the world at a given time

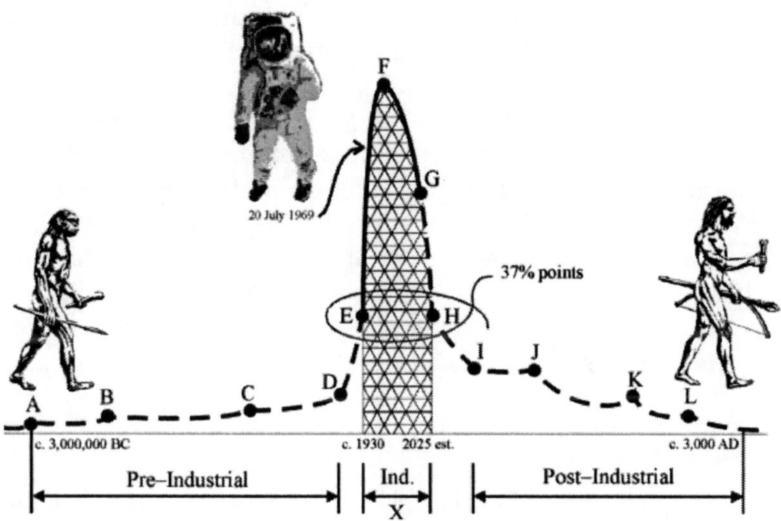

FIGURE 7.1 Average oil consumption per capita (AOCC) from the dawn of man to the projected fall of civilization.

and divide that number by the world's total population. This number is the average oil consumption per capita (AOCC). As shown in Figure 7.1, the peak value of the AOCC occurred in 1979. There are two points in time that fall at 37% of the peak AOCC. The first occurs during the Great Depression in 1930, and the second is projected to occur at about 2025. There is a point around 2010 where the AOCC falls off rapidly, thus the name "Olduvai Gorge." When this occurs, there are simply too many people demanding a portion of a scarce resource. The rapid fall of AOCC will trigger massive energy shortages, starvation, and rampant unemployment. Colin J. Campbell says this about the peak of the oil production:

> Although described as a production "plateau," it is likely to be anything but flat. It will more likely be a period of recurring price surges, recessions, international tensions, and growing conflicts for access to critical oil supplies, as the indigenous energy supply situation in the United States and Europe deteriorates.[26]

The pursuit of limited resources has been the most common cause of the world's armed conflicts. When people and families are faced with hopelessness and hunger, no option to relieve these conditions will sound unreasonable. These realities result in the devaluation of human life. In the aftermath of the AOCC drop-off, countries that are oil rich will have the revenues to build up their militaries to protect their valuable resources, and countries that are oil poor will be forced to respond and become more aggressive toward oil-rich countries.

Duncan does not say that his model is capable of predicting the future. Its value is to provide a glimpse of what could transpire if the world does not find a suitable replacement for the oil-based economy. What is clear is that the longer it takes to find that alternative, the divide between the rich and powerful countries and the disenfranchised peoples of the world will become deeper and more pronounced. This divide will breed hatred and create the forces that will drive proliferation.

7.6 CONCLUSIONS

The future proliferation of WMDs will be dependent on the evolutionary path taken by the global economy. Fair and equitable treatment of all the world's peoples would eliminate the reasons for nations to seek WMDs. As has been discussed, WMD technology will inevitably become available to those who desire it. These are forces that cannot be stopped but only slowed. It is imperative that the world endeavor to stop the destructive relationships in the Middle East and Asia.

In today's world, proliferation should perhaps be defined as the conversion of oil into WMDs. The part that an oil-based economy plays in the world's problems needs to be addressed. The U.S. is highly dependent upon oil, consuming 25% of the world's production, and the U.S. will need to take the lead in addressing this problem. As the burgeoning economic powers of China and India develop, the competition for the remaining oil supplies will lead to rivalries and exploitation. More money will flow into the Middle East, thus providing additional resources for the development of weapons of mass destruction and funds for terrorist organizations. One of the critical moves that can be made is to find long-term solutions for the replacement of oil. Extensive research in replacing the internal combustion engine is needed. This will wean the world off its oil-dependent economy onto a more long-term and stable pathway. Failure to do so will guarantee continuation of a world spiraling out of control and the proliferation and use of WMDs.

REFERENCES

1. Bohn, K., FBI: WMD Ingredients Readily Available, *CNN,* Apr. 4, 2003; http://www.cnn.com/2003/US/04/02/sprj.irq.fbi.wmd/index.html; accessed 5/10/04.
2. Christensen, G., Biological Terrorism, Lecture in Science and Technology of Terrorisms and Counterterrorism, Fall 2000, Nuclear Science and Engineering Institute, University of Missouri; http://prelas.nuclear.missouri.edu/NE401/l24.zip; accessed 4/28/04.
3. Menon, B., *Disarmament: A Basic Guide*, United Nations, New York, 2001; http://disarmament.un.org:8080/ddapublications/guide.pdf; accessed 4/28/04.
4. Sanger, D.E. and Broad, W.J., Pakistani's Nuclear Earnings: $100 Million, *New York Times*, Mar. 16, 2004; http://www.nytimes.com/2004/03/16/international/asia/16NUKE.html; accessed 3/18/04.
5. Ormerod, D., Ghosh, T., and Viswanath, D., Threats and Countermeasures, in *Science and Technology of Terrorism and Counterterrorism*, Ghosh, T., Prelas, M., Viswanath, D., and Loyalka, S., eds., Marcel Dekker, New York, 2002, pp. 433–435.
6. CNN, Officials: Pakistan Aided Libya Nuke Program, Jan. 6, 2004; http://www.cnn.com/2004/US/01/06/pakistan.korea.nukes/index.html; accessed 4/26/04.
7. CNN, Nuclear Scandal: Man "Confesses," Feb. 20, 2004; http://www.cnn.com/2004/WORLD/asiapcf/02/20/nuclear.malaysia/index.html; accessed 3/10/04.
8. Eisenstadt, M., Syria's Strategic Weapons, *Jane's Intelligence Review*, April, 1, 168–173, 1993; http://www.nti.org/db/nuclear/1993/n9315080.htm; accessed 3/10/04; Nuclear Threat Initiative, Syria Gets Nuclear Reactors from Russia, FBIS Document FTS19990530000096, 23 May 1999, NTI, Washington, D.C.; http://www.nti.org/db/nuclear/1999/n9919431.htm; accessed 3/10/04.
9. Gormley, D.M., Testimony before the Subcommittee on National Security, Emerging Threats, and International Affairs of the U.S. House of Representatives Committee on Government Reform, Mar. 9, 2004; http://cns.miis.edu/research/congress/testim/testgorm.htm; accessed 3/9/04.
10. McCloud, K., Ackerman, G.A., and Bale, J.M., Chart: Al-Qa`ida's WMD Activities, Center for Non-Proliferation Studies, Washington, D.C.; http://cns.miis.edu/pubs/other/sjm_cht.htm; accessed 10/08/04.
11. DHMO.org, Dihydrogen Monoxide FAQ; http://www.dhmo.org/facts.html; accessed 4/14/04.
12. Billings, M., The Influenza Pandemic of 1918, Stanford University, Stanford, CA; http://www.stanford.edu/group/virus/uda/; accessed 5/25/04; PBS, Influenza 1918; http://www.pbs.org/wgbh/amex/influenza/; accessed 5/25/04.

13. Transcript of Powell's U.N. Presentation: Part 9: Ties to al Qaeda, CNN, Feb. 6, 2003; http://www.cnn.com/2003/US/02/05/sprj.irq.powell.transcript.09/index.html; accessed 2/6/03.
14. Text of David Kay's Unclassified Statement, CNN, Oct. 2, 2003; http://www.cnn.com/2003/ALLPOLITICS/10/02/kay.report/index.html; accessed 3/29/04.
15. Arena, K., FBI Draining Maryland Pond in Anthrax Probe, CNN, June 10, 2003; http://www.cnn.com/2003/US/South/06/09/anthrax/index.html; accessed 5/10/04.
16. Broad, W.J., Johnston, D., and Miller, J., After the War: Biological Warfare; Subject of Anthrax Inquiry Tied to Anti-Germ Training, *New York Times*, July 2, 2003.
17. CNN, Libya Declares Mustard Gas Stockpiles, Mar. 5, 2004; http://www.cnn.com/2004/WORLD/africa/03/05/weapons.libya.ap/index.html; accessed 3/5/04.
18. Olson, K.B., Aum Shinrikyo: Once and Future Threat?, Centers for Disease Control, Atlanta; http://www.cdc.gov/ncidod/EID/vol5no4/olson.htm; accessed 4/28/04.
19. Prelas, M., Weaponization and Delivery Systems, in *Science and Technology of Terrorism and Counterterrorism*, Ghosh, T., Prelas, M., Viswanath, D., and Prelas, M., eds., Marcel Dekker, New York, 2001, pp. 95–108.
20. Bartlett, A., Arithmetic, Population and Energy, Department of Physics, University of Colorado, Boulder; http://www.hawaii.gov/dbedt/ert/symposium/bartlett/bartlett.html; accessed 5/12/04.
21. CNN, IEA: Oil Demand Seen at 16-yr High, May 12, 2004; http://www.cnn.com/2004/BUSINESS/05/12/iea.oil.reut/index.html; accessed 5/12/04.
22. Hubbertpeak.com, The Hubbert Peak for World Oil, Dec. 23, 2003; http://www.hubbertpeak.com/summary.htm; accessed 5/12/04.
23. Campbell, C.J., Forecasting Global Oil Supply 2000–2050, *Hubbert Center Newsletter*, March 2002, M. King Hubbert Center, Petroleum Engineering Department, Colorado School of Mines, Golden, CO; http://www.Hubbertpeak.Com/Campbell/Campbell_02-3.pdf; accessed 5/12/04.
24. CIA World Fact Book, Field Listing: Oil — consumption; http://www.odci.gov/cia/publications/factbook/fields/2174.html; accessed 5/12/04.
25. Duncan, R.C., The Olduvai Theory of Industrial Civilization, Institute on Energy and Man, Dec. 18, 1997; http://www.hubbertpeak.com/duncan/Olduvai.htm; accessed 5/12/04.
26. See note 23 above.

8

What Can Be Done To Limit the Impact of WMDs?

The unprecedented growth in science and technology over the past 70 years has brought many improvements to the quality of our lives, including social freedoms. Unfortunately, these great advancements in technology have also ushered in similar achievements in weapons technologies. Despite these significant advancements and the proliferation of weapons of mass destruction (WMDs), the world has seen very little actual deployment of these nuclear, biological, and chemical weapons (see Chapter 2). The combined effects of diplomacy, international cooperation, international pressure, and treaties have proved to be effective tools in limiting proliferation. As described in Chapter 7, an important reason why these methods have been so effective is the availability of oil, a widely available, cheap, highly energetic, and portable liquid fuel. Oil has fueled the world's persistent economic growth since the Great Depression of 1930. As long as there was hope of partaking in the prosperity that oil offered the world, the motivations for proliferation and the use of weapons of mass destruction could be controlled.

Prior to the fall of the USSR, bilateral and multilateral treaties were a successful means of controlling WMDs. These measures were successful, in part, due to the political stabilization brought about by two competing world superpowers. Other states were not willing to invest their resources to develop nuclear weapons (at about $9 billion or more, the investment in a WMD program is considerable). Knowing that they could not compete with the U.S. and the USSR, states chose instead to pit one power against the other in an international game of poker in a quest for aid and resources.

The decline of the USSR brought changes. Several states have reacted to the U.S. exertion of power and imperialism and have now chosen to invest in nuclear weapons technology. As a result, the world is entering a new and dangerous period. The rapid development of the Chinese and Indian economies has driven the demand for oil. On the other side of the equation, oil is becoming a scarce resource. In this environment, the tools for the control of WMD are diminishing in their effectiveness.

The 1973 oil embargo taught us the need for diversifying our energy sources. President Nixon presented the goal of achieving oil independence by 1985 by pursuing energy alternatives.[1] A number of factors challenged the achievement of this goal, including political pressures from special interest groups, such as the oil industry, the antinuclear movement, and the soft-energy movement, (alternatives to nuclear power, such as solar technology). As a result, the U.S. has been without a comprehensive national energy policy or vision that truly seeks energy independence from oil.[2]

At the time, many viewed Nixon's vision as impractical. Nixon promised to relieve foreign dependence by pursuing energy alternatives. With the decline of oil resources on top of increasing demand, the goal of oil independence is now more critical than ever. If this vision is to be realized, it must include all of the available resources — advanced coal systems, nuclear, renewable sources including solar, wind, ocean, geothermal, and hydroelectric — coupled with significant conservation measures. Any person or group that claims the energy problem can be solved solely by renewable energy sources or by any other energy sector alone does not fully understand the scope of the problem.[3] Special-interest groups have been a strong political force over the last 30 years. Their influence has cost the world, and specifically the U.S., valuable time in developing a far-reaching and comprehensive energy plan and has been a contributor to the forces that drive the proliferation of WMDs. Oil consumption will exceed the rate of oil discovery during the next decade. This, combined with increased demand driven by growth in the global economy, will lead to oil-price instabilities. As described in Chapter 1, this is a dangerous path. There is no time to waste in laying the groundwork for a diverse and comprehensive energy plan. Such a plan must have resources behind it. Further unfunded mandates and dependence on the free market to solve the problem is full of risk. The terrorist attacks of September 11, 2001 cost the U.S. economy trillions of dollars, and the bill for the second Gulf War is $200 billion and climbing. Can the U.S. afford to continue along a path of energy instability that foments terrorism and wars?[4] A significantly smaller investment would put the U.S. on the path of energy stability. It would also benefit the global community because the new energy technologies that the U.S. develops could be very attractive to other countries as well.

A second avenue is the development of new methods and motivations to stem proliferation of WMDs. These new methods are needed to supplement those that have been successful. Indeed, the changing world political climate demands that new approaches be developed. We must work toward an equitable global economy where all peoples of the world have an opportunity to benefit from globalization. The underlying causes of armed struggle and asymmetric warfare and terrorism must be addressed. The increasing availability of WMDs makes the prospect of winning even a limited war remote. History provides many examples that long-term political objectives cannot be achieved by force. Long-term peace can only be realized when all peoples are provided with the basic needs of life and the ability for self-determination. This would require an effort to improve education, health and hygiene, infrastructure, industry, nutrition, and government for the underprivileged. The international commitment and investment required to achieve these goals would be substantial. However, we contend that it would be well worth it to the global community as a nonproliferation measure. The benefits would be multifold. First, it would help to quell the hopelessness that might motivate people toward terrorism and violence. Second, it would give the global community additional avenues of economic growth. Third, it would reduce the motivations of governments to struggle for resources and influence, a factor in the pursuit of superior weapons.

A third avenue to deter proliferation involves the need for an international security structure. The weight of the international community is required to established expectations for sovereignty and accountability for the security of individual nations, both rich and poor. Though idealistic, some aspects of this are already in place within the charter of the United Nations, and this will need to be expanded into a workable framework. The balance between the sovereignty of nations and the good of the global community can be managed by positive motives rather than by fear and distrust.

The fourth consideration is the need to continue scientific development for the betterment of mankind. This is true despite the fact that knowledge is a double-edged sword, in that any good that comes from a technology is counterbalanced by the potential harm that it can cause. Biotechnology is an excellent example. This technology will dominate the 21st century, with the potential to solve the plagues of the prior centuries (e.g., disease, pestilence, hunger, and poverty). People once wrongly believed that nuclear weapons would destroy mankind. Unlike technologies of the past, which did not possess the capability, biotechnology does have the capability of destroying mankind. We must learn a lesson from the misguided antinuclear movement, which made claims about nuclear technology that grossly overestimated the technology's risk. If or when an antibiotechnology movement begins to seriously impact the biotechnology industry, the proactive way to combat the misinformation that such movements generate as a means of scaring and persuading people is through education. It is important that biotechnology research be embraced. If an antibiotechnology movement were to succeed in halting research due to an irrational fear of the technology, the knowledge derived from prior research would eventually find its way into the public domain, and weapons would be developed for which we would have no defense. On the other hand, if research were unhindered, then given that there is a lag time between new developments and the migration of knowledge to the public, research would always be ahead of applications. Thus, if weapons were developed from biotechnology, advancements would be available to counter those new weapons. This — coupled with efforts to reduce motivations for the development of weapons from biotechnology, such as plentiful energy resources, true globalization of economic benefits, and international security — would lead to a workable framework of nonproliferation measures.

REFERENCES

1. Miller, A.S., Energy Policy from Nixon to Clinton: From Grand Provider to Market Facilitator, *Environmental Law,* 25 (3), 715–731, 1995.

2. Sterzinger, G., OPEC and US Energy, *Harvard Int. Rev.*, 25 (4), 2004.

3. Ghosh, T.K. and Prelas, M.A., Energy Systems and Resources, to be published; see http://prelas.nuclear.missouri.edu/ne315/index.html; last accessed 5/16/04.

4. Martin, S., Enemies Key to U.S. Energy Needs: Clashes Likely to Continue, Senators Told, *Washington Times*, Sep. 18, 1996, p. 15.

Index

C

D

E

F

G

H

I

M

N

T

U

V

W

X

Y

Z